Winnebagos on Wednesdays

Winnebagos on Wednesdays

How Visionary Leadership Can Transform Higher Education

Scott Cowen
with Betsy Seifter

Princeton University Press • *Princeton and Oxford*

Published by Princeton University Press,
41 William Street, Princeton, New Jersey 08540

In the United Kingdom: Princeton University Press,
6 Oxford Street, Woodstock, Oxfordshire OX20 1TR

press.princeton.edu

Jacket art courtesy of CSA Images

ISBN 978-0-691-17461-7

British Library Cataloging-in-Publication Data is available

This book has been composed in Plantin Std

Printed on acid-free paper. ∞

Printed in the United States of America

10 9 8 7 6 5 4 3 2 1

I dedicate this book to my precious grandchildren—
Louise, Toby, Henry, Joey, and Mara.
I hope they will have the opportunity to grow and
develop through higher education and lead a life of
fulfillment, kindness, and happiness.

Contents

Acknowledgments

My motivation for writing this book emanates from my deep commitment to higher education as a transformative experience for those fortunate to experience it. In my mind, immersing oneself in life and learning in a college environment creates personal and professional opportunities that are hard to come by in any other setting—its impact and value are boundless. I hope this book will advance the dialogue about the current state of higher education and its future by focusing on a series of key issues that are shaping the education sector.

This book would never have become a reality without the valuable assistance and contributions of many people. At the very top of my list of those who significantly contributed to this effort are Betsy Seifter, acknowledged on the title page, and Heide Winston, my director of communications and civic engagement at Tulane.

Betsy is a superb writer and editor with a true gift for words. She has an endless curiosity and passion for knowledge, which inspired me to think more broadly and deeply on many of the topics covered in this book. Her unique insights were invaluable in shaping all aspects of the final product.

Heide is an outstanding researcher and fact finder whose remarkable editorial skills and thoughtfulness aided this project tremendously. Heide's work is impeccable, and she and Betsy were formidable team members in shaping the content and tone of this book. *Winnebagos on Wednesdays* would still be a figment of my imagination if Betsy and Heide were not involved.

During my time at Tulane I have been blessed to work with remarkable individuals, many of whom provided valuable guidance and assistance in the preparation of this book. Chief among them has been Michael Bernstein, Tulane's former provost, who read the entire manuscript and offered invaluable comments and insights. Michael is an outstanding provost (now at Stony Brook) and scholar. Other current and former Tulane colleagues who provided valuable assistance were Katie Busby, Barbara Moely, Amanda Kruger Hill, Amy Barad, Nicole Jolly, Earl Retif, Mike Goodman, Becky Ancira, Mike Hogg, Jeff Schiffman, Faye Tydlaska, Roger Dunaway, John Christie, Laura Levy, James Stofan, Ana Lopez, Agnieszka Nance, Johanna Gilligan, Rebecca Otten, Anne Baños, Yvette Jones, and Kathleen Kent.

Tom Burish, provost at the University of Notre Dame and former president of Washington and Lee University, also read and commented on several chapters in the book. His comments were always insightful and helpful as we did subsequent edits of the manuscript. Debbie Bial, the founder and CEO of the Posse Foundation, was generous with her time in describing Posse's genesis and philosophy.

Karen Oye, Sue Nartker, and Laura Watt, all former colleagues of mine at Case Western Reserve University, helped refresh my memory of referenced topics related to my time in Cleveland and at CWRU as a professor and dean. Elisabeth Hahn, a doctoral student at Harvard, and Tim Miller, a doctoral student at George Washington University, interviewed me for their respective dissertations about my Katrina experience and forwarded their interview transcripts, which were useful in recalling details from Katrina.

Our initial book proposal greatly benefited from comments by Mary Amicucci and her team at Barnes & Noble. Their comments sharpened all aspects of the project and pointed me to Princeton University Press as a possible publisher.

Peter Dougherty, director of Princeton University Press, and his assistant editor, Jessica Yao, guided and supported me throughout the publication process. I want to offer a special thank you, as well, to Lauren Lepow, whose meticulous copyediting strengthened the book immeasurably. It has been a delight to work with Princeton University Press.

Even though this project has truly been a team effort, I accept all responsibility for the views represented herein and any flaws you may detect.

Finally, I want to thank my wife, Marjorie, for her unwavering support of me throughout my career. She is a remarkable person who keeps me grounded and reminds me to have a life outside of my work. Whatever professional successes I have had in my career are in large part attributable to Marjorie. She has always been my most honest critic.

Winnebagos
on Wednesdays

Introduction

Here's the situation: I've just offered our talented football coach, Tommy Bowden, a higher salary than he's been offered by Clemson University, which has a Goliath of a program compared to Tulane's David. True, we're coming off an undefeated season, but that's an extremely rare event at Tulane—the last time was sixty-nine years ago—and I want to keep him. With this offer on the table, I feel I have a shot at it.

Tommy is clearly taken aback. He says, "It's not the money. You can't give me what I want."

"What do you want?"

"Winnebagos on Wednesday."

"Say again?"

Tommy explains: "I want a school where the program is so great, people start bringing their Winnebagos on Wednesday—for the Saturday game."

And I thought: So this is what we've come to. Tulane, a major research university, is somehow, for various crazy reasons, involved in the entertainment business—and we're not on the A-list.

I've carried that story in my head for over eighteen years; it comes to mind every time I'm confronted by one of those situations that feel both insoluble and also faintly ludicrous. The

Winnebagos story raises, in highly condensed form, a fundamental question: What is the ultimate purpose of higher education, and how is it changing over time? The long history of higher education in the United States is marked by the singular moment in 1862 when the Morrill Act established the land-grant colleges in every state in the union (later expanded to include the Confederate States and historically black colleges and universities). The Morrill Act created a uniquely American model, very different from the European system's focus on educating professional and military elites. In the United States, the overarching mission of colleges and universities was to prepare masses of young people for meaningful employment and engaged citizenship in a participatory democracy. But over the past hundred years, that original aim has been joined by another mission, the solving of social and global problems through research and innovation. Higher education's challenges—poverty, urban decline, income inequality, increasing diversity, racial and gender inequities, job loss, climate change, and a host of other issues—are the nation's challenges. The sector can't solve those problems in isolation; public understanding and continued investment of both private and public resources are necessary if the nation is to address its knottiest problems and remain a beacon of enlightened progress in a troubled world.

But in recent decades, we seem to have lost sight of our fundamental goals in a distracting sideshow of arguments and crusades. Somehow, we end up talking about Winnebagos. And athletics aren't the only flash point. Rival constituencies confront university presidents with a whole array of contradictory demands: protection of free speech vs. provision of "safe spaces"; the norms of shared governance vs. the need for nimble leadership; the requirements of medical training vs. the primacy of clinical services; investment in basic research vs. commercialization of medical discoveries; the pressure of media-generated rankings vs. adherence to institutional mission; and, the ultimate conundrum, preserving high quality vs. ensuring low cost. Add to this list of warring values the out-of-control admissions game, the amenities arms race, the all-digital craze, grandiose global ambitions, and the overriding insanity of spiraling costs and graduates without jobs. Some believe we've reached a point of no return—"The End of College"—but in my view, we need repair and reimagining, not demolition. We can do better, and the way to begin is by getting down to cases and taking a hard look at the facts.

This book consists of stories about those thorny situations—everything from athletics to the selection of a university president—that demand, but don't often get, rational assessment and decisive action, and about the leadership we need to remake higher education as a powerful, affordable, and meaningful agent of self-realization and social progress for the coming generation. I want to acknowledge, up front, that these stories don't always tell the whole story. In cases where an incident never received a full public airing, insiders privy to the undisclosed details may find its portrayal here oversimplified and partial. I've also sacrificed some degree of nuance and detail because I wanted to describe the entire landscape of higher education, in the belief that the wide-angle view reveals features that the close-up sometimes misses. Taken together, the examples will, I hope, convey a sense of the big picture—what is happening widely and variously in the sector.

I was moved to write this book because of my own forty-year experience in higher education as a professor and academic dean, and as president of Tulane University when Hurricane Katrina hit New Orleans, and the known world—of the institution, the city, the region, and beyond—shifted dramatically. Since that time more than ten years ago, I've often been asked to speak about leadership in times of crisis. Here I want to speak not about crisis leadership per se, but about "transformative" leadership—the kind that creates positive, fundamental change through judicious action at key decision points and offers a vision of hope that inspires others to join in. My views on leadership and organizational change are also informed by my experiences as a board member and consultant to many for-profit and nonprofit organizations during the last four decades. A crisis requires a series of urgent choices and actions, but the daily life of an organization also demands crucial decisions that affect the character of the entire institution. You don't need a hurricane to know which way the wind blows: the times are a-changing, and every academic leader needs to focus on the arc of the future.

The change that we're undergoing is, if not a crisis, a tipping point. I remember long ago as an undergraduate reading Thomas Kuhn's *The Structure of Scientific Revolutions*, and it seems to me that its central insight applies here: when data accumulate that can no longer be explained by a traditional model, a new paradigm emerges to accommodate the wave of new information. In the realm of higher education, we are awash in data of all kinds—metrics that measure pedagogic practice, graduation and retention rates, jobs and salaries, and a host of other things—and these indicators may point the way to a new paradigm for education. That's the position that the prophets of digital learning take: they predict a totally new kind of college experience in the "University of Everywhere," as students soak up information from online courses on a range of subjects, many of them with a technological and vocational emphasis. Their basic argument is familiar to anyone who has a degree in business administration: innovate or die. We all know the cautionary tales of Kodak and Smith Corona, and many more (may they rest in peace): companies that didn't see which way the wind was blowing and, by ceasing to adapt to new realities, became dinosaurs.

On the other side of things are the traditionalists who defend the value of the system we have and, even while admitting the necessity to adapt, warn against throwing the proverbial baby out with the proverbial bathwater. They say there's no substitute for residential colleges, the liberal arts curriculum, and flesh-and-blood teachers in brick-and-mortar classrooms if we're to continue to produce educated and sophisticated thinkers and innovators. You can add bells and whistles and tinker with the details, but the basic model should stay the same. The answer of the all-digital crowd to the defense of the liberal arts is to decry the two-tier elitism inherent in a system that provides immersion in high culture and critical thinking for those who can afford it, and sends the rest to community colleges, with few resources and poor track records, to acquire vocational training.

Let me say at the outset, and it's hardly a unique or novel position, that I strongly believe in the inherent value and aspirations of higher education. I also support efforts to expand access and affordability. Let me also say, despite the sense of an impending revolution and talk of new paradigms, I am skeptical of universal remedies that fail to take into account some key facts, chief of which is the intricately woven tapestry of our schools—some four thousand of them across the United States. It's one of the splendors of the American system of higher education that so many diverse schools are pursuing so many distinctive paths to educating young people, who themselves have widely various backgrounds and learning styles. One result of this rich complexity: different institutions exhibit different strengths and suffer from different ills. That is, the successes and failures of our institutions are specific to people, places, and circumstances.

This book is about people, places, and circumstances—what's actually going on inside the ivy-covered halls in the second decade of the twenty-first century. I hope to avoid the one-size-fits-all problem by drawing from our vast array of schools, public and private, large and small, to tell specific stories about leadership and institutional mission in the context of contingent events and social trends. The stories of leaders at moments of decision on matters of importance—from athletics to medicine to research to community engagement—reveal the approaches, realistic and practical but also innovative and courageous, taken all across the country by committed educators and administrators. Some of these stories are, sadly, about presidents derailed and initiatives abandoned—equally instructive as we try to get at what works, what doesn't, and who we need at the helm.

I am taking this inductive approach because I believe we can arrive at a true assessment of higher education only by looking hard at individual narratives when something changed for the better (or sometimes, regrettably, for the worse). Among the many people I'll be describing in the coming pages are truly great leaders who through their vision, persistence, and character transformed their schools. To name a few: Norman Francis, who recently, after forty-seven years, stepped down as president of Xavier University, a small Catholic historically black school in New Orleans, having during his long tenure turned it into a major pipeline for black doctors, scientists, and pharmacists; Steve Sample, who in the space of nineteen years transformed the University of Southern California into a world leader in the fields of communication and multimedia technologies, while also creating innovative community partnerships and solidifying its reputation as one of the nation's leading research universities; Diana Natalicio, the president of the University of Texas at El Paso, who over the last twenty-nine years has increased the endowment, expanded research expenditures, grown the graduate degree program, and upped enrollment from fifteen thousand to over twenty-three thousand in a low-income minority population; and Judith Rodin, president of the University of Pennsylvania from 1994 to 2004, who in addition to increasing research funding, endowment, and enrollment and consolidating the university hospital and medical school into one organization, significantly enhanced the ties between the university and the surrounding community through public safety initiatives, university alliances with small businesses, and the revitalization of city buildings and public spaces.

It's by getting down to cases of individuals like these that I attempt to parse the phrase "transformative leadership." Significantly, all these leaders had substantial tenures, ranging from a decade to nearly half a century; meanwhile, the average length of a presidency is now seven years (with many terms at troubled institutions as short as a year or two). These long-standing presidents suggest that transformation rarely happens in a blinding instant, but rather unfolds through years of persistent effort. In addition to presenting the portraits of others, I also occasionally refer to my own experience, to give a view from the inside out; and, throughout, I stress the importance of context, collaboration, and mission in any successful leadership initiative.

My own understanding of transformative process was deepened by Hurricane Katrina, which threatened the very existence of the university and at the same time was one of those "blinding instants" that unleashed the possibility of transformation, both as a strategy for survival and as a way to reset the university. More change could be effected in a short space of time because of the diminution of shared governance in the midst of a bona fide disaster and a concomitant rise in presidential power and autonomy. The transformation was also aided by an influx of resources, both financial and humanitarian, that helped bring us back from the brink, allowing us to reimagine what Tulane could become after this critical event in its history. One of the chief lessons of that time is the extent to which contingency and context influence outcomes. No one, however powerful and autonomous, can exert total control over events. And though I ultimately made the hard decisions, I consulted with an in-group of other university presidents who helped guide me through the roughest passages. Bottom line: as we think about the future of our institutions, we need to reexamine how we govern them—to consider the modes of leadership and the kind of change needed, incremental or transformational, according to various contingencies.

Before Katrina, I had learned something about leadership of the incremental, day-to-day kind. My background, including the military, athletics, even a learning disability diagnosed in my twenties, prepared me for the hard choices implied by "the buck stops here," and I also have the temperament for it—an innate resilience (my wife, Margie, would say, "thick hide") and tenacity (Margie would say, "stubbornness.") A set of core values stemming from my identification with Judaism has served as a kind of internal compass in my life, both personally and professionally. Plus, probably a compensation for my early learning disability, I'm the sort who learns by doing: I grew into my jobs.

To give you just two points on my learning curve: the first involved a situation when I was a new dean of the business school at Case Western Reserve University, and a young one, thirty-eight years old, and feeling a little precarious, as though I were the child now managing all the adults. It was maybe in my second or third year that I received an anonymous note informing me that a prominent member of our faculty, a distinguished chaired professor who had helped me get promoted and supported me for the deanship, had a fraudulent résumé. Given that the letter was anonymous, I could have brushed it off as malicious, but something about the way it was written seemed genuine to me. I had a trusted assistant review the professor's CV item by item, and significant discrepancies emerged—significant enough to warrant further inquiry. At that point, I called him into my office to inform him of a formal process of review. He tried to talk me out of it. It broke my heart to pursue it, but pursue it I did: I convened a faculty committee, and they issued a report confirming the falsehoods. The university dismissed him, thus ending what was once a flourishing career.

This, to me, felt like firing a father figure but taught me, in my bones, that I had responsibilities that superseded personal relationships and focused me on the best overall interests of the organization, no matter the consequences to me and perhaps others. I was indebted to him for past kindnesses, but I did not owe him a career based on a tissue of lies.

Another kind of bone-deep learning occurred early in my presidency at Tulane, when students organized a protest against the university's investment in companies accused of using sweatshops in Asia. The protesters took over the main administration building; ironically, many of them were wearing athletic clothes manufactured by these same companies. It was the first sit-in I'd confronted, and I felt some uncertainty, though I did know I wanted to avoid a 1960s scenario of open hostilities and outside policing. I asked the students to research the companies and collect data on how they might fix the problem, and also to consider their own choices and what personal sacrifices they were willing to make. Then I brought administrators at Tulane together to address the ethical issue the students had raised. After a week or so, the students decided to end the sit-in, and we all met to discuss an effective strategy. The end result: Tulane became a charter member of a group of schools fighting horrific labor conditions in these specific countries—an exercise in conflict resolution for the students and also for me.

When to stand firm, when to yield, how to compromise: these are the sorts of decisions that you make every day. Transformative moments come, most obviously, with crises, but they also come at quieter junctures: when business-as-usual falters for financial or other reasons, or simply when traditions have ossified and a deadening complacency has set in. I focus on these moments of change throughout the coming pages, in the belief that these stories will illuminate the practices that define effective leadership.

The book's structure reflects the most pressing questions confronting our institutions. Chapter 1, "On Impact," describes ratings and metrics, often drawn from media outlets and sometimes misleading, that are being used to evaluate our colleges and universities, and also considers the human meaning of the word—how higher education qualitatively changes the lives of graduates. Chapter 2, "Door Wide Open," is about the burning issue of access and affordability, and looks at schools that are doing a remarkable job of educating low-income, first-generation, and minority students and thus providing upward mobility. Chapter 3, "Keeping the Ship Afloat," is about financial sustainability and prospects for survival, and focuses on innovative strategies, other than the annual rite of tuition hikes, that generate funding. Chapter 4, "The Tail Wags the Dog, Part I: Athletics," details the problem of escalating costs and risks associated with big-time sports programs. Chapter 5, "The Tail Wags the Dog, Part II: Medicine," describes the collision between a new health-care system founded on principles of efficiency and economy and the training and research programs associated with academic medical centers. Chapter 6, "Brave New World," underscores the significance of the discoveries and innovations emerging from our major research universities, but also proposes increased support for an emerging scholarship of engagement that addresses urgent societal issues. Chapter 7, "Can We All Get Along?," is about governance and stakeholder issues in higher education—how implosions and cabals weaken an institution, and how the process of finding consensus works (when it works). Chapter 8, "The Ivory Tower," describes the historic tensions between town and gown, and presents cases of institutions of higher education that embrace their role as anchor institutions and have become deeply engaged in their communities. Chapter 9, "Who Are We?," tells stories of schools pursuing unique missions and of schools that for lack of clear identity and purpose are heading toward failure. Chapter 10, "Presidential Leadership," recapitulates the central theme of transformative leadership, proposing a theory of change that synthesizes insights from all the preceding chapters, and offers recommendations for recruiting, evaluating, vetting, and hiring university leaders.

In each of these chapters, leaders of all kinds try to solve the problems that confront them and to strengthen their schools for the future. Though I present these subjects discretely, many topics overlap and many themes recur. Among the recurring themes are three that suggest a "tipping point": widespread misperceptions based on misleading metrics and data; mounting financial pressures affecting adherence to mission; and increasing social and global challenges that present both risk and promise. As the future unfolds, the threats and opportunities will likely change, but the basic issues outlined here—the most urgent problems in higher education, requiring creative and courageous leadership to solve—will, I believe, remain much the same. Likewise, the traits required to meet the unknown head-on and create meaningful progress will remain the same. I do believe the best university presidents share certain essential qualities: an ability to grasp the realities in front of them; to contextualize the facts to their particular institution; to sense the possibilities inherent in the situations they face; to intuitively understand other people; and to be true to a set of beliefs and principles. The last is really "character," in the old-fashioned sense of internal strength and integrity, and the most inspiring of the stories to come are about character in action.

The book's closing analysis of leadership underscores a fundamental point. To carry on the work of higher education, we need to find the next cohort of leaders: people of character and vision who can make the right decisions, time after time, in instance after instance, and so reawaken the American dream of opportunity for future generations.

1

On Impact

*If many of the rankings are misleading and many of
the measures irrelevant, how can we construct a nuanced
and accurate portrait of a school's impact? How can we
get a real picture of how graduates are doing, not just
economically but in their lives as a whole?*

I remember the day—I'm thinking it must have been mid-April
1964, since that was when most letters went out—that I learned
of my acceptance to college. I can still recall the thrill of seeing a
thick envelope in the mailbox: that was the telltale sign that the
school had a lot of things to say to you, rather than a paragraph
of perfunctory explanations beginning with "We regret . . ." I'd
already had one of those from an institution that shall go un-
mentioned, and was beginning to really worry. And there was
the additional issue of money, something my family didn't have
much of. But in that thick sheaf of paper from the University of
Connecticut was further good news: not only an acceptance, but a
student-athlete scholarship that would allow me to actually attend.

For me, as for so many young people, college was the door-
way to everything else, but in my case it wasn't by any means a
given. My sister and I were the first in our family to go to college
(statistics say that the chances of someone from a "no degree"
family going to college are less than half that of someone from a
two-degree family).[1] Also, I wasn't exactly a scholar: I struggled
in school in the early years with undiagnosed dyslexia—no such
diagnosis back then. But the narrative changed when I went off
to UConn on my football scholarship. In the mid-1960s, amateur

status meant amateur, so though I was an offensive and then defensive lineman, I could count on actually getting an education despite my obligations to the football team. (I should add for the sake of transparency that I had a fairly undistinguished career as an athlete that ended after two years because of an illness.) By the time I graduated, it was the height of the Vietnam War; I deferred entrance into graduate school and enlisted in Infantry Officer Candidate School, serving three years in the army. Then I went back to school on the GI Bill, getting a master's and then a doctorate in business administration.

I think it was a combination of disparate experiences—my love of learning, an appreciation for the world around me, athletics, and the military (both of the latter, by the way, helping foot the tuition bills)—that ultimately gave me competence, confidence, and the ability to embrace different points of view. These are experiences and attributes that I would draw on over and over again in my life. But particularly because of my dyslexia, schooling was a critical part of my evolution as a person. Early on, the learning disability made me feel I couldn't make my way in the world, especially in academics, and I struggled with failure, developing other capacities—what back then were called "interpersonal skills"—to compensate for my weaknesses. At some point, supported by caring teachers and mentors, I mastered the world of letters and was able to go on with my general education and then to launch an academic career, which ultimately brought me to Tulane. Education transformed my life. If this isn't impact, I don't know what is.

Mine clearly isn't a unique story. Most graduates, even ones who profess to hate their schools, are shaped by their experiences at college and graduate school. These experiences occur in the crucial years of transition from adolescence to young adulthood, at a time of rapid development of brain and body.[2] Learning in these years is vivid and lasting partly because young minds are fertile ground for novel stimuli. If we're going to talk about the "impact" of postsecondary education, the intense immersion in a community that offers exposure to many domains of knowledge and many differing perspectives is inevitably going to have a substantial effect on the minds and lives of graduates.

I've begun with my own story because the impact of education is, at root, personal—critical events that shape who you are and hold the promise of economic security, mental and physical well-being, a satisfying career, and meaningful participation in society. The higher education sector has held these truths to be self-evident. It's the story we've been telling about higher education since time immemorial; unchallenged, we didn't feel it was necessary to flesh out the particulars.

But then the price of a degree rose, and rose, and rose. As the cost increased and institutional missions expanded, legislators, journalists, and the general public began to question the old assumptions and to look for evidence that proved the worth of higher education. Social science researchers and, more particularly, the media began to develop metrics to determine quality and impact, gathering data that allowed observers, including parents and prospective students, to get a look at who was doing what, and how well a given institution stacked up against others. And hence were born the rankings, generated by a number of publications, most notably *U.S. News & World Report*. As we'll see, those rankings have taken on a life of their own, driving decisions about how universities allocate resources, recruit and accept students, and conduct a host of other activities, from research to athletics.

The point is not simply to decry the rankings, but to consider how complicit we've become in trying to nudge the numbers. It would be wise to look within—define "success" in our own terms, then measure it appropriately and collect the data to support our claims.

One reason we haven't accumulated revealing data is that the most relevant information isn't always readily available; another impediment is an overwhelming volume of random data that requires sorting and analysis. I remember that when I came to Tulane in 1998, the Office of Institutional Research was a tiny place. In the nearly twenty years since, the explosion of information about every aspect of academic institutions has made it hard to keep pace. But now is the time not only to marshal the available facts, but to reclaim our narrative and reframe how we in higher education determine our quality and impact—not for those ranking us, but for ourselves and our own efforts at self-improvement. As we'll see in the ensuing discussion, in letting others decide on the metrics and the data points, we've lost control of our own story and occasionally strayed from doing what is best for our students and the communities in which we exist. To make the case to the public, we need to tell it in our own words, using reliable evidence and metrics that will convince skeptics of our worth.

Before wading further into the issue of data, metrics, and rankings, I'm going to take a moment to describe the influence a college or university has on its community and society at large. At most institutions this kind of impact has begun to be evaluated statistically, using data about the economic and social effects colleges and universities have on their town, city, or region. For example, a 2015 report on Tulane's economic impact enumerates the full-time students, hours of community service, patients treated by medical faculty, licensing agreements, start-ups, and jobs associated with the university. Bottom line: as the largest private employer in New Orleans, the university has had over a $1 billion impact on our community and the state's economy, attributable to wages, purchasing, construction, research funding and operational costs, and visitor and student spending.[3]

The story of how the university came to have such significant impact on the city hinges on Katrina. The school's story has a "before" and "after," with our mission undergoing an evolution in response to the catastrophe that befell us. When I first arrived in New Orleans in the late nineties, Tulane was a midsize research university lacking the resources of some of the wealthy public universities and the Ivies, but with the capacity to be as influential as institutions more richly endowed. What was needed, I felt, was a creative, hands-on, entrepreneurial approach that would make the school noteworthy, distinctive, financially sustainable, and attractive to students, faculty, alumni, parents, community leaders, and donors—the latter a crucial element, because there's no playing in the big leagues without the funds to compete. I focused on practical goals precisely because I wanted us to be highly competitive and distinctive. Among the many strategic aims of my first two years as president of the university—which included getting to know people, letting them get to know me, and building consensus toward the creation of an institutional vision and strategy—I oversaw a financial restructuring that involved the establishment of a decentralized management model and embarked on an active fund-raising campaign and pursuit of research grants.

Then, seven years into my tenure, Hurricane Katrina hit New Orleans, almost destroying the university and causing damage to Tulane that amounted to $650 million. I won't repeat all the details of the Renewal Plan we constructed to save the university, but the basics involved merging seven undergraduate colleges into one, eliminating several undergraduate and graduate programs, downsizing the medical school, suspending half the athletic programs, and ultimately letting go about eight hundred of our full-time faculty and staff. These decisions—and they were difficult, controversial, and painful—grew out of the fiscal analysis years before, which had identified programs with relatively weaker impact in terms of enrollment, revenue, and productivity.

Perhaps the key decision post-Katrina—the one that signaled an evolution in our mission—was the integration of public service into the core curriculum for all undergraduates, with a greater emphasis on community engagement, social innovation and entrepreneurship, and experiential learning. Through the Center for Public Service, social innovation and social entrepreneurship programs, Tulane City Center[4] at the School of Architecture, the Cowen Institute for Public Education Initiatives, Tulane Community Health Centers, and a host of other new research and educational programs, the university has markedly enhanced its impact on the entire community, contributing through learning, service, and research to health, education, housing, culture, the environment, and the economy.

We reached out to the city, as well as to communities around the globe, in unprecedented ways after Katrina and, in so doing, reinvented the school's identity. Tulane had always been considered a good school (along with Vanderbilt and Duke, it's been called the "Harvard of the South"), but it also had a reputation as a party school; it is in New Orleans, after all, where the good times roll. Our aim was to make the Tulane of the future a deeply committed anchor institution for New Orleans, where students would become active leaders and citizens of the city, and later the nation and world, through thoughtful engagement with communities outside our walls. If our graduates went forth in the world as agents of social change and community solutions—if they contributed to the public good and the enrichment of our culture—we would be doing our job of creating the next generation of committed and thoughtful participants in the democratic society of the future.

Ironically, it was a disaster that helped us sharpen our sense of mission and led to the development of service learning and community engagement. At the same time, we preserved our discovery mission as a research university, continuing our commitment to scientific investigation and progress. Tulane University actually started as the Medical College of Louisiana, founded in 1834 and chartered in 1835 by a small group of young physicians in response to a cholera and yellow fever epidemic in New Orleans. In 1847, the Medical College merged with the newly established University of Louisiana, a public entity, and expanded to include an undergraduate school and other graduate programs. In 1884, with an endowment from philanthropist Paul Tulane, the university was rechristened in his name and privatized. Today, Tulane has a robust and significant commitment to research in all fields, anchored by a health science complex that includes the Tulane University School of Medicine, the School of Public Health and Tropical Medicine, the Tulane Primate Center, the Tulane Hospital and Clinics, and segments of our School of Science and Engineering. This complex, like similar ones at other universities, is conducting research and caring for patients, with a significant impact on the lives of people locally, nationally, and around the globe.

Biomedical research has a very personal meaning to me because my wife, Margie, who has Parkinson's disease, is a beneficiary of that research. Though there's no cure for Parkinson's, levodopa, the "miracle drug" that quells tremor and eases rigidity, emerged from clinical trials in the 1960s at the Universities of Vienna and Montreal, and later Brookhaven National Laboratories in New York. The impact of our research institutions on millions of lives is hardly news, but sometimes forgotten when we begin doubting the ultimate value of higher education. To name just a few examples of research at our universities that have changed our world: sequencing the human genome, stem cell therapies, targeted immunotherapy for cancer, HIV combination therapy, minimally invasive surgery, transplant surgery, bionic prostheses, functional magnetic resonance imaging—the list goes on.

Tulane's story is a narrative of rising impact associated with a transformed mission. It's true that institutional stories are told in many ways—brochures, websites, mission statements, press releases—but in our "evidence-based" age, reports like the one Tulane issued on its economic impact, full of graphs and tables and statistics, carry significant weight. What stories do the numbers tell? Katie Busby, Tulane's former assistant provost for assessment and institutional research, had the job of supplying information to the Tulane community and to outside organizations like the Association of American Universities and a host of accreditation and data-gathering agencies. She supplied the data, on everything from student-faculty ratio to graduation rates to alumni giving, so that impact could be measured. One of the chief recipients of data from Tulane (and from most other colleges and universities in the United States) is *U.S. News & World Report*, which publishes an annual ranking of schools from first to worst. And here we come to the issue I mentioned at the outset, that others have seized control of the story line and established a powerful, though distorted, narrative of institutional value. Rankings based on trivial metrics often exert a strong influence on applicants and donors and sometimes radically alter an institution's strategic aims.

Katie describes *USNWR* as "the devil you have to dance with"; it's an arms race you can't get out of precisely because everyone else is in it.[5] When she herself was asked, "Why is college so important?" she responded with some version of "Your son/daughter is going to grow and develop," considering this the primary impact of higher education. Meanwhile, many metrics focus on employment and earnings rather than assessing student satisfaction, intellectual growth, or the ability to solve problems and make constructive decisions.

Apart from the variable meaning of the word "impact" and the variable means of measuring it, Katie Busby's chief problems were insufficient data on students, who as seniors often have "survey fatigue," and inadequate information about alumni, whose post-collegiate lives are even more difficult to track. Without a good clearinghouse that includes longitudinal data, it's hard to measure the impact undergraduate school is having (or has had) on graduates' careers, happiness, contributions to society, socioeconomic status, or anything else.[6]

In social science realms, impact studies sometimes have a tendency to prove the obvious, but an essential function of impact measurements is to do just that—provide credible evidence of what is known in order to defend against critics, advertise worth, and fortify institutional values. For example, Tulane social scientist Barbara Moely has been studying community engagement since 2003, with a focus on whether service learning helps produce civic-minded graduates. After Hurricane Katrina, the university's inauguration of a public service requirement gave her a rich source of data. Her findings, though not surprising, are reassuring: students engaged in service learning, compared to those not so engaged, showed increases in plans for future civic action, positive assessments of their own interpersonal, problem-solving, and leadership skills, and a belief that societal factors influence individual outcomes (a social justice perspective).[7]

University presidents are inundated by reports that describe impact, because it's our job to make decisions about allocation of resources based on hard data. Who is productive? Where is the dead wood? What works? What doesn't? Most important of all, what strengthens institutional mission and what subverts it? In the case of Tulane, increased community engagement was a way to heighten the university's impact, not only because of the proven effectiveness of service learning, but also because of the distinctive purpose it conveyed: "We are the school engaged in the rebuilding of New Orleans and taking the lessons learned to other communities around the globe."

Generally speaking, for leaders to make good decisions, we need reliable measures and a clear sense of mission in order to sustain and improve quality, but "quality" is a slippery notion in the mind of the public. As I've said (more than once!), inadequate metrics and questionable data plague many of the rankings currently out there—those articles purporting to assess the "Top 100 Schools" or "The Best Colleges for Innovation." *U.S. News & World Report* is a chief culprit, oversimplifying the varied landscape of colleges and universities, comparing apples with oranges (with little sense of the distinctive missions of different schools), using obsolete data, and measuring the wrong things.

The questions parents and students are most likely to ask when evaluating a school include such things as "What is the quality of teaching and how much do students learn? Do they get jobs after graduation? Are they prepared to live a productive life, personally and professionally? How good is the financial aid? If the school is residential, what is the quality of residential life? Does the school produce leaders and engaged citizens?" *U.S. News & World Report* does not answer a single one of these questions. The questions *USNWR* does ask (e.g., "How many classes of under twenty students do you have? How many applicants do you reject [so-called selectivity]? How many of your faculty have doctorates?") are not an acceptable substitute for the more searching concerns of families. The significant weight (22.5 percent) that *USNWR* gives to

"Reputation," which is in essence a popular opinion poll based on surveys of people likely to be influenced by the rankings in the first place, is particularly misleading for students looking for reliable measures of quality.[8]

The rankings verge on the cartoonish and are almost always a distortion. One case close to home—actually *at* home—is the slide Tulane experienced in the rankings after Katrina, when retention and graduation rates (the most significant factors in the ranking) declined after the school closed for an entire semester, and over 20 percent of the entire student body failed to return. It took nearly a decade to flush out the bad data, and Tulane is once again climbing back to its proper perch, but for years people focused on our slip in the rankings rather than on how the university had transformed itself to the betterment of students and the communities where we live and work. During the ten-year rebuilding process, *USNWR* never made any attempt to acknowledge or weigh the circumstances, or even provide an asterisk.[9]

The rankings can also lead institutions astray. One example: Clemson, a public land-grant institution in South Carolina, made changes that allowed the school to move into the top twenty-five of public universities on the *U.S. News & World Report* list, coming in at number 22 in 2009 and holding steady at number 23 in 2017. Some of the changes were a shell game, like decreasing average class size by increasing the size of other sections and rating all other schools lower than Clemson on the administration's survey questionnaire. But the chief change was a policy of rejecting all applicants who were not in the top third of their high school graduating class. To win its higher ranking, Clemson became a much more exclusive school, privileging merit over access in a poor state—and thus, it could be argued, violating its mission as a public land-grant institution.[10]

Reed College, a small liberal arts college in Portland, Oregon, took the opposite approach; the school stepped out of the rat race of rankings altogether, finding the metrics meaningless to its core purpose, and in the process strengthened its identity as an institution prizing academic excellence and serious intellectual inquiry.[11] Reed could successfully retreat from the arena of competition because its applicant pool is sui generis: intellectually superior, off-the-beaten-track, sophisticated. No major research university could ever retire from the lists with equal impunity. Top-ranked universities don't tend to complain about the rankings that put them at the top, and leadership at the Association of American Universities and the Association of Public and Land-grant Universities have been largely reluctant to critique *U.S. News & World Report*.

You could also make the case that *USNWR* does, at least, point you in the general direction of self-improvement, if you read the tea leaves right. In my own case, though I dismissed our fall in the rankings after Katrina as an artifact of the storm, I did take to heart the problem with retention and graduation rates (themselves artifacts of the storm), and worked to ameliorate those troubling numbers to the best of my ability.

If many of the rankings are misleading and many of the measures irrelevant, how can we construct a nuanced and accurate portrait of a school's impact? How can we get a real picture of how graduates are doing, not just economically but in their lives as a whole?[12] The story I began this chapter with—the time-honored story of personal transformation and growth—can also be told another way, with data that influence policies and perceptions.

One promising approach is suggested by the Gallup-Purdue Index, a survey of thirty thousand young adults—with a bachelor's degree or higher, living in the United States—which attempts to measure workplace engagement and general well-being among alumni. One example of the kind of detail that the index pursues: the finding that six experiences in college are linked to superior outcomes for graduates. Three of these have to do with personal relationships with teachers: "a professor who made me feel excited about learning," "professors who cared about me as a person," "a mentor who encouraged me to pursue my goals and dreams." Three others are related to high-impact, engaged activities: "worked on a project that took a semester or more to complete," "had an internship/job that allowed application of classroom learning," "was extremely active in extracurricular activities and organizations." Insights like these help inform decisions about resources, policies, mission, and culture; among other things, they strongly encourage investments in faculty and small student-faculty ratios.[13]

One example of high-impact curricular design is Tulane's TIDES (Tulane Interdisciplinary Experience Seminar) program: all undergraduates participate in a one-credit-hour TIDES seminar during their first year at Tulane. These courses, bringing together small groups of students and faculty to explore the city of New Orleans from multiple academic perspectives, emphasize intellectual challenge, active learning, and social cocurricular activities. The exposure to the culture, history, politics, and ecology of the city, all in an interactive and relational setting, is the kind of immersive experience associated with "superior outcomes" on the Gallup-Purdue Index.

Another nuanced analysis of impact is the Higher Education Quality Council of Ontario (HEQCO) study of Canadian post-secondary performance. The study includes a much broader set of indicators than is common in US metrics, going beyond "inputs" like tuition, expenditures, and access, to "outcomes" like value-to-students and value-to-society. Value-to-students looks at student engagement, literacy and numeracy skills, employment rates, life satisfaction, and physical and mental health. Value-to-society considers job creation, new discoveries (research funding and impact), magnet for talent (prestigious scholarships, international enrollment), and engaged citizens (voting and volunteerism). The study has produced a highly readable chart of outcomes, showing in graphic form the spread between "High performance/low cost" and "Low performance/high cost," with data for all thirty-two indicators reported across all Canadian provinces.

The HEQCO is something for us to aspire to in the States: nuanced qualitative data, plus reliable quantitative data, plus clear communication of clear outcomes, plus nationwide application. The Canadian study, in essence, turns our own metrics upside down. Instead of focusing on inputs to define a school's quality (the "before" snapshot of student achievement or internal features like class size and amenities), the Ontario group emphasized outputs (student satisfaction and public engagement as well as employment and wages) to paint a full portrait of a school's worth.

In contrast, a strictly quantitative approach is being pursued by UMETRICS, an alliance dedicated to "measuring the impacts of research on innovation, competitiveness, and science" in universities. UMETRICS brings together science researchers with university vice presidents from the Midwestern Big Ten plus the University of Chicago[14] and uses data from the federal STAR METRICS project (Science and Technology for America's Reinvestment—Measuring the EffecTs of Research on Innovation, Competitiveness, and Science). STAR METRICS provides detailed information about federal science investments: number of people and time associated with a project, purchase of supplies and equipment, sources of funding and disbursements, and subcontracts with other institutions.

The key purposes of UMETRICS are to create coherent measures through the collaboration of eleven research universities, and to quantify the impact of university research on student flows (the postgraduate lives of students), on regional and national economic spillovers, and on public value (social issues ranging from education to energy to science policy). Ensuring that the data are reliable and accessible is another crucial aim, in order to help administrators decide what to fund and to help individual scientists identify promising research areas or collaborators.

Involved in all this data collection and data mining is Julia Lane of the American Institutes for Research, who was a founder of STAR METRICS. She focuses on quantifying impact through revealing statistics and smart metrics—and "smart" is the operative word. For example, she doesn't believe that counting publications is a useful measure of scientific productivity, because it biases scientists to get on a treadmill and simply keep pumping out more articles—not a very good indicator of creativity, innovation, or impact. Rather than look at numbers of academic papers, she thinks a better measure of the real impact of research is "student flows": trained graduates and postdocs moving into, and enriching, other areas of the economy with their knowledge.[15]

All these efforts, from the qualitative survey to a strict focus on graduates' salaries, help us evaluate and measure school performance. But it does seem to me that while we're awaiting better metrics and more reliable data, we still can talk intelligently about impact, in the ordinary sense of a substantial or meaningful effect, and perhaps change public perceptions about the value of a degree. I'm going to focus on a few cases here because I believe the stories of institutions—large and small, with various student populations, diverse missions, and distinct regional cultures—are profoundly revealing of what is working well in our colleges and universities, and what isn't.

My first example is a fellow New Orleans institution: Xavier University of Louisiana, a historically black school with an enrollment of three thousand. That Xavier is small and highly distinctive only makes its social contribution all the more remarkable. The only Catholic institution among the one hundred or so historically black colleges and universities in the country—all founded in response to the segregation of higher education prior to *Brown v. Board of Education* in 1954—Xavier has a "facts and figures" page on its website that is the very definition of impact. (Xavier, like most institutions, does use rankings to make its case, but in contrast to some of the spurious ratings out there, these are truly illuminating numbers.) A few excerpts will suffice: Xavier leads the nation in awarding degrees to African American students in the biological and medical sciences and in physics and the physical sciences. It also leads in the number of African American graduates who go on to complete medical school; it is number 3 for graduates who go on to earn a PhD in science and engineering, and among the top four colleges of pharmacy in graduating African Americans with a doctor of pharmacy degree.[16]

Little school, big impact. In a sense, the school's remarkable achievements are a sad comment on the state of educational equality in this country. Though the percentage of African American students attending graduate schools has increased in the last decade,[17] our flagship public universities and elite colleges have largely been less effective than tiny Xavier in promoting upward social mobility among black Americans. Two things account for Xavier's success: first, an intensely focused mission that sparked innovation and clarified decision making; and, second, a truly transformative leader who had the vision and the persistence to fulfill that mission. Norman Francis, who stepped down in 2015 after forty-seven years as president of Xavier, hired J. W. Carmichael to head the premed program back in the 1970s and created a science curriculum that has bred these astonishing results. Recognizing that most of Xavier's students came (and still come) from low-income families and from high schools that prepare them poorly for college, Francis and Carmichael developed a mentoring system using study groups to encourage shared responsibility for success, and established a uniform curriculum in freshman chemistry and biology using faculty-written workbooks that break down complicated material and specify information in stepwise increments.[18] Without huge resources or fancy buildings or equipment, Xavier has consistently been one of the nation's largest conduits for black doctors and scientists, a genuine contribution to the public good. It has kept its tuition low ($19K) because so many of its students have limited financial resources, and provides financial aid to 87 percent of its undergraduate student body.

Xavier's "facts and figures" page is full of numbers, but the subtext is a narrative. The school's mission of bringing black students into the middle class by means of professional training produces measurable results, but it also changes lives, addressing an issue of enormous societal importance student by student, year by year.

If Xavier has accomplished much with little, the opposite end of the spectrum—big school, big impact—is also revealing of what is actually working in our universities. Stanford, though once a rural backwater, is now the epicenter of Silicon Valley, and that relationship between a large research university and world-changing technology is an essential aspect of higher education in a competitive global setting. From the outset, Stanford had a nontraditional approach. It accepted women as well as men at a time when most private universities were all male; it was nondenominational, as opposed to the mass of schools that had religious affiliations; and its aim, pointedly practical, was to produce useful citizens rather than turn out cultured members of an intellectual elite. When the school opened its doors in 1891, its first president, David Starr Jordan, said to the inaugural class, "It is for us as teachers and students in the university's first year to lay the foundations of a school which may last as long as human civilization . . . It is hallowed by no traditions; it is hampered by none. Its finger posts all point forward."[19]

Over the decades, the "finger posts" have pointed the way to astonishing new frontiers, largely through a burgeoning relationship between research scientists and entrepreneurship. A condensed description of how that relationship developed: Frederick Terman, an MIT-trained electrical engineer and former chair of Stanford's engineering department, became provost in 1955 and instituted a program of "steeples of excellence." At a time when the university had a poorly paid faculty and little room for growth, Terman saw the government's growing support of research as an opportunity; he drew top-notch scientists to the university who then went on to win government funding and grants, thereby allowing the hiring of more outstanding faculty.

The connection to industry goes back to 1939 and the almost-mythic founding of Hewlett-Packard by two Stanford graduates, literally in a garage (and Terman was there from the start, bringing Bill Hewlett back to Stanford from MIT to join forces with Dave Packard, who had been working for GE). HP's first product, born in that garage, was an audio oscillator. The "start-up" model held over the next six decades, leading to a series of groundbreaking innovations: in the 1950s, microwave electronics; in the 1960s, semiconductors and integrated circuits; in the 1980s, the rise of personal computers; in the 1990s, the explosion of the Internet. Over the last five decades, Stanford faculty and graduates have started twelve hundred companies, and over 50 percent of Silicon Valley products have originated in the companies of Stanford alumni—among them such innovations as Google and Yahoo. The university has generated numerous patents, and members of its faculty sit on multiple tech company boards or serve as consultants or chief technology officers.[20]

Stanford has achieved this level of impact, fulfilling its fundamental mission of producing useful citizens—"useful" is an understatement—by creating an environment that rewards creativity, disruptive thinking, entrepreneurial risk, and teamwork. Other factors contributing to the successful partnership between the university and Silicon Valley are the significant number of PhDs, the availability of venture capital, university and government support of research, faculty leave of up to two years to take industry jobs and then return to the university, law firms specializing in technology, open forums for exchange of information among competing companies, nonhierarchical organizational structures that reflect a collaborative spirit, and—big plus—the quality of life that California offers. By now, there is an established feedback loop, whereby Stanford faculty who departed for industry come back later and train grad students, who push the frontiers themselves.

And there is room for the trial and error that characterizes a research orientation. One example: Sebastian Thrun, a Stanford faculty member, left to found Udacity, a purveyor of MOOCs, massive open online courses, meant to be a pathway to a degree for those who can't afford the full price of a residential college. Courses had a fee of $150, and San Jose State University launched an experimental partnership with Udacity to count these courses for credit. After a year, the failure rate was high and the dropout rate even higher, so SJSU ended the Udacity contract. After this defeat, Thrun rethought the proposition that online courses could replace conventional classrooms and reconfigured Udacity. Now it offers "nanodegrees" in highly technical areas like software coding, giving both high school and college graduates high-demand market-ready skills.[21]

It should also be said that Stanford is more than "Startup U." It has a robust liberal arts environment that features interdisciplinary majors like CS+X, combining the study of computer science (CS) with a humanities discipline (X), and a broad-based emphasis on critical thinking, problem solving, and design.[22] The university has also made strides in access and diversity, making the list of top twenty schools on the College Access Index on the basis of two figures: the percentage of freshmen who are Pell recipients and go on to graduate, and the net price paid by students whose families make between $40,000 and $75,000 per year.[23]

Another top-ranked school on the College Access Index is Amherst, one of the most prestigious liberal arts colleges in the country (and often number 1 on the *USNWR* rankings of small colleges). Founded in 1821 as a school for "the education of indigent young men of piety and talents," it has stayed true to its mission of helping the needy, and in the last fifteen years has instituted policies that guaranteed a more diverse student population than almost all schools in its category (small, liberal arts, selective) across the country. First in the nation to eliminate loans for low-income students in 1999 under the leadership of dean of financial aid Joe Paul Case, Amherst began to replace all student loans with financial aid scholarships in 2008 and extended need-blind admission to international students. The school is also strongly committed to community engagement and has significant economic impact locally, apart from its excellence academically.[24]

I've picked a few schools to name, plucking examples from a hat, but there is a plethora to choose from. I merely wanted to illustrate the wide range of highly effective schools, from historically black college to large research university to small liberal arts college, and to give credit to visionary leaders, including Norman Francis at Xavier, Frederick Terman at Stanford, and Joe Paul Case at Amherst, who crafted meaningful and transformative policies that substantially changed things.

The larger point: higher education, though clearly not a monolith, is adding to the public good in myriad places in myriad ways.

We're not a system on the brink of extinction, as some suggest. It's true we have genuine problems: spiraling costs, rising debt, employers doubting that graduates have the skills they need, and graduates unemployed or in low-wage jobs. Because of these problems, critics offer sweeping pronouncements about the end of college and offer various cure-alls: we need to go all digital, we need more vocational programs, we need to abolish tenure, we need a financial restructuring of the whole system. I agree that the problems are real, but the rhetoric is exaggerated. The sweeping pronouncements are too sweeping. We aren't looking at the things we do well. We aren't addressing specific problems in specific ways. And we're ignoring our history.

Beginning with the Morrill Act of 1862, which, as mentioned earlier, funded state colleges with public land grants, our system of higher education has been a global leader in educating the nation's citizenry—a crucial element for a democracy, and a matter of "public justice," according to Justin Smith Morrill's argument for passage of the bill on the floor of Congress. (The land grants were extended to the Confederate States after the end of the Civil War, and expanded to include separate land grants to institutions for people of color—the historically black colleges and universities—in the second Morrill Act of 1890.) Originally dedicated to "agriculture and the mechanic arts," practical knowledge that would improve communities, these acts have been the foundation of our prosperous middle class and the expansion of opportunity to all. We cannot cease investing in this realm if we're to continue our preeminence in the world economically and as leaders in innovation and research. We need to realize the dream of opportunity and upward mobility for another generation, through nuts-and-bolts problem solving, continued financial investment, and creative leadership.

And, yes, we need to measure our impact "holistically" and with greater precision—to pinpoint exactly where we're succeeding and exactly where we need to improve. We need to expand our longitudinal data to take into account what happens after graduation; to collect qualitative data that illuminate personal satisfaction and contribution to society; to use valid and appropriate metrics and give less weight to categories like "reputation" and "alumni giving"; and, a vital point, to consider the mission of an individual institution when assessing its value and impact. "Be true to your school" isn't just a pep rally slogan; it's crucial advice to those making decisions about a university's future directions—a reminder to respect the core identity of the institution. Though some parameters like retention and graduation rates are relevant to everyone, other measures of success are specific to a school's unique character.

And a final caveat: some things that count can't be counted. Metrics will never be the whole answer to our problems; their prime importance is that they help to tell a story of value and impact, a story that university presidents need to reclaim. Leaders tend to use the best evidence available but also a creative intuition—call it a vision—of what will work; they're the ones who make the decisions and forge the path ahead. It is those stories of character in action that you will find in the coming pages—stories that illuminate the problems and celebrate the accomplishments of our priceless array of colleges and universities, still the envy of the world.

2

Door Wide Open

If the sector doesn't find ways to reflect the varied
segments of the population and at the same time make
college more affordable, our institutions will become
bastions of privilege and tradition rather than incubators
of fresh perspectives and necessary innovations.

I was recently reflecting on my early years as president of Tulane when I stumbled on materials relating to the university's mission, vision, and strategy, including an action plan from July 2000 entitled "Creating Tulane's Future: A Distinguished University as Distinctive as New Orleans." In those years, my emphasis was on making the university precisely that: "distinguished" and "distinctive." I worked to enhance the quality of academic programs and research, raise the profile of incoming classes, boost fund-raising, organize the many complex systems involved in the smooth operation of the university's day-to-day life, and partner with the communities in which we lived and worked. In the strategic report of 2000, "diversity," the subject of this chapter, is the charge given to a university-wide Diversity and Equity Task Force in order to ensure an environment of openness and inclusiveness at the university and to pursue hiring policies that reflected that aim.

Looking at this document from more than seventeen years ago, I'm reminded of one of the disappointments of my presidency: in my sixteen years as president (1998–2014), I was unable to significantly enhance the diversity of the full-time student body, staff, and faculty. Forces pushing the school in other directions included, first and foremost, the intense focus on redefinition after

Hurricane Katrina and the urgent task of reestablishing the university's reputation and distinctiveness. My failure to strengthen campus diversity remains a regret. Why couldn't Tulane significantly change the composition of the full-time student body, especially in terms of young people of color?

We did try to move the dial on diversity in several different ways. For example, we started a summer transition program for local high school students, many of whom were African American, to help them prepare for the demands of a four-year college or university. We also entered into partnerships with several national college access and completion programs and expanded our need-based financial aid offerings through a no-loan scholarship and microscholarships that students can accumulate during their high school years.

Still, despite these efforts, Tulane's full-time undergraduate student body remained almost three-quarters Caucasian, and the number of students of color, particularly African Americans, and of students who are eligible to receive Pell Grants did not increase significantly. The only true success story was our School of Continuing Studies, which targets part-time students, approximately half of whom are minority students. But the question remained: Why weren't our intentions and actions translating into manifest results in the full-time undergraduate student body?

I turned to Tulane's head of admissions to help me unravel this. One set of data that he shared with me stood out. Compared to our peer institutions in the South, we were doing fine when it came to the number of applications from students of color, and we were accepting a higher percentage of students of color than most of our Southern peers. Unfortunately, many of the applications we received were incomplete and consequently couldn't be processed.[1] But the fundamental problem for us was not applicants but student yield, that is, the number of African American applicants who got accepted and actually decided to enroll at Tulane. We found ourselves near the bottom when we compared our black enrollment numbers with those of our Southern peer institutions.

In all likelihood, the black students who were accepted to Tulane but chose not to come had also received acceptance letters from higher-ranked schools, or they had been offered better financial aid packages elsewhere, or they chose schools that were known to have a more inclusive culture than Tulane's. The perception of exclusivity is very difficult to change; that elitist reputation, though perhaps accurate historically, did not reflect our newer efforts to become a more diverse and welcoming environment. At the same time, to be frank, we were not courageous or innovative enough to move the dial on diversity. Another reason for Tulane's homogeneity was, as mentioned, the goal of being recognized as one of the outstanding private research institutions of higher education in the country, a subset of schools celebrated precisely for their selectivity and exclusivity. We were vying with our competitors for resources, the best and brightest students (typically determined by SAT/ACT scores and high school grades), and boast-worthy spots in the rankings, however flawed such lists may be. (You'll remember from chapter 1 that "selectivity," a measure of how many applicants are rejected, is a key metric in the *USNWR* standings.) This race to the top is, practically speaking, the name of the game, but at the same time a barrier to innovation and, in many cases, to diversity, especially in the area of undergraduate admission standards. The truth is we had contradictory aims that, in the end, subverted the goal of diversifying the student body. The goal of enhancing Tulane's academic reputation and rising in the public's estimation determined the choices we ultimately made, to the detriment of our other aspirations.

Reflecting on my own participation in this arms race, I've thought about the reframing that's required by all schools in the United States as we confront a newly emerging reality. When I talk about a paradigm shift, or a tipping point, in higher education, diversity is one of the areas where such a shift is most evident. The population of our country has changed over the last decades, with a rise in people who identify as Hispanic or Latino (we will soon be a majority-minority nation, demographers predict); growing income inequality (along with sky-high costs for college); and a resurgence of identity politics, with individuals defining themselves by party affiliation, religion, sexual orientation, race, ethnicity, and socioeconomic class. Recent political shifts in the United States have highlighted a neglected demographic of low-income students who come from rural, economically depressed areas of the nation.[2] Mission, vision, and strategic plans from fifteen or twenty years ago are inevitably outdated given this era of seismic shifts, and university leaders all across the country are now confronting critical issues of recruitment, admission, and inclusion of students from disadvantaged and nontraditional backgrounds. If the sector doesn't find ways to reflect the varied segments of the population and at the same time make college more affordable, our institutions will become bastions of privilege and tradition rather than incubators of fresh perspectives and necessary innovations.

At Tulane, our most effective step toward transforming our full-time undergraduate student body was a partnership with the Posse Foundation, founded by Debbie Bial. Her story, in brief: Lamont, a former student of hers at an after-school program in the Bronx, was back on the streets after a brief stint at an elite college, where he'd won a scholarship. Debbie asked what happened, and Lamont said, "I never would have dropped out of college if I'd had my posse with me." That one remark was the germ of Posse, a nationwide college access program that seeks out and then supports underrepresented students with proven leadership abilities, sending them in groups of ten ("posses") from major US cities to partner schools across the country. Many top-tier institutions are using partnerships—with Posse and other programs that identify academically qualified but disadvantaged students—to help solve the problem of homogeneous campuses while maintaining and continuing to improve retention and graduation rates.

Our results with Posse students have been outstanding, suggesting that success in college depends on more than test scores and where you went to high school. The challenge now is to bring these results with Posse or similar initiatives to scale, even though such attempts may have an adverse impact on rankings. Efforts to increase diversity and access also require resources, especially because a disproportionate percentage of underrepresented students also overlap with those in the lowest socioeconomic levels. What's needed is a major financial commitment by schools that makes diversity a primary institutional goal. Letting go of policies that win a school top rankings comes at a price, and changing direction takes courage and a sense of purpose. I believe that spelling out one's commitments in a strategic plan is a first step: pick the words you intend to live by, and then live by them.

The stories in this chapter describe leaders in distinctive circumstances who have committed themselves to initiatives that focus on urban youth, low-income students, applicants from rural backwaters, high achievers whose résumés are atypical, and other groups underrepresented on college campuses. Their efforts illustrate four strategies that are having a significant impact: first, improve the pipeline by collaborating with high schools and community colleges as they help students navigate college prep courses and the complex application process; second, change the methods of assessment in order to recruit and enroll talented students overlooked by the current system of admissions; third, develop novel approaches to funding and scholarship aid that will make it possible for underrepresented students to afford a college degree; and, fourth, learn from what the innovators are doing to address the issue of diversity. Some of those innovators may even be at your own college or university.

Though old habits die hard, and though the arc of change is long, the stories that follow indicate we are in a transformative moment, one that will open the door to the diverse young people who are the nation's future. The battle about diversity is being fought on all fronts right now, including our electoral politics. It's my belief, forged in my own unsuccessful struggle with this issue, that higher education should be in the forefront of social change, meeting new realities and constructing a path that is both necessary and right.

Before describing current efforts to increase diversity and access, I want to sketch the history behind them. How did we get to this "tipping point"? Fifty years ago, the word "diversity" primarily signified race.[3] The notion that we are postracial, an idea expressed by Supreme Court Chief Justice John Roberts, has not been borne out by recent events, including police shootings and the #BlackLivesMatter campaign, many incidents of racial unrest on campuses, and the affirmative action case argued before the Supreme Court in 2016. "Affirmative action"—first used by John F. Kennedy to describe active measures to end job discrimination in the federal government, and later applied to admissions policies in higher education—rests on the notion of the state's compelling interest in a vibrant diverse society that adheres to its founding belief in equality. Apart from the phrase itself, the idea goes back to the Civil War; during Reconstruction, General William Tecumseh Sherman awarded every freed slave in Georgia "forty acres and a mule" in recompense for the grave injustices that slaves had endured.

But redressing historical injustice wasn't simple then—Jim Crow laws undid much of the work of Reconstruction and nearly a hundred years elapsed before the desegregation of schools and the passage of the Civil Rights Act—and it isn't simple now. The notions of redress, fairness, and equitable representation are inevitably influenced by the cultural moment, and we are now, as mentioned, living in the midst of a notable demographic shift. Affirmative action emerged in the 1960s, at the same time as the black power movement, and the focus on African American prerogatives reflects that specific time. Even then the policy faced opposition, including legal challenges: Supreme Court decisions starting in the 1970s and continuing to 2003 suggest an ongoing tension between the desire for racial justice and strict adherence to the equal protection clause of the Fourteenth Amendment, which leads opponents to charge reverse discrimination.[4]

The most recent Supreme Court case, *Fisher v. University of Texas* (2016), a suit brought by Abigail Fisher alleging an infringement of her rights as a qualified nonminority candidate, highlighted, among other things, the theory of "mismatch," which proposes that affirmative action is ultimately harmful to students admitted to elite colleges and universities, because they tend to be at the lower end of the grade distribution in most courses, and either drop out or fail to succeed in their chosen profession.[5] However, an amicus brief filed with the court in 2013, written by a group of leading social scientists and statisticians, has convincingly discredited the original paper on mismatch because of a host of invalid comparisons, false assumptions, and unwarranted causal inferences. The brief cites evidence of higher earnings for minority graduates of elite institutions,[6] and other research suggests that students, both black and white, are most likely to graduate if they attend the most selective institutions that admit them.[7]

Many offer personal testimony about the extensive benefits of affirmative action, for individuals and for society as a whole. Carole Carmichael, for example—one of seventy-seven students admitted to NYU as a Martin Luther King Scholar after King's assassination and currently a visiting journalism fellow at the Russell Sage Foundation in New York City—writes, "We discovered that our NYU degree was the first step on a ladder that allowed many of us to rise to the pinnacle in the professional fields of law, medicine, education, technology, engineering, aerospace, public service and journalism, leaving a lasting imprint on America. We defied failure. We stayed in school and earned our degrees."[8]

In addition to personal accounts like these, research points to enhanced learning for both minorities and nonminorities in a diverse setting. Students reported increased intellectual engagement and performed better on tasks like essay writing and reading comprehension, which involve complex cognitive processes, and on standardized tests of critical thinking. They were also more likely to continue civic engagement activities (voting and participating in political or community groups) after graduating.[9]

Whatever its benefits, the fate of affirmative action is still not completely settled. Some states have decided to ban affirmative action at public flagship universities (Michigan, Arizona, California, and elsewhere); among private institutions, uncertainty remains about which admissions policies will be deemed legal in the future. One novel approach: the University of Michigan has made substantial efforts to offset the negative effects of the ban on affirmative action—African American enrollment at Michigan has dropped 33 percent in recent years—by increasing its "yield," that is, the number of accepted minority students who ultimately come to the university.[10]

Another approach to the problem of increasing diversity without using race as a factor is to substitute socioeconomic class for race, given that poverty and minority status go hand in hand, and given the increasing economic inequities of our society. Low income is clearly a disadvantage: only 9.4 percent of students from families with income below $33,000 receive bachelor's degrees from four-year institutions. Some observers suggest that class is a more important determinant of disadvantage than race.[11]

QuestBridge is a college access program that focuses solely on high-achieving low-income students: the financial requirement is that the household income is below $65,000 (and often less than $50,000) for a family of four; and the academic criteria include high GPA in rigorous courses, class rank in the top 5–10 percent, SAT scores above 1270 and ACT above 26, and strong essays and recommendations. The initiative was fueled by the fact that significant numbers of low-income students are academically outstanding yet often fail to apply to top-tier schools.[12] QuestBridge is one of those partnerships used by premier institutions—places like Columbia, Princeton, Swarthmore, and Amherst—to recruit diverse students who are academically qualified and desirous of success; their College Match program for seniors allows students and schools to find each other through a ranking of preferences.

The efforts of QuestBridge to bring outstanding first-generation students to a range of campuses have brought needed attention to the area of socioeconomic disadvantage. However, according to some researchers, substituting class for race as the chief marker of disadvantage seems to come at the cost of racial diversity. Several studies, including a review of Israel's class-based admissions policy, suggest that such a policy doesn't increase minority representation on campuses, and in fact reduces it.[13] Some efforts in the United States focusing on income have apparently failed to improve minority enrollment. (Though some have: Vassar College, which won a million-dollar award for increasing economic diversity, has increased its percentage of students of color from 20 to 33 percent, even if its demographics still aren't where they should be.)[14] Dennis Parker of the American Civil Liberties Union Racial Justice Program is among those who argue that socioeconomic diversity is ultimately an inadequate proxy for racial diversity. As he puts it, "The significance of race goes far beyond just the color of your skin. It deals with opportunities you have. It deals with barriers you have faced. And it's unrealistic to say that you can deal with discrimination by pretending that it doesn't exist."[15]

In short: it's complicated. Though it's tempting to reach for across-the-board solutions, there is no single method that will ensure broad equitable access nationwide. The problem admissions offices face is how to slice the pie—who deserves what, who gets what—when not all agree on the definition of "disadvantage" or "diversity," when the research is still unclear, and when no admissions policy in the country can fully represent, or satisfy, the many segments of the nation that suffer from some form of discrimination or hardship.

Despite the complexities and questions, efforts to be more inclusive are continuing on campuses across the country in order to keep pace with an inarguable social reality. At this moment, income inequality is much in the news: recent shifts in the political climate have focused attention on the white working class, which, primarily because of a loss of manufacturing jobs and the rise of a tech economy in an era of globalization, has experienced significant financial distress. But race, too, remains a burning issue. The 2014 shooting of Michael Brown, an unarmed black teenager, by the police in Ferguson, Missouri, along with other such deaths in other cities, touched off the Black Lives Matter movement, and a student protest at the University of Missouri criticizing President Timothy Wolfe and involving a threatened boycott by the predominantly black football team ended in Wolfe's resignation. Since then racial strife has been roiling our campuses, with students sitting in, going on hunger strikes, and presenting lists of demands to administrations. In response, administrators at Mizzou and elsewhere have been holding town halls to hear complaints, organizing committees to investigate "campus climate," offering sessions on diversity and inclusion, and reexamining their recruitment practices.[16]

A few cases will illustrate how college and university leaders are attempting to respond to this latest crisis. At Amherst College—interestingly, one of the most diverse liberal arts colleges in the country, where only 42 percent of the student body is white, and which, as noted earlier, ranks at the top of the College Access Index—student protesters calling themselves the "Amherst Uprising" generated a list of demands during a sit-in at Frost Library, where many minority students spoke eloquently of chronic slights and insults. Canceling a scheduled trip, President Carolyn "Biddy" Martin returned immediately to the campus and met with students. Soon after, in an open letter to the community, she responded with admirable sensitivity and clarity to the issues at hand. Referring to the students who spoke of their experiences of prejudice, she said, "That pain is real . . . What we have heard requires a concerted, rigorous, and sustained response."

Martin, invoking the principle of shared governance, encouraged thoughtful deliberation about the conflict between cultural sensitivity and free speech: "The commitments to freedom of inquiry and expression and to inclusivity are not mutually exclusive, in principle, but they can and do come into conflict with one another. Honoring both is the challenge we have to meet together, as a community. It is a challenge that all of higher education needs to meet." She concludes with a list of steps the administration will take—more diverse staff and faculty, innovative ways of teaching, support of dialogue and reflection, the provision of spaces for interaction, and the establishment of a committee on race and racial injury.

In response, the Amherst Uprising sent a letter acknowledging that the demands were made "in haste," in a moment of "urgency and emotion," and announcing the end of their sit-in after meeting with President Martin and realizing that their goals "would be best met by collaboration with administrators, faculty, and staff over an extended period of time, rather than through immediate action."[17]

In short: reason prevailed. And in a development soon afterward, the Board of Trustees took action on one of the students' original demands, the removal of Lord Jeffery Amherst as the unofficial mascot of the school. The protesters regarded "Lord Jeff" as a proponent of genocidal germ warfare: as a commander in the French and Indian War, he wrote a letter recommending the eradication of Native Americans through the distribution of smallpox-infested blankets. Cullen Murphy, chairman of the Board of Trustees, said of the decision to drop the mascot that the board wouldn't try to impose its position on anyone else. "Beyond that, people will do as they will. The college has no business interfering with free expression, whether spoken or written or, for that matter, sung. Period. We hope and anticipate that understanding and respect will run in all directions."[18]

At Yale, another school striving for cultural sensitivity, an email from an associate master about excessive policing of Halloween costumes caused an outcry, with students itemizing the "microaggressions" they met with every day on campus. Jonathan Holloway, the first black dean of Yale College, reflected that this generation of students seems to be somewhat less resilient than past ones, but thinks feelings of anguish are understandable—perhaps inevitable—in an environment where privileged students come together with those from very different circumstances against a background of persistent racial inequality.[19] Working-class and first-generation students are sometimes antagonistic to campus movements devoted to identity issues, considering such preoccupations self-centered and self-indulgent. It should be said, though this is a particularly precarious moment, that our campuses have always been the scene of uprisings and protests, marches and rallies. The college years mark a time when students are moving out of adolescence and into adulthood—a time when, very often, idealism is tinged with self-righteousness and moral absolutism.

How can university leaders help everyone get along? Not just in a spirit of kumbaya, glossing over differences, but in a deeper way: considering other points of view, engaging in dialogue, emerging with a capacity to think deeply and acknowledge more than one truth. Right now, Tulane is holding town hall meetings where students can air their grievances and express their feelings—a first step, but clearly not enough. In addition to emotional catharsis, there's a need for engagement, discussion, and self-reflection. As at the University of Missouri, we need task forces, committees, conversations both formal and informal, and a set of concrete actions to move beyond diversity as measured by enrollment to an inclusive, integrated environment.

We also need to change university culture, which, on many campuses, has devolved into "affinity groups," "themed living arrangements," and "self-affirming enclaves" that isolate students from each other. Davidson College in North Carolina has made attempts to integrate these subgroups through campus organizations and off-campus trips that orchestrate exchanges between diverse students, black and white, religious and atheist, Republican and Democrat. Denison College in Ohio uses special funds to support campus groups that host events with dissimilar groups and is reexamining the layout of the school with the idea that "quads" could become "public squares" where students cross paths and mingle.[20]

Meanwhile, ironically, historically black colleges and universities, founded in the nineteenth century in response to segregation, are losing funding and enrollment because students have migrated to supposedly integrated campuses—which, in practice, consist of separate, and largely self-created, "safe spaces." Framingham State University has coined a pointedly contrary phrase, "Brave Spaces," for a program focused on inclusion that encourages intermingling of disparate groups.

I've made a wide circuit, encompassing the history of affirmative action and the problems that arise when diverse students come together on a campus, but to return to my main theme: How do we get such students on campus in the first place? One approach (the first of the "four strategies" I mentioned at the outset) is to collaborate with secondary schools in order to prepare disadvantaged students for college and help them navigate the application process. The problem of qualified students who don't apply— addressed by the QuestBridge mission, as described above—has been the focus of an initiative at the Cowen Institute at Tulane University. Amanda Kruger Hill, current director of the institute, founded a consortium for high school counselors in order to discuss and implement best practices, with a first aim of getting more students to complete the FAFSA, the Free Application for Federal Student Aid. Amanda helped develop a website that serves as a portal for seniors from all New Orleans and Atlanta high schools, where counselors can see online how many of their students have completed the FAFSA, and redouble their efforts if the number is low. Counselors also have access to an online "best practices" tool kit, including guidelines for hosting an evening with parents to help them complete their tax returns, a requirement of the FAFSA. This might sound a bit unspectacular as a step toward greater diversity, but the truth is, the FAFSA is a daunting first hurdle for large numbers of high-achieving low-income students.

Another approach to improving the college readiness of disadvantaged students is "early college." Stephen Tremaine, founding director of Bard Early College in New Orleans, points to the disconnect between secondary and postsecondary institutions and cites "one of the most disastrous statistics in American education: In 2009, 89% of first-generation college students left college before earning a degree."[21] At Bard Early College in New Orleans (BECNO), eleventh and twelfth graders spend half of every school day as undergraduates of Bard College, enrolled in demanding for-credit college courses; these students complete the first year of a Bard education during the last two years of high school. Over 98 percent of BECNO alumni have been accepted to colleges and universities, schools such as Emory, Bates, and Swarthmore, as well as first-tier institutions in Louisiana. Since 2011, over 95 percent have remained enrolled in college and on track to graduate. The average financial aid and scholarship award to a BECNO student applying to college is $30,240.[22]

Other initiatives provide college preparation for high school students through wraparound academic and social services. College Track—founded by Laurene Powell Jobs and Carlos Watson, with branches throughout California, two in Colorado, and one in New Orleans—provides after-school and summer programming from ninth to twelfth grade for low-income students, covering study skills, standardized test preparation, extracurricular enrichment, tutoring, college application guidance, financial advising, and college matching, plus a dedicated adviser, once the student is on campus, who helps access university support services. High school counselors are themselves becoming more proactive in some parts of the country, for example rural Texas, where efforts are being made to match outstanding students with the Ivies, through help with applications, phone calls to admissions offices, trips to the East Coast, and oral history projects that encourage those who do graduate from top schools to return to their local communities.[23]

One more approach to bridging the gap between high school and college is an "articulation agreement," a feeder program whereby graduates of two-year associate degree programs at community colleges are guaranteed acceptance at state universities as transfer students.[24] The arrangement makes financial sense: students pay low tuition for their first two years and save on housing and travel costs, and community colleges and state schools save by sharing support services, faculty, and facilities. It also makes educational sense, giving students a gradual introduction to college-level work, with time to gain confidence, refine their focus, and extend (or discover) a love of learning.[25]

A second strategy for building diverse student bodies focuses on how admissions offices assess ability. These programs move beyond the current definition of "merit," offering ways to identify talents not always evident on a standard application form. To go back for a moment to Debbie Bial, the founder of the Posse Foundation: she had the insight that the tests for diversity, whether racial or economic, had an aura of charity, so that the beneficiaries were in some sense victims in need of support—they were "at risk," "needy," "disadvantaged." She decided to go toward already-existing strengths and the many thousands of diverse high school students from a range of ethnic and socio-economic backgrounds who were not "at risk" but outstanding, with proven merit—although not always by the conventional metrics of test scores, class rank, or quality of secondary school, measures that overwhelmingly favor white and Asian students. Why not find, recruit, and support these students on the basis of their demonstrated merit and leadership ability rather than on the basis of need? Why not educate them at elite institutions so that, en masse, they could radically change the workplace—so that senators, CEOs, presidents of universities, law partners, heads of departments of medicine, and so on, across all disciplines and careers, could cease being more than 90 percent white and male and become more representative of our increasingly diverse society?

To achieve these aims, Posse has developed an assessment process to identify talent and intellect that standard measures sometimes fail to capture. Debbie Bial points out that admission decisions are, in practice, far from objective, with committees weighing class composition—the need, say, for a violinist for the orchestra—against class rank or test results. Posse's Dynamic Assessment Process was created with a more nuanced understanding of ability than "plays the violin" or "has a 4.0 GPA." The DAP sets up an environment where observers evaluate kids performing tasks "on the fly" alongside peers—making robots out of Legos, developing a conversation about genetics testing in four minutes, quickly putting together a public service announcement in front of a hundred people. Activities like these show sophisticated thinking, creative improvisation, teamwork, leadership skills, and problem-solving ability.[26]

The Dynamic Assessment Process is not an effort to take over college admissions but an attempt to help recruiters find the diverse kids they claim they want. To widen the net of opportunity even further, the foundation has established Posse Access, a database available to admissions offices at Posse partner schools that lists the names of Posse candidates who didn't win scholarships but are nonetheless outstanding leaders and motivated learners.[27] And the program has achieved notable success. Posse publications are filled with stories of newly elected scholars who are leaders of their high schools and communities. To take a single example, Janeya Cunningham from Chicago's South Side (DePauw University, class of 2019) organized a peace march at her high school in response to local gun violence that has since become an annual community event, and is herself the subject of a documentary on student activism. Once at college, Posse Scholars continue to shine, winning Fulbrights, fellowships, internships, and research grants and assuming leadership roles on campus.[28]

Posse may be a harbinger of change in admissions policies across the country. A number of schools are experimenting with innovations in how they assess applicants. Goucher College offers the option of submitting a two-minute video, plus essays, rather than a standard transcript; Bard College invites applicants to submit four twenty-five-hundred-word essays in response to questions (an online "Entrance Exam") as an alternative to a regular application; and Bennington College provides the opportunity to submit a "Dimensional Application" consisting of a student's portfolio, with or without high school transcript and with the sole requirement being that the submitted work creates "a portrait of what you bring to the Bennington community."[29]

A program at Southern Vermont College, Pipelines into Partnership, is specifically modeled on Posse but with modifications accommodating the fact that Southern Vermont (unlike Posse partner schools) is not considered an elite institution. In 2011 Karen Gross, an education reformer and president of SVC at the time, announced a plan to identify promising students who were being overlooked by other colleges—students with "fire in the belly"—and reached out to colleges, foundations, and specific schools and community organizations ("sending institutions"), among them KIPP (Knowledge Is Power Program) charter schools in places like Harlem and the Bronx (with nominations from Jane Martínez Dowling, executive director of KIPP Through College) to create the Pipelines program. Among the seventeen students in the program's first year, all were black, Latino, or of mixed race; 94 percent were Pell eligible; and 65 percent were the first in their families to go to college. The cohort's average SAT score was 865, with an average high-school GPA of 2.66 (with individuals ranging from 1.18 to 3.36). All but one student reenrolled the following fall, holding out promise for a high retention rate.

A typical story at Southern Vermont involves a student from the Academy for Young Writers in Brooklyn, who was strongly recommended by the principal because of her evident talent in spite of a traumatic background (both parents had died of drug addiction) and low SAT scores. Her performance at SVC has been outstanding. Basically, SVC bets on the whole person and offers the refuge of a private college, far from the city and from intense family needs. It also supplies money: full scholarships come from a combination of Pell Grants, private donors, and the Helmsley Charitable Trust.[30]

The search for "the whole person" has led some schools to lessen the emphasis on scores and statistics in the evaluation process. More than eight hundred colleges and universities are now "test optional": these institutions do not require SAT or ACT scores, though they will consider them if the student wants to provide them. Forty-six percent of top-tier liberal arts colleges and a significant number of large research universities are in this group, ranging from Temple and George Washington Universities to Wesleyan, Brandeis, and Bryn Mawr. Test scores, as Debbie Bial and others have noted, are stacked in favor of those who go to excellent secondary schools and who have the background to excel on a test with cultural and class biases, plus the means to hire tutors and take the test multiple times.

Minority applicants increase at many test-optional schools, and the policy can be seen as an attempt to widen the pool of applicants in the hope of enhancing campus diversity.[31] A test-blind approach—in which admissions officers don't consider test scores even if applicants submit them—is an even more committed step toward a nonstatistical admissions process, but it's not an easy or cost-free step. Sarah Lawrence College was test blind for ten years but went back to test optional because being unranked in *U.S. News & World Report* put it at a major competitive disadvantage in relation to its peers. Because of its particular niche as a small, selective liberal arts school, the rankings (and attendant national recognition) proved to be a decisive factor in the policy reversal.[32]

In contrast, Hampshire College, a small school in Amherst, Massachusetts, and among the first in the country to go test optional, is now firmly committed to a test-blind admissions policy because of studies showing that entrance exams are biased against low-income students and lack any predictive value in terms of college performance. The school has added two essays and a graded high school paper to the application requirements, allowing a look at the whole student instead of simply scores and grades. The first year was a great success according to Meredith Twombly, dean of enrollment and retention, with a rise in number and yield of applicants and an increase in minority and first-generation students with an average GPA of 3.5, the same GPA as prior classes admitted using test scores as a factor. Twombly says it's "the best class in decades, using a truly holistic admissions process." As she puts it, "Tests aren't part of Hampshire's pedagogy"—the school uses year-long projects and narrative evaluations rather than tests and letter grades—"so why would we use a test to determine which students will thrive here?" She makes the case that the SAT is a snapshot of one day, when academic records, civic engagement, essays, and recommendations "trump anything the SAT could tell us." And, she adds, financial aid should be used to support those "who most need assistance, not to reward those who are good test takers."[33]

That Hampshire apparently feels it can afford to go unranked may be because of its off-the-beaten-track appeal to a self-selected pool of applicants, much like the attraction of Reed College, which, if you remember, decided to exit the rankings altogether. Still, it's hard to step away when everyone else is playing the game. A recent paper on admissions from the Harvard Graduate School of Education, "Turning the Tide," encourages stepping away, strongly urging admissions offices to look for more than academic achievement. Instead of assessments focused on test scores, class rank, GPA, and résumés overstuffed with extracurriculars, the Harvard report suggests priority be given to essays and references that attest to meaningful community service and family responsibilities. By selecting for compassionate service, admissions offices will almost certainly open the door to many high-achieving disadvantaged students, who are often active in their communities and are also likely to be caretakers of siblings, parents, or grandparents. The writers of the Harvard report also underscore the behavioral economics of admissions policies: the subtitle of the report is "Inspiring Concern for Others and the Common Good through College Admissions." That is, new admissions practices not only reward people for what they're doing but encourage people to do it.[34]

It's an inspirational message: higher education has a duty to be forward-looking and lead the way in a complex mutable world. Colleges and universities, by making a strong commitment to new practices of assessment, can be a powerful tool in creating a better future for all the diverse citizens of the United States.

Again, we need resources and will to make it happen. We need more, better-trained, and possibly somewhat older admissions officers. We need administrators willing to "dig for the gold," as Frank Bruni puts it, reading application essays for embedded narratives that reveal character and compassion. We need college and university presidents to support significant change in the admissions process even if it means bucking the traditional measures that influence rankings. We need Harvard itself to implement the

Harvard report. And—if we truly want diversity—we need to be willing to pay for it.

Which brings me to the third strategy for increasing diversity: new models of financial aid. Among the practices that have led us to a staggering student loan debt, $1.3 trillion in 2016, are bidding wars for students, with merit-based aid handed out to the affluent; an arms race to maximize tuition revenues at the expense of other values; sticker price inflation that allows the dispensing of small awards; "gapping," the provision of insufficient aid for poor students so they either take on debt or don't attend; and a shell game that uses Pell Grants for low-income students and funnels institutional money to the rich.

The explosion of student debt isn't all due to misallocation of college resources. It's also the inevitable effect of economic policies that overwhelmingly favor the wealthy and punish the poor and working class, producing enormous pressures on middle- and lower-class families.[35] But the cases that follow suggest that colleges and universities are trying to shoulder their share of the responsibility. If their efforts aren't always successful, I believe that's because we're in a moment of crisis in terms of changing demographics and widening income inequality. Higher education should, as a sector, be ahead of the curve, not behind it, but when you look at financial resources, there's a sense that the sector didn't see the storm coming. Some schools are playing hurry-up and catch-up, only to backtrack; some are relying on partial or simplistic solutions. But some are beginning to find innovative ways to provide need-based aid to diverse students.

Schools that have tried to increase accessibility include, notably, the University of Virginia. Access UVA started a policy in 2004 of awarding grants to low-income students instead of relying on loans, and the yield of low-income applicants jumped to 61.8 percent in five years. But the model was pinched by its own success: doubling the enrollment of the target group proved to be a huge financial burden, with the cost of the program leaping from $11.5 million in 2004 to $92 million in

2012. And the results of the experiment have been disappointing. UVA remains homogeneous, with a culture perceived as exclusionary, and no significant increase in socioeconomic diversity or minority representation. (Pell Grant recipients constitute only 13 percent of the student body.) When the university rolled back its no-loan policy in 2014, costs were reduced by more than half. The school did initiate a substitute program, Affordable Excellence, that offers a high-tuition, high-aid approach as a way to help decrease borrowing, but loans—the driver of student debt and diminished economic prospects—are now back in the picture.

Considerable internal debate has ensued, with UVA's student newspaper criticizing recent construction of a $12.4 million squash court as indulgent compared to need-based scholarships, and a board member, Helen Dragas, questioning the school's priorities in regard to a $17.5 million line item for advertising and communications in a draft of the university's projected spending, with no mention of future money for Access UVA. Some have charged that UVA, by ending the program, has returned to its original elitist ways. Bottom line: other aims took precedence, and an initially well-intentioned effort failed to achieve its announced goals.[36]

Another case of good intentions gone awry is Kenyon College. Led by then president Georgia Nugent, herself a first-generation college graduate, the school made a commitment to meeting 100 percent of financial need. Nugent was also an outspoken national leader in the fight against merit awards. But despite her beliefs and her activism, in the end the school remained caught up in the merit wars, with one eye on tuition revenues, primarily because of Ohio's shrinking population of college-age students and increased competition for top scholars all across the state.[37]

A school that has achieved significant success in opening the door to diverse low-income students is the University of North Carolina; its Carolina Covenant program commits to no loans, period. Chancellor Carol Folt says, "Covenant literally means promise. It's a promise we have always made, that Carolina's worthy students are granted admission regardless of financial status. It is part of who we are."[38]

UNC has thus far made the program work financially by drawing on federal aid to students living 200 percent below the poverty line and by including a work component, with all recipients required to take a federal work-study job. Low tuition has helped sustain the no-loan policy, as has the availability of a state grant program for need-based aid—but that program was recently capped by the state board of governors of the public university system. Private funds will be needed to continue the Carolina Covenant, which James Johnson, a faculty adviser, considers the core of the constitutional mandate to serve the people of North Carolina. Chancellor Folt has said that funds for the program will be a top priority in the coming capital campaign. The difference between UVA and UNC comes down to the latter's commitment to be "all in." UNC considers need-based aid central to its identity, underscoring the critical importance of mission and message: spell out a purpose and then live by those words.[39]

Vassar and Hamilton College convey the same lesson and are particularly notable because of their persistence in the face of the economic downturn in 2008.[40] Both schools not only stuck with need-blind and no-loan policies but beefed up their need-based aid, even in the face of declining endowments. Monica Inzer, dean of admission and financial aid at Hamilton (and, interestingly, also a first-generation college graduate), points to the school's origins as a seminary begun by Presbyterian missionaries, whose religious convictions and sense of purpose are part of Hamilton's identity. But she also says that the policy has a practical aim. The US Department of Education projects that by 2021, the number of Hispanic students will jump by 42 percent, those who are African American will increase by 25 percent, and white students will inch up only 4 percent. Inzer puts it this way: "Most companies don't know who their customers will be in five years, but I do, because they're in the seventh grade."[41]

An outstanding example of a school that has been steadfast in its financial commitment to diverse students is Davidson College, an early adopter (since 2007) of no-loan and need-blind admissions, with no preview of financial need beforehand and an absolute promise of finding funding for those accepted. The result: in 2012, 22 percent of students were minorities, with 45 percent of students receiving aid from the Davidson Trust (up from 33 percent in 2008). This progress came at the significant cost of $20 million a year, requiring an additional endowment of $70 million. A $15 million pledge from the Duke Endowment helped, but fund-raising and good management of investments will be key to the trust's continued viability. Davidson kept its need-based commitments through the recession and remains prepared to make cuts in other areas in order to protect financial aid. I find Davidson particularly worthy of admiration because, as a small school with a small endowment, it may need to make genuine sacrifices.[42] Bigger, wealthier schools can be generous without sacrificing other programs and goals.

I'm going to take a moment to describe a few "niche strategies" that help low-income students stay in school and complete their studies. Georgia State University's Panther Retention Grant program provides microgrants—small amounts of money ranging from a few hundred to a few thousand dollars, depending on the circumstances—to those who are in good standing but in danger of dropping out because of issues like a month's rent or the purchase of a textbook. The City University of New York provides textbooks, subway passes, and intensive advising that has doubled its three-year graduation rate for associate degree students and boosted transfers to four-year institutions. Microscholarships are another interesting approach: Raise.me, a social enterprise website, allows students to earn scholarship money starting in the ninth grade by increasing their GPA, taking an AP course, earning an A, taking on a leadership role in an extracurricular activity or sport, or taking two or more foreign languages. (Amounts for each item are specifically named by each college registered on the site.) Sum totals can be applied to tuition at the partner colleges offering the awards. In essence, microscholarships are both a college prep program and a savings program.

This chapter has grown long, but the length attests to the volume and multiplicity of efforts all across the sector to meet the urgent demands confronting us right now, especially the needs of low-income, first-generation, and minority students. The first three strategies—improve the pipeline, develop new methods of assessment and a new definition of merit, and change the financial model—are all works in progress, but that is in the nature of a paradigm shift. A new world is emerging, but it hasn't yet coalesced.

I want to stress, in closing, the fourth, and most transformative, element in this sea of programs, initiatives, and experiments, and that is the power of leadership to create new possibilities. I could go back through this chapter and repeat the names of those who led the way to significant change, but instead I'll add one more story, about the University of Texas at El Paso.

President Diana Natalicio, who has been at the helm for almost thirty years, has changed UTEP into a tier-one school by sheer force of will. Since 1988 the annual budget has increased from $65 million to nearly $450 million, and research expenditures have grown from $6 million to over $84 million a year; doctoral programs have grown from one to twenty in that same period of time. The school, 78 percent Mexican American (with another 5 percent commuting from Ciudad Juárez, Mexico, right across the border), has increased its enrollment from 15,000 to 23,000 students. As Natalicio puts it, "We look like El Paso now." Her enrollment of students from the region, based on her conviction that American universities should educate the newest wave of immigrants, has added substantially to the net diversity of schools across the nation.

Natalicio has an unwavering devotion to the talented students her institution serves. She takes issue with the six-year graduation rate, one of the metrics used by *U.S. News & World Report* to rank schools. Given that transfer students, a large contingent at UTEP, aren't included in graduation rates, and that almost the entire student body comes from low-income households and nontraditional backgrounds, with work responsibilities and family stresses that lengthen the time to graduation, the six-year rate is misleading as a measure of the school's quality. Natalicio considers other measures of value more important and more accurate: degrees awarded (in 2012, forty-three hundred, up from twenty-two hundred ten years earlier); affordability (tuition at UTEP is the lowest in the United States of any research university); successes in engineering and science (the National Science Foundation designated UTEP as a Model Institution for Excellence and twice ranked UTEP as the number 1 graduate engineering school for Hispanic students); and the improving economy of El Paso, which is in large part due to its college-educated young.[43]

If we're going to change the landscape of higher education, we have to mean it, and then do it. We have to reclaim our own story from the list makers and pundits with a return to basic values. The core of Diana Natalicio's strategy and vision is simple: look at the community, see what they need, and respond. And demographic changes mean that many colleges will be in a situation like UTEP's. They will need to educate a new and different kind of student, or they will be circling the wagons against an emerging reality and creating a dual-class system, a most un-American idea.

To be clear, not every college is the University of Texas at El Paso. A school like UTEP—an open-admission public university specifically devoted to serving local young people—is by its very nature different from a Tulane, a research university in country-wide competition with other elite schools for virtually the same students, including the same diverse students. But every institution, whatever its strategic aims, can begin to focus more on diversity. The schools cited in this chapter illustrate, to one degree or another, an evolution in their sense of mission, as institutions of every size and shape try to make diversity one of their highest priorities. University leaders are rewriting the stories of their institutions to include this central objective; resisting the lure of rankings and the glitter of publicity, they are creating new pathways for those who have been marginalized and forgotten. Nothing could be more important. These efforts to diversify reflect the deepest aspirations of our educational system: to mirror and serve young

Americans, to influence their lives, and to have a lasting impact on society.

Critically (to repeat the point), achieving greater diversity requires not only commitment but cash. How institutions handle their resources in order to achieve their purposes, no easy thing in the current financial climate, is the subject of the next chapter.

3

Keeping the Ship Afloat

*I do see challenging times for a number of schools in
the years ahead, and I suspect there will be a winnowing—
though maybe that sounds a bit too apocalyptic. A better
word might be "pruning": gardeners cut away the weaker
undergrowth in order to allow healthy plants to flourish.
It's possible that the overall landscape of higher education
will improve with judicious, continuous cutting back.*

In 2013 I wrote a letter to the Tulane community about "the new
normal" confronting higher education. That year I was chair of
the Association of American Universities, an organization of sixty-
two leading research universities, and participated in particularly
somber discussions focused on future challenges to all colleges
and universities in an era characterized by constrained budgets,
increased government scrutiny and regulation, and pressure from
the public for more accountability and for proof of the value of a
college degree. A major area of concern was whether the financial model of higher education was sustainable in a world where
expenses were certain to outstrip revenues unless new sources
were tapped and productivity increased. It was also a world where
middle-class incomes had been stagnant for years, making access
to higher education even more difficult to attain.

Unsettling news, to say the least, and a tricky moment, because
what we were experiencing then were symptoms of an impending
crisis, not the crisis itself. When I expressed my doomsday message at Tulane, it was meant to set the terms of a conversation
about an emerging reality that had so far been met largely by

denial, evasion, and wishful thinking. My aim was to wake people up—students, parents, faculty, board members, alumni, donors. I began with the positive, stressing Tulane's long-term planning, remarkable recovery from Hurricane Katrina, and continuing efforts to remain distinctive, qualitatively excellent, and financially strong despite the seismic shifts ahead. But I also underscored some basic truths: that there would be no return to the status quo; that change would have to be institution-wide; and that budget and value were not synonymous. As each year has passed, my concern for the financial well-being of the higher education sector has deepened, in part because universities and colleges still don't fully grasp the new world we're living in.

The current fiscal crisis of spiraling costs and stagnant revenues wasn't the first I'd encountered at Tulane. On my arrival in 1998, financial issues that had been accumulating since the 1980s were at the top of my agenda. We significantly improved our finances by 2004, mainly by transitioning from centralized to decentralized decision making and budgeting that increased productivity and accountability, which allowed us to directly assess the performance of individual departments. Then, in 2005, Katrina presented us with a full-blown crisis, fiscal and every other kind, which led to a fundamental reimagining and restructuring of the university in the interests of basic survival and a potentially brighter future. Our Renewal Plan, as mentioned, was controversial because it involved the consolidation and elimination of several academic programs and administrative functions, a rightsizing of the faculty and staff head count, and the suspension of half of our athletic programs along with a third of our doctoral programs.

But my letter of 2013 was meant to address a lingering concern bigger than any one of us. The present upheaval affects the whole sector, and, not to be dramatic, I would predict that only the strong will endure. Schools that are either highly differentiated or low cost are the most likely candidates to weather the coming storm because, for different reasons, they're both at the least risk. According to business theory, a high-value product has pricing freedom, while a serviceable commodity relies on low price and high volume. But the large "middle," some two thousand institutions across the country—schools that have high price tags but aren't at the elite level—are going to need to adapt, innovate, and focus in order to weather the sea change that's at hand.

The financial choices schools make going forward will depend in large part on their particular mission, or, in more commercial terms, their "brand." Tulane, for example, is built for "high distinctiveness and value." We're not likely to ever compete on the basis of price, and our target will continue to be the high end of clearly differentiated schools. In contrast, many community colleges as well as schools that are less distinctive are on the commodity end, providing a lower-cost option, with affordability as their main mission. Loyola University, Tulane's next-door neighbor in New Orleans, represents a school in the middle, with a relatively high price tag but unclear differentiation; like other schools in this middle range, Loyola has begun to make significant efforts to distinguish itself from the crowd.

Higher education also has its own "1 percent," immune to the stresses affecting the rest of the sector because the wealthiest universities, as nonprofit organizations, garner huge financial benefits from endowment gains and landholdings that aren't taxable. Basically, the rich are getting richer and the poor are getting poorer. One example: in New Jersey, Princeton University's endowment tax advantage—in a sense, a form of public funding—was $105,000 per student in 2013, far exceeding the $12,300 per-student public appropriations received by Rutgers University or the $2,400 per student received at neighboring Essex Community College.[1]

Because of these disparities in wealth and niche, institutions across the country can't all do the same thing to address problems with revenues and costs.[2] But perhaps the most significant divide in the sector is between public and private. Many small private colleges are facing declining enrollments and financial issues relating to the steep discounting of tuition in order to attract students. Public universities are suffering from significant reductions in state funding as well as increased demand for enrollment; they are seeking out-of-state and international students who will pay full tuition to meet their shortfalls.

How will four thousand institutions with widely various financial stresses, characteristics, and histories survive in a period of economic uncertainty? I am somewhat reassured by the burgeoning efforts of some schools to confront the challenge head-on. The failure of old financial models—for private institutions a primary dependence on tuition and for public universities a heavy reliance on state funding—is beginning to inspire institutions to create new ones, and, in the process, to rewrite their mission statements, reach out to underserved populations, and explore new technologies and pedagogies. We've seen in the previous chapter how financial decisions reflect the mission of diversity: to pick one example, UVA's reversal of its no-loan policy in contrast to UNC's redoubled efforts to preserve that same policy. Money and mission are inextricably linked, and current financial pressures are reshaping schools across the country as they seek ways not only to survive, but to reinvent themselves.

Nonetheless, I do see challenging times for a number of schools in the years ahead, and I suspect there will be a winnowing—though maybe that sounds a bit too apocalyptic. A better word might be "pruning": gardeners cut away the weaker undergrowth in order to allow healthy plants to flourish. It's possible that the overall landscape of higher education will improve with judicious, continuous cutting back.

The facts of the crisis are these:[3]

- An increasing number of schools are operating at a loss and have significant debt. Long-term debt at institutions of higher education is growing by 12 percent a year.
- Annual interest expense and the costs of administrative and student services are growing significantly faster than instructional costs.
- Average annual tuition has been increasing at several times the rate of inflation.

- The high-tuition, high-aid model, where full-pay students help pay for low-income students, is failing because there aren't enough affluent applicants to go around, and the money often gets recycled as merit aid rather than need-based aid.
- Student loan debt has now surpassed total US credit card debt, a trend that clearly shouldn't continue, and is also unlikely to do so as applicants look for value and affordability.
- Higher education's ever-expanding list of amenities in response to consumer demands and societal expectations—a list that includes everything from mental health services, sustainability initiatives, and food pantries to more "decorative" offerings like rock-climbing gyms and hot tubs—comes with an enormous price tag, straining the budgets of schools across the country.

Schools most at risk of existential failure are those where admissions yield has fallen, tuition revenue has declined, admissions standards have been lowered, and faculty have been cut; where the endowment is in the millions and not billions, and a large percentage is restricted; and where government funding and financial aid have been reduced. Overall, the aim should be to decrease waste and inefficiency, enhance revenue streams, outsource functions, and monetize assets. And, a critical point, make "the core"—institutional mission and values—the litmus test for decisions. Cut from the outside, build from the inside.

The forthcoming cases, which include successes and failures, as well as intriguing if still unproven experiments, examine the problem in more detail. Which schools are the innovators in cost containment and revenue production? Most importantly, which are focusing successfully on the "core," thus proving that value is not necessarily synonymous with budget size? It's not simply how much money there is, but where the money goes. As I tell the stories in this chapter, I will try, as often as I can, to put names to the leaders who are forging a path that others can follow; those who, through their strategies and visions, are tending the garden, minding the store, and ultimately—one hopes—saving the ship. Though strategies vary and missions are particular to institutions, one common thread that unites all the efforts described below is a focus on continuous innovation, which has become, of necessity, the "new normal" in higher education. To reinvoke the garden metaphor, those institutions characterized by flexibility and creativity are likely to flourish, while all others will wither and may even die away.

When financial pressures mount, the quickest route to a balanced budget, if not the most ingenious or remarkable, is simply to cut costs. But rarely are there simple and sustainable fixes for serious financial issues at an institution. What's needed is a holistic analysis of the organization, including its strategy, organizational structure, processes, and financial position, plus a review of the relationship between administrative and academic functions. And last but not least, ongoing attention to two fundamental issues: what is a school's mission and how does it sustain its identity through the financial choices it makes?

In recent years, universities have increasingly turned to external consulting firms to conduct a detailed institutional appraisal, with recommendations that will lead to better financial health. However, a recent report suggests that the use of consultants is one of those quick fixes likely to disappoint. Consultants seem to have a single aim, to cut costs, and by and large come up with the same set of proposals.[4] Though the point of hiring consultants is to reduce nonessential spending so more dollars can go to where they count, the consultants themselves tend to miss the forest for the trees. Their focus is almost always on administrative costs, with a tendency to shy away from the sacred cows of academe: the academic enterprise, athletics, libraries, nonproductive faculty, and institutes and centers that aren't self-sufficient and fail to significantly advance the institution's mission. In an overview of twenty-one consultants' recommendations, all advocated centralizing information technology services, computerizing human resource processes, modifying equipment to reduce energy costs, and consolidating vendor contracts.[5] But consultants tend to overestimate savings while underestimating both actual costs and the time frame needed to accomplish the goal. Meanwhile, the academic enterprise, fertile ground for savings, is an "untouchable" area because it is virtually synonymous with core mission, and also because of the likelihood of faculty protests. One recurring theme throughout this book is the clash of constituencies, a hallmark of shared governance, and, as we'll see again and again, financial decisions are a chronic source of conflict between faculty and administration.

Recommendations relating to overall organization—for example, eliminating management layers, creating shared services for learning centers and institutes, or utilizing assets more efficiently—have achieved results in some instances. UC Berkeley's Operational Excellence project eliminated three hundred administrative positions by terminating supervisors who oversaw three or fewer direct reports and saved the university $20 million a year. The State University of New York regrouped its sixty-four campuses into regional Campus Alliance Networks to develop shared services plans and placed three presidents in charge of two campuses each.[6] In an experiment in classroom utilization at the University of North Carolina at Chapel Hill, the administration offered to pay departments for technology upgrades if they would agree to standardize class schedules (no half-hour schedules colliding with on-the-hour classes) and allow nondepartmental usage of their classrooms—a good deal all around, with no need to build or renovate.[7]

But in general, changing organizational design is difficult for institutions to achieve and sustain, even when consultants recommend it. Instruction, which includes faculty salaries and benefits—the largest expense category for institutions of higher education—is by far the hardest to reduce without impinging on educational mission. Some institutions have replaced fulltime faculty with part-time or adjunct teachers in an attempt to contain salaries and fringe benefits, but studies suggest that such a move negatively affects degree-completion rates.[8] And any attempt to eliminate programs or faculty inevitably comes at a human cost in jobs lost and doors closed, and hence is almost always contentious.

A recent example is UC Berkeley, where the chancellor, Nicholas Dirks, wrote an open letter to the community to announce an overhaul of the university's workforce and academic structures in order to offset a $150 million deficit, resulting from declines in state appropriations and increasing costs of employee pensions and health care. In an Academic Senate meeting described by the *LA Times* as "testy," professors claimed that the university's plans to consolidate resources and possibly merge or eliminate academic departments were secretive and being pursued without faculty participation. Many professors sharply suggested cutting the number and pay of administrators rather than shrinking the academic program, and basically defended the core, the "comprehensive excellence" that makes the university a "top-ranked global brand."[9] The principle of shared governance is often a bar to timely, effective financial planning; faculty need to be brought aboard and educated about a domain very different from their area of academic expertise. Dirks has since resigned as chancellor, in large part because of his handling of university finances. Although he avoided a no-confidence vote, the Academic Senate blocked his plan to merge some graduate programs and possibly eliminate others.[10]

One of the consequences of a major existential crisis is the tendency of the entire community to come together in the face of an emergency, allowing suspension of some of the complex rules of academic organizations. At Tulane after Katrina, our academic and financial survival was primarily dependent on changes in vision, strategy, and organizational design. As previously described, we eliminated and consolidated academic programs based on objective criteria, merged schools, terminated faculty both tenured and untenured, and reenvisioned the entirety of the undergraduate student experience—exactly those things consultants shy away from in favor of more politically correct cost-saving measures, most of which focus on downsizing the university's administrative overhead. We reshaped our mission and strategic plan on strengths and core activities. We also tried to eliminate "mission creep" and to reallocate resources to high-priority and high-performance programs and activities. Mission creep is one of the biggest challenges for all of higher education: we are constantly adding courses, programs, centers, and institutes to our portfolio of activities, while rarely eliminating anything. The "creep" may have value but is often not worth the expenditure of time and resources.

The dramatic changes made at Tulane in 2006 resulted from a bona fide man-made and financial crisis. In the fall of 2005, our institutional survival was at stake and our faculty and staff were dispersed throughout the country. In essence, shared governance was suspended during the height of the disaster. I've often described my presidency in the period immediately following the hurricane as a benevolent dictatorship; the hurricane created both the necessity and the authority to make radical and timely changes. Though there were dissenters, the Renewal Plan generally won the backing of a deeply engaged and committed campus.[11]

Some schools are currently garnering the benefits, ironic though they are, of a life-or-death juncture. The crisis and subsequent reorganization that occurred at Sweet Briar College, an exclusive women's liberal arts school in rural Virginia, has made it the poster child of resurrection in the face of fiscal calamity. Known for its equestrian program as well as its academics, and one of only forty-four women's campuses remaining in the country, Sweet Briar represents a not-uncommon case of declining revenue and modest resources. Sweet Briar's endowment dropped from $96.2 million in 2011 to $84 million in 2015 because of steep operating expenses and insufficient tuition revenue, a problem compounded by escalating merit aid. Of the remaining endowment, a whopping $71 million was restricted to specific purposes such as scholarships or faculty chairs, leaving little for operating expenses. The school also carried $25 million in debt.

Facing the possibility of default, the college closed amid much anguish in the spring of 2015 only to reopen in the fall, saved by wealthy alumni who rode (as it were) to the rescue and raised $28.5 million in less than four months. The newly installed president, Phillip Stone, hired two hundred people—the entire terminated faculty—overnight, "sight unseen" (even though not all consented to come back); persuaded the head of the engineering department (one of only two women's engineering schools in the country) to stay; and convinced 240 students to return. The intense media attention has attracted applicants, with more than a thousand students applying for the 2016–17 academic year; the alumnae coalition is continuing to raise significant funds; and the school is actively recruiting full-pay international students.[12] The crisis evoked an outpouring of school spirit, alumnae activism, and a "we-can-do-it" mentality. Still, the multiyear decline in enrollment and the expensive model, highly personalized education with small class sizes, may well mean continued financial vulnerability.

Apart from a crisis that allows a comprehensive restructuring, what inventive strategies are colleges and universities pursuing to reduce costs and increase revenue? It turns out that the most innovative colleges are often ones nobody ever heard of. Among these is Trinity Washington University, a historically all-female Catholic school in Washington, DC, founded in 1897. Twenty years ago, enrollment had fallen to three hundred students, and its financial situation looked dire. President Patricia McGuire, told she had to repair the school's fortunes or close it down, began to transform the recruitment target from affluent Catholic women to low-income women of color. Some questioned the change in the school's mission, but McGuire maintained that educating those for whom a degree was truly transformative—a way of achieving the economic power that would allow them to take care of their children—was aligned with the meaning and spirit of Catholicism.[13]

In the 1990s, a researcher looking at Trinity's new policy suggested that the school was "the canary in the mineshaft," doomed to die, but the canary has, instead, thrived. By reinventing the student body, changing the curriculum, and developing sustainable financial aid, Trinity grew its student body to two thousand by 2015. The financial rescue of the school rested not just on tactics but on moral commitment and vision. McGuire, in her 2016 acceptance speech for the Hesburgh Award for presidential leadership, said, "A true commitment to access and success for new populations of students is not to let a chosen few in with the expectation that they alone will bear the burden to conform to our language and customs, but rather, that the institution, itself, will learn their language and customs as well, and incorporate those into a new canon of learning and institutional life. That's the essence of transformation . . . If higher education can't do social change well, who will?"[14] The lesson here is that changing priorities and taking a holistic institutional view—with curriculum, aid models, and human resources all conforming to an overriding vision of justice coupled with a grasp of new realities—can work financially and even save a school from extinction. Sweet Briar doubled down on its original demographic and mission and, for the moment, seems to be alive and well, waving the flag of tradition. But change is occurring all across the nation, and those like Trinity that accommodate to it, those "canaries" in the forefront, may be the ultimate survivors.

Another school that has switched demographics in order to survive is Paul Quinn College in Dallas, a historically black college founded by circuit-riding preachers from the African Methodist Episcopal church. In 2007, when Michael Sorrell, a lawyer in a prestigious Dallas law firm, assumed the presidency, the school was in debt and struggling with declining enrollment, anemic alumni donations, and a campus in grave disrepair. The first thing Sorrell did as president was end the football program, which he considered unaffordable. The first thing students did was exit in droves, reducing the student body by half, to 445, one year after he made this move. Then the Southern Association of Colleges and Schools took away Paul Quinn's accreditation, which meant no state or federal aid. The student body shrank to 171.

Sorrell's turnaround began with a slogan, "We Over Me," which became the name of a vegetable farm planted on the former football field. Though the farm just about pays for itself by selling produce to local restaurants, it has become a stirring symbol of reinvention. Sorrell also instituted a dress code: shirts and dress slacks for men, suits and dresses for women, with clothes donated by local black churches and stored in Paul Quinn's Career Clothes Closet (84 percent of Paul Quinn students are eligible for Pell Grants, and unable to afford new wardrobes). Sorrell shifted the mission of the school to urban entrepreneurship and instituted a required course for freshman, Introduction to Quinnite Servant Leadership, to teach the guiding principles.

Donors have been impressed by the mission, the farm, and the new commitment of students; fund-raising has increased, with donations coming from corporations and wealthy Dallas investors. But perhaps the most critical factor in the reinvention of the school has been its embrace of new demographic realities. "If we're in Texas, how would we not have more Hispanics?" Sorrell says. He is on the leading edge of a curve. Fifty years ago, the students at HBCUs across the country were black; now a quarter are Asian or Hispanic, with the largest growth among Latino students. The debate now is about a loss of identity and historical roots, but Sorrell is firm in his belief that HBCUs "provide opportunities for students who have some type of disadvantage in their background . . . I'm not insecure about our institutional heritage. I'm not insecure about our African American heritage. In fact, I'm so secure about both that I can welcome others as well, and it doesn't diminish mine." His latest slogan for Paul Quinn: "You can be our kind and not be our color."[15]

As Trinity and Paul Quinn attest, the move to increase tuition revenue and improve financial stability by responding to the needs of low-income and Latino students also promotes meaningful social change. In attending to its fiscal woes, higher education can also serve as a catalyst of social justice and an economic engine for restoring a thriving middle class. Both Trinity and Paul Quinn, in transforming their missions in order to expand enrollment, have significant overlap with the schools described in the previous chapter, on diversity. Sometimes the quest for fiscal health comes first, leading to demographic expansion and the search for underserved students, and sometimes the quest for diversity takes priority as an ethical imperative, with financial innovations and commitments that reflect this aim. The point is, fiscal health and diversity are not mutually exclusive by any means, and in fact are often synergistic.

In the face of dire predictions—Moody's that college closures will triple by 2017 and Clayton Christensen's that half of all colleges could be in bankruptcy within fifteen years[16]—many liberal arts schools across the country are pursuing innovative paths to financial health. An overview of nine such institutions confirms the energy and activity across the sector.[17] The executive summary issued by the Council of Independent Colleges identifies six overarching themes found in these change leaders: a bias for action, a drive to connect locally and regionally, realistic self-assessment and adaptation, structuring for innovation, assertive leadership within shared governance traditions, and alignment of mission and innovation.

These relatively abstract concepts emerge in living detail in a story like that of Benedictine University, a Roman Catholic school in a suburb of Chicago, which adopted a "go where they are" approach similar to that of Trinity and Paul Quinn. The school recruited new and diverse populations, including Muslim students (now 30 percent of the student body); developed innovative models for graduate degrees, including online and hybrid teaching approaches and an affordable $10K MBA program; and built new facilities to accommodate their growing enrollment. According to William Carroll, who stepped down as Benedictine's president after two decades in 2015, the established mission of a school has to be "broad enough . . . It's a warrant. It gives you permission . . . A closed mission is a dying institution."[18] Some schools have underscored, rather than expanded upon, their singular identity in order to accentuate their distinctiveness. For example, Stetson University in Florida has instituted a variety of innovations, including increasing faculty pay to ensure quality instruction and focusing on a "dare to be excellent" goal. President Wendy Libby said, "We just felt that leading with quality—every time—was the way to recapture the essence of the university and reestablish our strengths in the marketplace."[19] And some schools have focused on creating institutional processes that facilitate change and innovation. New England College in Henniker, New Hampshire, has set up a strategic planning process whereby the entire faculty can meet within a day's notice. By actively engaging faculty, the school has been able to rapidly implement across-the-board curricular redesign, including experiential learning in every course.[20]

These schools and others have been successful in increasing enrollment, and hence revenue, and remaining competitive in the marketplace. All have a bias for action along with a willingness to learn from failure. But all of them, it should be noted, are private colleges. What about the publics? I've suggested that the low-cost option in higher education is a safer bet than many private institutions with heftier tuition rates, but state budgets remain a huge factor in the fate of public colleges and universities. Those budgets have been cut in every state in the union except for Alaska and North Dakota, both oil rich and with money to burn. Public community colleges, especially those serving African American and poor populations, seem especially vulnerable to funding cuts. One case is Chicago State University, a predominantly African American school on the South Side, which faced closure in the summer of 2015. Chicago State's long-term financial problems led to $50 million in deferred maintenance, a 15 percent cut in the workforce, frozen travel expenses, and renegotiated contracts, but none of these stopgaps were sufficient to halt the oncoming crisis, caused by the Illinois state legislature's failure to pass a budget.[21] As of this writing, CSU remains in crisis, facing continued budget deficits and resorting to paid lobbyists to seek state funding.

Large state universities are not immune to draconian government reductions. Given that state budgets include everything from K–12 schools and roads to Medicaid and prisons, higher education often seems the easiest item to cut when revenue falls. Arizona, where funding fell by more than 40 percent in recent years—the deepest state cuts in the nation—has become a tale of two campuses. The University of Arizona—home of rooftop infinity pools and luxury apartments, Pinkberry and Chick-fil-A, student spas and personal trainers—is part of a trend nationwide to cater to affluent students who can afford full tuition. Basically the university has pursued the Law of More by increasing merit aid to attract affluent high achievers from out of state, who pay double the in-state tuition. As the state budget shrank by nearly half from 2002 to 2013, tuition revenues grew from $179 million to $455 million, and out-of-state students increased from 32 percent to around 38 percent.[22] (Along with the fancy amenities designed to meet the needs of this influx of wealthy students have come some surprising developments, like campus food pantries frequented by students from low- or middle-income households, who are spending so much on tuition that they can't afford basic subsistence.)

Arizona State University has taken almost the opposite route, developing creative strategies to generate revenue and reduce costs by increases in scale, expansion of online offerings, and structural reorganization. Michael Crow, president of ASU, touts his school as the "New American University" in a recent book by that name, describing it as "a complex and adaptive comprehensive knowledge enterprise . . . accessible to the broadest possible demographic."[23] The language may sound like a string of buzzwords, but in point of fact, the school has increased its enrollment by 50 percent, from 55,000 when Crow arrived to 83,000 at last count, including 13,000 in online degree programs. The result is a student body that reflects Arizona's demographics. Between 2002 and 2013, the number of African American students grew by 107 percent, Hispanic students by more than 130 percent, and low-income students increased from 219 to 919.[24]

Another tactic Crow has used to increase efficiency and productivity is the consolidation of academic departments into larger units. For example, biology, microbiology, and plant, molecular, and cell biology merged into the School of Life Sciences, with similar consolidation occurring in schools with impressive names like Human Evolution and Social Change, Earth and Space Exploration, and Social and Family Dynamics. Such mergers have saved millions of dollars in administrative costs. Other novel strategies include a public-private partnership model exemplified by the Starbucks College Achievement Plan. Jointly initiated by Starbucks and ASU in June 2014, the plan offers 100 percent tuition coverage for every part- and full-time benefits-eligible US Starbucks employee, with 24/7 tutoring, a choice of fifty ASU undergraduate online degree programs, a commitment by Starbucks of at least 25,000 graduates by 2025, and a promised investment of $250 million over the next decade, with no demand to stay with Starbucks after graduation.

And in April 2015, ASU together with EdX, an online instructional company, announced the Global Freshman Academy, which offers first-year courses (no transcript or application needed) to incoming freshmen, adult learners, and educators who can use the material to supplement the standard curriculum. On completion of a course, students who pass the final exam can pay $200 per credit hour to get college credit for the course; eight courses in the series constitute a full freshman year at ASU. Students pay only if they pass, and even then only if they wish, meaning there is no financial risk involved. The academy costs less than half of regular in-state tuition ($4,800 for eight courses vs. $10K for a year's residential tuition) and offers a pathway for exploration and preparation to students who might not otherwise seek a degree.

ASU has also joined the University Innovation Alliance with schools like Michigan State, Ohio State, and the University of Texas at Austin to expand the number of graduates, especially low-income ones, share innovative tools, and lower the cost per degree. Michael Crow says states should pay not for enrollment figures, but for people, ideas, and inventions. And he says, "Scale is your friend. It allows you to do what you couldn't otherwise do."[25]

Skeptics suggest that students may be getting degrees but aren't getting much of an education, particularly because, as experience has shown, online learning often hasn't borne its promised fruit. Only time will tell how substantive these dramatic changes will turn out to be, and whether a "top-down" approach to transformation, without a "ground-up" mobilization of the faculty, will ultimately endure. But the seriousness and inventiveness of Crow and ASU are in many ways inspiring; the school is thriving and financially stable. The university is meeting an enormous need and generating opportunities for social mobility and economic growth. In contrast to elite schools, prone to complacency and often reluctant to try new strategies and practices, ASU has undeniably been a hotbed of innovation.

Another innovator is Purdue University in Indiana, where former Indiana governor Mitch Daniels has been president since 2013. A Republican who in his prior job reduced funding for higher education, Daniels, to the surprise of many, has proved to be an inventive and open-minded leader at Purdue.[26] In his first years in office he made it a point to listen and talk to students, faculty, deans, and board members. Skeptical faculty members were won over by the fact that he'd studied academic infrastructure and culture and had clearly come to view teaching and research as the primary mission of the school.[27] But he also was assertive in his aims. Invoking the Hoosier idea of thrift, three months into his tenure he imposed a tuition freeze, now in its fifth year, to assure that Indiana students could afford a Purdue degree, building "a culture of economy and students-first across campus." Any savings identified as part of the common effort go into a Student Affordability and Accessibility Account. Basically, Daniels turned the normal process upside down; instead of the institution doing whatever it wants and then sending the bill, he began with the idea of affordability, and by building support through conversation and consultation, got the buy-in he needed from the community.[28]

I want, for a moment, to talk about the tough decisions no one wants to make. Among the steps Crow took to shore up Arizona

State University in the face of state cutbacks were difficult measures that many of the schools mentioned in this chapter have had to take, actions that cut close to the academic core. He eliminated twenty-two hundred positions, some administrative and some academic, and increased faculty teaching loads; he hired adjuncts and merged departments. In the sector as a whole, CFOs have reported a much greater commitment to increasing enrollment and launching new revenue-generating programs than to deeper structural changes like administrative collaborations with other colleges, shutting down underperforming academic programs, or reducing administrative positions.

Another step schools tend to shy away from is any reduction in employee benefits and health-care costs. Northeastern University, a rare innovator in this area, has developed a health management initiative as part of a joint effort with the Boston Consortium for Higher Education. Called Healthy You, the program is designed to help faculty and staff "understand, improve and maintain their health and well-being."[29] Voluntary and confidential, Healthy You includes a personal health assessment to share with a doctor, lifestyle coaching, and outreach and resources including Blue Cross Blue Shield tools and education. Yes, it's good for everyone's well-being, but it is also intended to help contain health-care costs for both the university and employees, who pay a portion of those costs.

One group I haven't talked about here is the elites, those schools that are brands unto themselves, with enormous endowments, wealthy alumni, and a price tag no one will ever argue with. The traditional model of a residential undergraduate school offers many benefits—faculty as mentors, the opportunity to do research, a cross-cultural experience—that remain valuable even in the face of the "new normal." But it would be unwise for these schools, and I include Tulane among them, to become complacent; even they need to be aware of and adapt to powerful changes in society.

I was at a conference not long ago at one of these upper-echelon schools, where Jeff Selingo—the author of *College (Un)bound: The*

Future of Higher Education and What It Means for Students—gave an impressive talk about the extent of these changes. Back in the sixties, you got an education, found a job or a career, and stayed put until retirement. Now students repeatedly switch jobs (on average once every four years), reeducate themselves to find new jobs and adapt to new working environments, and learn on the job. Many take a long time to arrive at a "career," changing locales and directions and dropping out and returning to school. Institutions of higher education, Selingo suggests, need to respond to this new student profile and "unbundle" their offerings to include hybrid teaching, low residency, transfer of credits, competency-based pedagogy, internships and apprenticeships, and overall a more personalized experience that equips a young person for the new realities of our society.

When someone in the audience said, "Well, we don't have to worry about this," I suggested that maybe this elite school, and all of our elite schools, had better pay attention. As society changes, we risk becoming the relics, the typewriters in an era of smartphones. There is an old adage of leadership and management that the more successful an organization is, the more likely that the seeds of its destruction are being sowed. Success often leads to organizational arrogance and complacency. Even if the model has virtues that should be retained, we don't want to become irrelevant, a citadel of white privilege in a society that is increasingly diverse, segmented, and riven by economic inequality. The job-switching, mobile, adaptive graduate of the future is largely the "underrepresented" segment of applicants—nontraditional, low income, minority (though soon to be majority). And the elites would do well to embrace this surging population. Currently admissions practices are stacked against poor students so that, according to a True Merit report, "they actually punish the striver."[30]

To reiterate: financial stability and demographic expansion can, and often do, go hand in hand. One elite school that has done a remarkable job of increasing diversity while strengthening its financial sustainability is Vassar, under the ten-year leadership of Catharine Bond Hill (retiring in 2017), an economist of higher education. Since Hill's arrival in 2006, Vassar has expanded its recruiting efforts, partnering with QuestBridge, the organization that matches low-income students with elite colleges, as well as with community organizations doing outreach in poor neighborhoods, and also pooling recruitment with Bowdoin, Carleton, Davidson, and Haverford in order to meet with more low-income students. The school has doubled its financial aid budget while putting an end to merit aid and directing all aid to needy students. Fifty-eight percent of the student body receives some form of financial aid, 23 percent receive Pell Grants, and the percentage of students of color has doubled.

To make all this work financially required some painful cutbacks, including faculty and nonfaculty staff reductions, mostly through retirements and vacancies but also nonrenewal of contracts. Hill also changed the curriculum; before the recession of 2008, the school allowed classes with only two or three students to continue, but now such classes are no more. Vassar has also postponed renovation of buildings in order to reduce costs. Hill notes that 25–35 percent of Vassar's revenues come from government subsidies—Pell Grants and tax breaks for their nonprofit status—designed to help colleges promote social mobility for everyone.

Hill is blunt that part of Vassar's success was timing: the push started in 2006, before the countrywide economic crisis. "That buy-in was easier. The trade-offs didn't look quite as complicated." The hard part was sticking with the initiative once the meltdown happened, but, Hill said, "to say we're going to balance the budget by reducing aid to the families that were getting hit hardest by the crisis didn't seem like the right way to go."[31] The ultimate lesson is that assertive leadership can change the prospects of an institution. And lesson number two, as I've noted several times: financial sustainability does not preclude either social innovation or academic quality. In Hill's case, as in the case of Sorrell at Paul Quinn, McGuire at Trinity Washington, Carroll at Benedictine, Libby at Stetson, Crow at Arizona State, Daniels at Purdue, and in many other instances across the country, the driving force of transformation comes down to an individual with a vision.

Like the diversity initiatives outlined in chapter 2, the efforts of these leaders to embrace new populations and recraft their missions in order to put their schools on a sound financial footing indicate a liveliness and energy that the reports of doom and disaster don't capture. At the same time, I don't want to minimize or discount the difficulties accompanying such efforts. A survey of chief financial officers indicates that the most common method of achieving financial stability is to enhance revenue by an increase in enrollment. The least common method, which may offer the most promise, involves the "sacred cows": revising tenure, eliminating programs that don't measure up academically and financially, revisiting the core curriculum and course offerings, and, the most sacred of all, cutting athletics and restructuring medical schools. Which brings us to the next two chapters.

4

The Tail Wags the Dog, Part I
Athletics

Something that originated as an extracurricular activity
devoted to the ideal of "mens sana in corpore sano,"
a healthy mind in a healthy body, is in danger of
swamping the academic mission of higher education.
Why can't we stop the insanity?

Back when I was dean of the management school at Case Western
Reserve University and being recruited for the job of president by
several universities, the then president of CWRU, Agnar Pytte, gave
me a succinct piece of advice. "What you don't want," he said, "is
big-time athletics or a medical school and hospitals." In the end,
at Tulane, I got both. What Agnar was trying to tell me, and what
I now know well, is that sports and medicine are two giant enterprises that eat up an inordinate amount of a president's time and
attention, often to the detriment of an institution's other missions.

As a former student-athlete and sports fan, I want to say, up
front, that I enjoy and support college athletics. However, athletics, particularly football in the Division I Football Bowl Subdivision (a.k.a. Division I-A) and men's basketball in Divisions
I-A, I-AA and I-AAA are becoming increasingly problematic and
would seem to demand a thorough review, both financially and
from the perspective of university mission. Big-time football and
basketball have increasingly abandoned the amateur model for
something very close to professional sports, and consequently
have exposed many universities to reputational risk because of

scandals and improprieties. These two sports, played at the highest levels, are the focus of this chapter. They can disrupt the entire community, generating anguish and rage when things don't go well and overshadowing an institution's mission of learning, discovery, and community engagement.

The rage of sports fans is another thing I know well. I have a vivid memory, perhaps the most indelible of my tenure before Katrina, of looking up from my desk and seeing myself hanging in effigy outside my office window.

I will get to the story of how I ended up hanging from a lamppost, but my story is only one of many. Almost all presidents of large universities have a hair-raising story about athletics because the situation is so combustible. As John Gerdy, a former administrator at the Southeastern Conference and the NCAA, puts it, "Expecting academic institutions to continue to fall on a financial sword for athletics in the name of alumni ego and a national profile based on sports is, quite frankly, irresponsible."[1] Big costs and headaches tend to accrue to sports like football and men's basketball, which generate significant revenue and offer the potential of a professional career after college. Though the statistical chances of a postcollegiate career for any one athlete are small, Division I college football, with full cooperation from the NCAA, has in essence become a farm system for the NFL.

It's true that the amateur model of rounded development is often very effective in Division III, intramural, and Olympic sports, contributing to student-athletes' personal growth as well as to institutional distinctiveness and school spirit. But in the case of Division I-A and I-AA schools, where the NFL and NBA go for their draft picks, the tail often wags the dog. Something that originated as an extracurricular activity devoted to the ideal of "mens sana in corpore sano," a healthy mind in a healthy body, is in danger of swamping the academic mission of higher education. Why can't we stop the insanity?

A complex history has brought us to this place of dysfunction. In the case of football, from the very beginning of the twentieth century the sport had an uneasy alliance with colleges. Fans and alumni loved it, but the game was extremely violent and dangerous; the "flying wedge" sent players into massive collisions that ended with flailing heaps of bodies fighting for the ball. One statistic that attests to the carnage of that early era: between 1900 and October 1905, forty-five college football players died from injuries ranging from broken necks to broken backs to concussions. So many young athletes were dying that the *Cincinnati Commercial Tribune* published a cartoon of the Grim Reaper perched on a goal post. One result was that some schools switched from football to rugby, and some wanted to ban it altogether.[2]

President Teddy Roosevelt, a fan of "manly sports" and strenuous physical activity, wanted to reform the game rather than ban it. He called together leaders from Harvard, Yale, and Princeton, forming a committee to change the rules. In 1909, sixty-eight colleges founded a new organization that acquired the name National Collegiate Athletic Association. New rules allowed for a passing game that spread players out across the field, and when a player fell on the ball, the game stopped, preventing the bloodshed and mayhem of the former free-for-alls. Flash forward to 1951: in response to two scandals—counterfeit grades for football players at the College of William and Mary and a basketball point-shaving conspiracy involving five schools—Walter Byers, the NCAA director, created an infractions board, giving it the power to suspend players and whole teams. In 1952, money started pouring in when the NCAA developed an eleven-game rationing system for TV football coverage (too much TV, so the thinking went, would compete with gate receipts) and made an exclusive deal of $1.4 million with NBC for the Game of the Week.[3]

Ultimately the schools themselves sought control of the money. In 1981, a coalition of sixty-two of them with major football programs pushed for an independent contract with NBC involving $180 million over four years. A landmark 1984 Supreme Court decision, *NCAA v. Board of Regents of the University of Oklahoma*, citing antitrust principles, freed football schools to market their games independently. Byers was furious over the loss of TV revenue and, on his retirement, denounced the idea that the NCAA should enforce amateurism rules when the universities were capitalizing on what looked a lot like professional athletics.[4] With the passage of time, it's become clear that his concern was prescient.

In the current era, the notion of "student-athlete" has come under fire as an empty catchphrase designed to help the NCAA fight liability cases brought by injured players.[5] My own experience as a student-athlete at UConn in the 1960s was more in line with the amateurism that the NCAA was originally designed to protect. We weren't allowed on the varsity squad in our freshman year, giving us time to adjust to the complicated task of juggling athletics and academics, and athletic scholarships covered the entire four years.[6]

Since my day, the whole operation has become more and more commercialized and professional looking, breeding all kinds of ethical and financial issues, causing a fissure between different conferences, and widening the financial gap between the "haves" and "have nots" of Division I. Football head coaches' salaries have ballooned since the 1984 Regents decision that gave TV revenue directly to colleges and universities, with a 70 percent increase in Division I-A salaries since 2006, to an average of $1.64 million.[7] An NCAA rule from 1973 confining scholarships to a one-year commitment, unilaterally renewable (or not) by the schools, has had the consequence of kicking young, predominantly black students out of school for good. (The National College Players Association scholarship data from 2008–9 showed that 22 percent of players on top Division I basketball teams failed to get their scholarships renewed in that year.)[8] Questions of race and exploitation continually hover over the whole discussion of athletics. As Sonny Vaccaro, former Nike executive, says of the NCAA, "The least educated are the most exploited."[9]

At the same time, scandals continue to break out over grade inflation and cheating among athletes. (One such scandal occurred in 2014–15 at UNC–Chapel Hill, with collusion from professors and a blind eye from administrators, continuing into 2016 with charges of a shadow curriculum and fake classes dating back to 2011.) The rise in football concussions and the dangers of punishing workouts in college programs, the lack of due process in

NCAA disciplinary hearings, and congressional discussions of antitrust suits against the NCAA have all been in the news in recent years. A culture of "one and done" in men's basketball—draftees putting in a mandatory year of play after high school graduation as required by the NBA and then turning professional—and inconsistent transfer rules, which sometimes force young players to sit out a year after being "run off" by a new coach and sometimes give them immediate eligibility elsewhere, have created chaos in the sport and further erosion of the amateur model.[10]

So that's an overview of the intricate, intertwined histories of an advocacy organization—though you do have to wonder, sometimes, who the NCAA is really advocating for—and the many colleges and universities involved with sports, sometimes against their own best interests. The reason so many schools stay in this bad relationship is that they can't get out.

To illustrate: The year I assumed the presidency of Tulane, in 1998, the football team, the Green Wave, was undefeated. New to the territory, I thought, oh, good, this must be the way it is around here. I was an immediate booster and fan, with an annual ritual of dyeing my hair green for games (thereby giving students many photo ops). Let me say right here how much I love college sports, from the athlete's high I experienced as an undergraduate player, through years of vicarious thrills on football Sundays, to the elation I felt every time the Tulane squad took the field. And let me say also that I understood what football spirit did for the school, creating a powerful sense of identity and emotional attachment in students, faculty, alums. I also got caught up in the hype—hence my green hair.

But as luck would have it, despite the cheering and the banners and the display of school colors, we weren't winning many games after that 1998 season. And it wasn't just bad luck. You'll remember, we lost our head coach, Tommy Bowden, to Clemson, because of Winnebagos on Wednesdays. It took a few years of regular losses to send me back to the record books: it turns out that 1998 was only the second time in 105 seasons that the team had had a perfect record.[11]

Green hair and fandom aside, I planned to assess the athletics program as part of a larger financial review of every aspect of the university, undertaken early in my tenure at Tulane. It took until the spring of 2003 to get around to athletics, when the board was shocked to learn that the school's sports programs were running an annual deficit of $7–10 million.[12] Attendance at the Superdome, where the Green Wave played, rarely topped 20,000 and often dipped to the low ten thousands—way under the current national average of 43,800.[13] The huge drain of resources and the lack of attendance raised an inescapable question: Why are we doing this, and who are we doing it for? We formed an ad hoc committee to consider arguments pro and con and review the options.

The arguments in favor of big-time athletics included the prospect of more donors, more applications, lower acceptance rates, and more prestige (i.e., a higher place in the *U.S. News & World Report* college rankings). A stronger argument was that competitive football and basketball programs would enhance diversity on campus, given that the majority of players in the revenue sports, and especially in skills positions, are African American. If we could attract gifted young African American men and women to Tulane as student-athletes and they graduated at the same rate as students from privileged backgrounds, we would be contributing to greater equality and the public good. Need-based scholarships were part of our budget in any case; athletics was simply another, and some would say better, way to make an investment in underprivileged youth.[14]

Arguments against big-time athletics are chiefly financial: the fifty-thousand-dollar price tag of athletic scholarships per student, escalating outlays for coaches and facilities (otherwise known as the "arms race"), and number and amount of subsidies provided by universities to their athletics programs. Ultimately the donor and applicant arguments aren't very persuasive as offsets to the big financial drain. Donors may earmark their gift for athletics and take it away if the program isn't successful, the number of applicants doesn't necessarily improve the profile of enrolled students, and Tulane applicants list athletics way down on surveys of what they want at Tulane. Plus, the icing on the dismal cake, there's been an occasional threat to treat proceeds from athletics as "unrelated business income" taxable by the US government, despite the fact that until now the NCAA has had tax-exempt status because of the supposed amateur status of athletes.

The subversion of academic aims, a consequence of the financial drain, also influenced the Tulane committee on athletics. To be honest, I was president of Tulane, not Ohio State, so we didn't have nearly as much at stake. Bottom line: I thought we could transform the model after the review was complete. Though no final recommendation had been made, word leaked out that we were considering a change from Division I to Division III, which would mean a less visible program, less commitment of resources, and an end to athletic scholarships. In fact, Tulane had already been accepted in a Division III conference, with schools like the University of Chicago, Brandeis, and Emory, so we were set to go once we'd brought the community into the decision-making process.

Then all hell broke loose. I couldn't leave my office without first passing a dummy-me hanged in effigy on a campus lamppost. Emails stuffed my inbox, articles appeared everywhere, and fans staged protests. At a town hall meeting to discuss the issue, someone in the audience posed the question, in a voice dripping with disdain, "Why would you want to be in a conference with the University of Chicago?" I felt the irony of the Chicago reference. A founding member of the Big Ten conference, winner of six football championships between 1899 and 1924, the University of Chicago dropped its varsity football program in 1939 after a decline in success and out of a growing concern for the school's rigorous academic standards.[15]

I knew I was in trouble after that town hall question; emotions were running high and reasoned discourse was all but impossible. The tendency to live vicariously through the victories (and, unfortunately, the defeats) of beloved teams is a fundamental feature of sports psychology.[16] Team competition brings out powerful passions and intense attachments; in the Deep South, football is not just a game—it's practically a religion.

In the face of stakeholder outcry, we made the reluctant decision to stick with Division I, even though the outcome was likely to be less than gratifying over time given the continued divide between the "haves" (the power, or "autonomous," conferences) and the "have-nots" (everyone else, otherwise known as "the group of five"). A case could be made that the NCAA needed schools like Tulane, to remind it of its original mission of allowing college student-athletes to compete at the highest level while also receiving an education that would help them become productive citizens and leaders. So I decided that, if we were going to do this, we should try to make our program more viable financially, which meant making it more competitive.

A first step was to take aim at the Bowl Championship Series. Brand-new in the 1998 season, the BCS had been created as a way to determine a national champion, but it was stacked in favor of the power conferences—back then, Atlantic Coast, Big East, Big 12, Big Ten, Pacific-10, and Southeastern. These dominant sports schools had a lock on the most lucrative bowl games primarily because of television rights that dated back to the 1984 Regents decision, which, you'll recall, gave sixty-two schools exclusive rights to marketing of their football teams. Non-BCS teams from conferences like Tulane's Conference USA, or the Western Athletic, Mid-American, Mountain West, or Sun Belt conferences, were virtually barred from a Rose Bowl or Orange Bowl because, despite Division I-A status, they didn't have the money to support truly competitive programs. Small private institutions like Tulane, with sixty-seven hundred undergraduates, also had much more stringent academic requirements for student-athletes than big public universities with power teams.

In 2003, in an op-ed in the *New York Times*, I itemized some of the glaring failures of the NCAA and college sports generally, including for some highly competitive schools a dismal graduation rate of 20 percent for student-athletes as compared to Tulane's 80 percent. I invited fifty-four non-BCS colleges to join a coalition demanding a fair shot at the postseason bowl games. And I testified to Congress on antitrust aspects of the Bowl Championship Series: the sixty-two powerhouse BCS schools used income from television contracts to pay for their athletes' cost of attendance (not just tuition but many other expenses, including health insurance and transportation), and thereby created a monopoly on both talent and access to competition. I argued that a play-off system of eight or sixteen teams—a version of basketball's Final Four—would be more equitable, minimize branding damage, and also generate plenty of television excitement (and revenue) by allowing underdog teams with storybook seasons the well-earned right to compete at the highest level.

In the end, the BCS made some adjustments, with more money going to non-BCS programs, and the door was opened a crack for these "have-not" Division I-A teams to make it all the way to the top. In recent years Boise State, Utah, Texas Christian University, Hawaii, Northern Illinois, and Central Florida have all competed in the prestigious bowl games. A new play-off system (albeit only four teams) has now replaced the BCS system, but the problem of runaway athletic costs remains for everyone, especially for those universities not in a Power Five conference. Likewise, the autonomous conferences control the College Football Playoff (CFP) and now have a dominant position in the NCAA. In my view, these developments do not bode well for the future.

Back at Tulane we made the somewhat quixotic decision to build our own stadium—obviously a big thumbs-up for football and an apparent about-face from our initial plan to reduce spending on sports. But once the community made its will known, we had to do what we could, which was to help athletics pay for itself. At the Superdome, home to our football team ever since the demolition of the old Tulane Stadium in 1979, our only proceeds were ticket receipts; concessions, sponsorships, parking, and seat licenses all went to the Superdome. We hoped to capture the fruits of our investment, almost all from private sources, by tapping these subsidiary sources of income. You could ask, why not take that money and give it to the English or political science department? And the answer would be, because the donors wouldn't have given the money for that purpose. Yulman Stadium, named for the major donor, a member of the board of trustees, opened September 6, 2014. Now homecoming is literally at home, and our stadium also serves the wider community. However, it remains to be seen whether this investment results in the projected returns, competitively and financially. The Glazer Club, named for another major donor, has a six-figure membership fee, payable to the university, which then allows the member to purchase tickets for premier private seating on the fifty-yard line; the club has sold out. Serious economics are at work, and the hope is that over time the stadium will generate sufficient resources to mitigate the school's costly subsidy of the athletic programs. At other universities with Division I-A, I-AA, and I-AAA athletic programs, football and/or men's basketball could serve as the mainstay of all athletics, including Olympic sports like track and field and lacrosse.

I want to address one final point: you could ask why I didn't make another attempt to move to Division III football after Hurricane Katrina, when the school was reinventing its mission, cohesion and spirit were at an all-time high, and I had the goodwill of the community behind me. One reason is that it had been only two years since I'd acceded to the will of a majority of stakeholders and recommitted to a Division I program, and it didn't seem morally right to backtrack so quickly. Another reason had to do with symbolism. The Tulane football team, as well as other fall sports, carried on through the fall of 2005, playing away games all over the country; they were, in essence, the face of Tulane at a moment when the university was shuttered and its very existence was in doubt. Tulane games were a rallying point and a source of hope for the scattered members of our community, and the Green Wave's heartening message was an instance of what football does best: tap into emotions and lift spirits. The metaphoric value of having a home team to root for, then and in the years to come, seemed far more important than resetting the course of athletics.

So what did I learn from my failed attempt to reform athletics at Tulane in 2003? First, absent a bona fide crisis or an overwhelming set of facts that prove big-time athletics is damaging your institution, it is almost impossible to make a change that repositions your football program from the Football Bowl Subdivision (formerly Division I-A) to something less visible. Ironically, not only have there been no transitions in recent decades from the Football Bowl Subdivision to the Football Championship Subdivision (formerly Division I-AA) or a lower division; we are actually witnessing a trend for more schools to upgrade from FCS to FBS despite the imprudence of such a move. These schools have convinced themselves that such a move is akin to finding the Holy Grail. There is nothing like athletics and the excitement it can bring to people to cloud good judgment.

Of course, Tulane is not alone in struggling with this issue. According to *USA Today*, more than one hundred Division I-A schools currently subsidize intercollegiate athletics by more than $10 million a year. One of these schools is the University of Alabama at Birmingham, home of the Blazers, a Conference USA football team. In December 2014, citing a review by Carr Sports Consulting that indicated spiraling expenses for NCAA football, president Ray Watts announced the final seasons for UAB football, bowling, and rifle in the 2014–15 academic year.

The immediate motivation for this step was undoubtedly the added cost of keeping up with the five powerhouse conferences—which now, since the institution of the College Football Playoff system in 2014, include the Big Ten Conference, the Big 12 Conference, the Atlantic Coast Conference (ACC), the Pac-12 Conference, and the Southeastern Conference (SEC) (collectively referred to as the Power Five Conferences). In August 2014, the Power Five, with permission from the NCAA, made a set of rules that increased the amount of support to student-athletes and allowed players to consult agents, meaning increased outlays for athletes along with facilities and coaches' salaries. UAB was already subsidizing $20 million of the $30 million annual athletic department operating budget, and Watts and his board decided it was time to wave a flag of surrender. But elsewhere the arms race continues, and at a time when high costs paired with widespread underemployment of recent college graduates are making students more price sensitive than in the past. Passing on athletic subsidies to students in the form of higher fees is increasingly unrealistic. Add to this a steady onslaught of stories about corruption and abuse in sports: phantom courses at the University of North Carolina, sex abuse at Penn State, and widespread cheating at other schools. This climate may well make presidents and trustees more inclined to withdraw from the escalating race to the top.

Reactions at UAB were pretty much in line with what happened at Tulane, but instead of lynching Watts in effigy, donors threatened to withhold support, and faculty, undergraduates, and graduate students fired off votes of no confidence in Watts. Football mania, again, though the Faculty Senate's resolution—"Recent decisions by President Ray Watts were exercised in a manner that demonstrates no respect for, or commitment to, shared governance"—suggests that faculty may have had a simmering distrust of Watts's leadership style before the football crisis. Although the board of trustees came out in full support of Watts, ultimately the football program was reinstated, following a review by a new consulting firm that concluded, "Both eliminating the football program and bringing it back would be financially viable."[17] You have to wonder about a conclusion that isn't exactly conclusive, but football fever, per usual, won the day.

Sound familiar? The narrative arc is fairly predictable. I've certainly been there. In my view, the board showed a lot of courage in raising the issue and backing Watts. That said, there may be a governance issue lurking here. If you're going to propose a radical change, you need to marshal all the facts and communicate effectively with stakeholders. But in practice, there are always debates about the "facts"; statistics can be misleading and proofs can suffer from bias. Even when you have the strongest possible evidence and the clearest possible data, emotions tend to overwhelm rational assessment. Part of the job of a university board and university president is managing, as opposed to being co-opted by, the excitement of athletics and the irrationality of those who don't care for the cold data about the pros and cons of big-time athletics.

Aside from issues of leadership and governance in battles over athletics, there's the basic human question: How do you survive it? I feel a kinship with Watts (who, it should be said, did survive as president of UAB). Though I didn't get a vote of no confidence, I got "lynched" right outside my office. The level of rage out there was pretty staggering.

Only time will tell whether the decision to retain football at Tulane was a wise one. If I had to guess, I would not be optimistic given the current arc of power consolidation in the NCAA and CFP. I still have considerable ambivalence about Tulane's athletics program. It would have been courageous, and liberating, to pull the trigger on Division I football. But many respected, well-meaning people felt it was a mistake to eliminate football, and it was difficult to ignore their views. To this day I second-guess myself about the final decision. Among other things, the UAB story underscores how difficult it is for one person's vision to prevail. What would it look like in a perfect world? How would a "designer" university—a Utopia U—deal with this problem? Most of us inherit schools with long, complicated histories. It's like the tax code or zoning laws: regulations build up over eons, with subordinate clauses and footnotes, until it's so tangled and arcane, with so many competing interest groups bent on keeping various parts, that no one can dismantle or simplify it. On campus, new programs develop, buildings get built, and faculty get hired. We know how to add, not how to eliminate, so growth and spending continue unchecked.

Ultimately, there's no escaping to Utopia. A real-world solution to the problem of commercialized, scandal-ridden athletics is possible, if university leaders and boards can free themselves from the byzantine demands and objectives of others. First and foremost, we need to reassess the role of the Power Five conferences in the CFP and within the NCAA, which have unduly influenced critical aspects of the NCAA governance system. Second, we must find a way to eliminate the arms race with respect to coaches' salaries and facilities, and to lower the cost of operating our athletic departments. The greatest hope in this area is the Knight Commission, which has fought for years for reform in athletics. Finally, we have to reverse the professionalization of athletics; provide more access and equity among all Division I schools, not just those in the Power conferences; further increase our support of student-athlete health and safety; and significantly diversify the ranks of coaches and athletic leaders.

The National Football League is, in a sense, the elephant in the room. Though statistics suggest that only about 1.6 percent of NCAA athletes become NFL pros, college football is itself professionalized, with college recruitment, televised games, and draft picks by the NFL grabbing big audiences and generating big money. The question of whether to pay college athletes—given the revenue they produce for universities, coaches, recruiters, and others—is highly politicized, with some charging the exploitation of athletes to enhance the visibility and appeal of various colleges and universities. The pay-to-play model is on the table—pay athletes as employees and abandon the pretense that they're students, deferring their education until after the football years, or, possibly, never.

The pay model, however complicated and problematic, could be the crisis that leads to a solution, forcing a change in business-as-usual. Imagine a scenario in which the courts rule that student-athletes can be paid and a bidding war breaks out as universities vie for top talent. The likely outcome would be a revolt of some Division I schools and a reconfiguration: pay schools, with their own new Division I group, and nonpay schools that uphold the amateur model and the original aims of the NCAA. Schools that I think would leave the NCAA at this point in favor of retaining big-time sports and their franchise are likely to be those in the Power Five conferences, while all others would attempt to find more rational and stable ground by reorganizing the NCAA to look more like the amateur model.

You could call the secession of pay-to-play schools, if it were to occur, the "Hurricane Katrina" solution: a crisis—not something you wish for—but also an opportunity to radically change the entire system for the better.[18] Such a moment would be a rare chance for presidents to realign athletics with their particular institutional missions and budgets.

Barring such a crossroads, presidents and boards, including the NCAA board, can have the courage to start saying no to changes that increase costs, put more pressure on student-athletes, or increase the professional look of college sports. If these leaders can't do it, I suspect legislators, lawyers, and athletes themselves may continue to rise up for reform. Presidents and trustees can also commit to step-by-step approaches that hold the hope of positive change in the long haul. Such steps might include reducing the number of games played, making first-year students ineligible to play in games, and improving the integration of student-athletes into the broader university. Another step is community-wide discussion of how dollars earned from athletics can be focused on the health, welfare, and academic needs of student-athletes in keeping with institutional mission. With more support from campus constituencies, schools lacking self-sufficient athletics departments might be able to return to Division III programs or join some other newly created division, and hence embrace more rigorous ethical and academic standards. Finally, the NCAA can reconsider transfer rules and ensure that student-athletes are getting academic degrees that will help them for a lifetime rather than just keep them eligible.

Amateur sports fits well with the mission of higher education: to expose young people to an array of formative experiences as they develop their intellectual capacities and grow into maturity. "Amateur" is the key word. Amateurism puts athletics in its proper place as one of many items on a rich and varied menu of possibilities, in preparation for a future that extends far beyond the years spent on the playing field. Nothing is a slam dunk in the arena of sports—feelings run high, arguments are endless—but I do know this: it's time for the dog to start wagging the tail.

5

The Tail Wags the Dog, Part II

Medicine

Though hospital ownership can be problematic, affiliation is problematic too, because hospitals and universities don't have the same goals. It's usually a marriage of convenience, and not always very convenient at that.

Medicine is another case of "the tail wags the dog": it can often be an administrative nightmare and a financial drain. However, it's different from athletics in that medical education, clinical care, and scientific research are fundamental missions of large universities. Medicine is the problem you have to solve.

In my own case, my involvement with the medical school didn't end when I stepped down from the presidency of Tulane. After my successor began his tenure, I continued the task of negotiating hospital affiliations for the university, first and foremost because it was an absolutely essential element of our medical training program. I also took on the job because I had the advantage of knowing the region's players after sixteen years in New Orleans, and because I wanted to take some of the burden off the shoulders of the new president. But after a year of unsuccessful negotiations, I'd had enough; with feelings of regret matched only by my feelings of relief, I retired from the search. If medicine is the problem you have to solve, it also often appears insoluble. The arduous search for functional hospital partnerships is occurring across the country, as universities try to deal with changes in health care while also pursuing the traditional objective of training the next generation of physicians and researchers.

Given the enormous percentage of a university's budget that goes to medicine, at least 50 percent and as high as 75 percent if it owns a hospital, and the equally large percentage of faculty who staff the medical school and health center, the question arises: Is the university a medical entity that happens to have ancillary schools—liberal arts, business, engineering, law—or is it a knowledge enterprise with a medical component? Hospital management in particular swallows up inordinate amounts of time and attention, requires a core competence that universities don't have, and entails considerable risk. If the hospital fails, the resultant financial crisis could bring down the whole university. Wouldn't it be better for all concerned to jettison hospital ownership?

Many outstanding institutions have done just that. Harvard University has one of the best medical schools in the nation but does not run its own teaching hospital. Instead it has partnered with local affiliates, including Massachusetts General and Brigham and Women's Hospitals, which are premier centers for teaching, research, and patient care. A similar structure prevails at Case Western Reserve University School of Medicine; faculty have admitting privileges and teaching responsibilities at a number of independently run Cleveland hospitals that pay physicians at the medical school for their clinical services.

Splitting off hospitals from the financial and legal structure of a university would be a no-brainer except that there's a tricky part: the university still needs to retain control over the hospital's arrangements with faculty, residents, and medical students in order to preserve the medical school's educational programs and research. That's one reason some schools, like Emory and Johns Hopkins, continue to stay in the hospital business; ownership gives them absolute authority to pursue an academic agenda. Though ownership can be problematic, affiliation is problematic too. Any such agreement has to be done correctly, because the hospital and university don't have the same goals, especially in the matters of cash transfers and academic priorities. It's usually a marriage of convenience, and not always very convenient at that.

The conflict plaguing these partnerships has only increased in recent years as health care has shifted from a fee-for-service model to managed care and a greater emphasis on cost containment, affordability, and prevention. Patients have become consumers of health care, with the Internet, drug company advertising, and iPhone apps giving them all kinds of information (including the unreliable kind) about their personal health status and what they should do about it. Independent physicians are a vanishing breed, replaced by HMOs and hospitals that supply clinical services in a very competitive market with narrow profit margins. Another development has been the rise of community clinics and outpatient care, and an accompanying decline in emergency room visits and hospital admissions at "big box" medical centers located in the downtown areas of inner cities.

And, finally, there can be no discussion of modern medicine without a mention of the "one trillion dollar problem," the annual cost of health care in the United States. The enormous price tag has been attributed to a number of things: overdiagnosis and overtesting; preventable behaviors and habits; heroic end-of-life measures; profiteering by insurers, hospital corporations, and Big Pharma. Whatever the cause, or causes, the net result of the sheer expense is a strong emphasis on cost containment and efficiency across the sector.[1]

All these alterations in the way health care is delivered have put significant pressure on medical schools. In a way, medicine is a test case of how universities adapt to social and economic upheaval. The idea of higher education as the preserver of traditional values against the ceaseless tides of change comes up against the equally important idea of the university as a source of innovation and evolution as the future unfolds.

The model of medical education that we are fighting to preserve has its origins in the teaching hospital. For centuries, textbooks and didactic lectures were the chief means of medical instruction, but Sir William Osler, often called the father of modern medicine, brought teaching out of the lecture hall to the bedside of the patient. As he put it, "He who studies medicine without books sails an uncharted sea, but he who studies medicine without patients does not go to sea at all."[2] Osler's early training in Europe introduced him to a teaching system, developed first in French hospitals, known as clinical rounds: a senior physician visits ward patients with trainees in tow, teaching diagnosis through the analysis of individual cases. On his return from Europe, after brief appointments at McGill University and the University of Pennsylvania, Osler became one of the first professors of medicine at the Johns Hopkins School of Medicine and the first physician-in-chief at Johns Hopkins Hospital. It was at Hopkins that he established the first medical residency program in the country, with young physicians as the in-house staff for the hospital, and developed clinical clerkships for medical students in their third and fourth years.

The primacy of bedside teaching in the United States—in particular, the thorough physical exam and patient history—originated with Osler, who famously said, "Listen to your patient. He is telling you his diagnosis." Beginning in the 1890s, well over a century ago, clinical experience became the bedrock of medical education, and an intimate link between medical schools and teaching hospitals was forged. (Osler's joint appointment in 1893 to both the school and the hospital formalized that link, setting a template for academic medicine in the United States.) Academic centers have also, historically, treated the indigent. An example from my own backyard is New Orleans's Charity Hospital, which was founded in 1736 and closed, amid loud outcry, only in the aftermath of Hurricane Katrina. For generations Charity was a hallowed training ground for physicians—a city hospital that admitted everyone, regardless of ability to pay, and where the house staff saw a wide range of disease, from garden variety to the rarest of the rare.

Though the numbers of the poor and uninsured have diminished with the Affordable Care Act, those numbers may again rise given the move to "repeal and replace" by the current Republican president and Congress. For now, academic medical centers will continue to treat the 5–10 percent of Americans who currently remain in that category, as well as undocumented migrant workers and other marginalized people. These are often the sickest patients with the most complex diseases. The academic medical center, with its subspecialty expertise, culture of investigation, and "safety net" mission of treating patients with complicated conditions, is a superb training ground for physicians and health-care professionals, but such centers are also under increasing financial stress as the landscape shifts to primary care and cost containment.[3] An added stress on the mission of medical education is the inadequate number of available residencies, falling far behind the number of medical school graduates, and the low pay of such residencies across the United States.[4]

Hospitals everywhere are now operating under incentives to deliver reliable cost-effective care, with physician training a distant consideration if it's considered at all. The surgeon and author Atul Gawande, in a *New Yorker* article several years ago, proposed the Cheesecake Factory, a restaurant chain, as a role model for hospitals because of its success in providing reliable service, quality control, reasonable prices, and customer satisfaction.[5] Many objected to the rosy picture he painted, pointing out the problems of "cookbook" medicine: the specter of personal liability, the loss of autonomy, and the possibility of new and different errors. But in this article, as well as other writings, Gawande has persistently tried to understand what-works-what-doesn't in industries like agriculture, the military, and the airline industry, seeking to apply those lessons to medical practice.[6]

One area he doesn't address is academic medicine, other than to acknowledge, in passing, that "we'll also have to figure out how to reward people for taking the time and expense to teach the next generations of clinicians."[7] As health care becomes a big business, we still have to train physicians and expand medical knowledge. Meanwhile, residency training has become much more about doing the job than about acquiring an education. The focus on "throughput"—admission and discharge of large numbers of patients within narrowly prescribed hours[8]—has resulted in an increase in errors, a decline in care, and widespread burnout among doctors in training. Faculty members, both clinicians and researchers, have little time left over for teaching—which, as Gawande points out, goes unrewarded in the current environment. (A joke among medical school faculty is that receiving teaching awards is the surest way not to get tenure.)[9] The notion of the triple-threat physician (i.e., great teacher, clinician, and researcher) is a thing of the past. Residents are left on their own to manage the hospital care of sick patients in an efficient, but often a fragmented, way. One example of the increasingly common collision between educational objectives and hospital management: an attending physician wanted to discuss the complexities of a lupus patient who had initially been admitted for a dermatologic problem, but he was cut short by the hospitalist,[10] who instructed the house staff to discharge the patient immediately now that the rash was gone, in order to free up the bed for the next admission.

A similar focus on generating revenue is affecting research: most drug company money goes to support clinical trials testing the efficacy of a potentially lucrative drug, device, or procedure that can be brought quickly to market. But basic science research, without immediate clinical applicability, has the potential to lead to breakthroughs in our conception of disease and hence to innovative treatment.

The academic environment is meant to nurture scientific exploration and to train medical minds. Hospitals, on the other hand, are narrowly focused on profitable procedures, including surgery, biopsies, and imaging.[11] When they pursue affiliations with academic institutions, what they really want is the branding that a university medical center offers and the pool of nationally known specialists that makes a hospital a destination for patients across the country. What kind of negotiation can succeed when medical schools have one objective, and hospitals a vastly different one?

For universities the question becomes: Is it better to own a hospital and hence have complete control over the education and research enterprise, despite the attendant financial risk and regulatory constraints? Or is it better to affiliate with a hospital system built for efficient and cost-effective delivery of care, despite the problems of integrating medical education into such an enterprise?

To illustrate some real-world approaches, I'll begin with Tulane University's efforts over the years to partner with a hospital that could serve as a teaching institution for its medical students. As I mentioned earlier, I have been involved in this search both when I was president of the university and then for one year as president emeritus. This won't quite be a tell-all because, as of this writing, the university is still engaged in negotiations to alter our current arrangements. Though I can't give every specific, I can describe the history that led to this moment, and what is at stake for us now.

Tulane formerly owned and managed its own hospital, but at the dawn of managed care in the 1990s, when hospitals started losing a lot of money, the increasing financial drain jeopardized the success of the university. In 1995, three years before I became president, the university sold majority ownership of its hospitals to the Hospital Corporation of America (HCA), a for-profit operator of health-care facilities, in a 75–25 percent split, but with a 50–50 split in governance—which meant the school could control faculty time devoted to clinical services and hence preserve its educational mission. Since that time we have reduced our equity ownership while retaining the original governance structure. In retrospect (always a tantalizing view), we might have done better avoiding a for-profit, with its objective of generating a return for its shareholders. However, at the time, the CEO of HCA, Rick Scott, currently the governor of Florida, had a vision of HCA partnering with an outstanding university and medical school and using that brand and capability across the entire HCA platform— an exciting prospect, with the potential to support more education and research with clinical dollars. But after Scott left the organization, others didn't share that vision, and Tulane University

Hospital and Clinic (TUHC) ended up as just another hospital in their portfolio, vulnerable to the changes in health care that are imperiling the mission of educating physicians. Despite this change, through the years, HCA has attempted to recognize and respond to Tulane's educational mission and support it within the contours of its own mission and goals. Without HCA, it is unlikely that Tulane's medical school and hospital would have survived in the aftermath of Hurricane Katrina.

Tulane is deeply committed to its educational, research, and practice mission. You'll recall that the school's first incarnation was as the Medical College of Louisiana, founded in 1834 by a group of doctors after an outbreak of yellow fever in New Orleans; today, the School of Public Health and Tropical Medicine—the only school of its kind in the United States—together with our Primate Center and medical school have made the university an exceptionally rich environment for the health sciences.

Despite the strength of its medical curriculum, the university faces many obstacles, some of them universal but some peculiar to the city of New Orleans, where health care is complex and competitive. For one thing, the city has two major medical schools, an unusual feature for an urban center of its size. How that came to pass is one of those colorful Louisiana stories involving Huey Long, the grandiose ambivalent figure who presides over a considerable swath of the state's history. He founded Louisiana State University Medical School in New Orleans—directly across the street from Tulane Medical School—rather than in Baton Rouge, home of all the other LSU campuses, as a pointed affront to Tulane. Incensed over some now-forgotten criticism of him from a Tulane professor, Long created a state institution that would be solely for Louisiana natives as a slap at Tulane's supposed elitism.

The two schools have had a rivalry ever since that time, but both have used Charity Hospital to train their medical students and residents. Since the demise of Charity after Hurricane Katrina, a new University Medical Center (UMC), run by Louisiana Children's Medical Center, has arisen in the downtown BioDistrict; though both Tulane and LSU will continue to use UMC as a teaching hospital, LSU has more influence at UMC because it is LSU's primary hospital in New Orleans, while for Tulane the primary institution is the Tulane Medical Center.

Apart from this background rivalry, the town's changing demographics make the fight for a medical footprint more intense. The decline in population after Katrina, an estimated loss of 100,000 people, has meant increased competition for patients among providers. At the same time, the health-care market in New Orleans is consolidating, with mergers that aim to create more beds in larger systems and thus achieve economies of scale at a time of cost pressures. In our own case, HCA is seeking to restructure its relationship with Tulane in order to expand and have greater control over its destiny, a not unreasonable position. As a city, New Orleans may ultimately have too many beds, given the new University Medical Center and a new VA hospital that opened in 2016. In contrast to a Boston or a New York City, we can't support a large number of training programs and care systems; regionally, we aren't an automatic destination as a center of excellence given our proximity to Atlanta, Birmingham, and Houston.

In terms of the educational mission of the university, Tulane's hospital center has too *few* beds, only three hundred—an insufficient patient population for faculty and students. Tulane's goal of enhancing its stature as an academic medical center justifies continued consideration of new and restructured affiliation agreements consistent with the mission of the university and medical school. The dealings with HCA are confidential, but the general outline is this: HCA, Tulane, and potential partners (public hospitals) are not always aligned as to goals, strategy, and culture. These facts, combined with politics and personalities, lead to difficulty in finding common ground in partnership agreements. Not surprising, given a crowded field of players jockeying for market share and enhanced reputation in a smaller market, plus misaligned objectives between the university and current and prospective affiliated hospitals. I do believe that eventually there will be alignment, because it will be in everyone's best interest to find common ground.

But how do you get it done? One case worthy of study is Vanderbilt. The Vanderbilt University Medical Center (VUMC) was previously owned and operated by the university, but faced with the rapidly changing health-care environment, the board of trustees opted in 2014 to reconfigure the hospital as a not-for-profit academic medical center financially distinct from Vanderbilt University. Immediate advantages included access to capital unavailable to them previously, a result of their adopting a more nimble organizational structure separate from the university's board and approaching the private equity market with an independently established A3 credit rating.[12] VUMC will also build on an existing affiliation (since 2011) with Vanderbilt Health Affiliated Network (VHAN), a regional entity that manages fifty hospitals in five states. As Jeff Balser, vice-chancellor for health affairs, describes it, given the consolidation occurring in health care, "we can either be part of a system or we can lead a system." Interestingly, Balser will continue to lead VUMC and serve as dean of the Vanderbilt School of Medicine, exactly the template established by William Osler in the 1890s at Johns Hopkins, suggesting that the link between academic faculty and the teaching hospital will continue despite financial and structural changes.

On the other hand, certain aspects of the merger imply that the new environment will be significantly less academic, despite the Vanderbilt brand name. The new Vanderbilt Health Affiliated Network is an "open" system in which the majority of physicians will be affiliated providers without faculty appointments at the School of Medicine.[13] The question is whether the faculty at the medical school will be under increasing pressure to provide competitive clinical services at the one academic medical center in the network, to the detriment of training and research programs. What drove this reconfiguration in the first place was a series of market factors: consolidation of hospitals, the decline in inpatient admissions, the undue burden of uninsured care on academic medical centers,[14] the evolving transition from big box hospitals to clinics in the community, the competition for patients, and the resulting emphasis on convenience, pricing, and amenities like Wi-Fi and food services.

Given that all academic medical centers will ultimately have to find ways to address the rising commercialization and consumerism of health care, the Vanderbilt reconfiguration is a notably creative attempt to deal with these realities head-on. The VHAN partner hospitals benefit by gaining access to Vanderbilt's medical specialists so they can expand their realm of care under the Vanderbilt brand; VUMC, the academic flagship, gains patient referrals that require a higher level of expertise, thus expanding its reach. A good deal all around, except for two sensitive areas: Will Vanderbilt faculty continue to have the freedom and time to teach and do research? And—a question that haunts every new deal and every step forward—what will happen to the care of the indigent?

I would propose that we all look long and hard at the Vanderbilt experiment; this might very well be the best model for academic medical centers in the future. It's true that all solutions (like all politics) are ultimately local. What works for Vanderbilt in the Mid-South, where the regional potential is wide open, might not work in densely populated urban areas.[15] But the model is a good one, which could possibly be adapted to fit other markets and cities. And the leadership exemplified by Balser is also instructive. You need a person with vision, but also with the interpersonal skills to bring others to the table. And you need someone with executive ability, the "get it done" mind-set that actually gets it done. Balser has all three of these capabilities and can be trusted, as dean of the medical school and chief of the hospital, to make the new affiliation work to the extent possible.

For universities struggling with their medical schools and hospitals, a good first step would be to seriously consider spinning off their hospital to create more nimble entities—both university and hospital system—with an ability to access capital and patients in a competitive market and to pursue their respective missions with more clarity and focus. But the second step is all-important: Get a good affiliation agreement, because a bad one will damage the medical school, the faculty, and the research and teaching enterprise.

For Tulane, the primacy of education and research is absolute as we look for a fruitful partnership with a hospital system that can increase our beds, utilize our brand name, and value and support the medical school's research and teaching missions. I not only believe this is possible; I believe it is necessary. The university's role in preserving knowledge, promoting innovation, and training the next generation of physicians cannot be abandoned even as economic priorities change and the marketplace grows more powerful. We need leaders, people like Balser and others, who can negotiate a good affiliation that respects the intellectual contributions of our best academic physicians, increases the patient population seen by trainees, and continues to protect the university's mission of education and research. Without such persistent vision, academic medicine will disappear, to be replaced by vocational training of a lower order and a one-size-fits-all approach to health care.

Of course universities can, on occasion, successfully administer their own hospital system. I've mentioned Emory and Johns Hopkins, but another outstanding example is Penn Medicine; created by Judith Rodin, university president from 1994 to 2004, Penn Medicine consolidated the Penn School of Medicine with the University of Pennsylvania Hospital into a single integrated system. In recent years J. Larry Jameson, executive vice president of the University of Pennsylvania Health System and dean of Perelman School of Medicine, has further strengthened the system. During Jameson's tenure, Penn Medicine has acquired Chester County Hospital and Lancaster General Health, built a new medical education center on the Philadelphia campus, and strongly emphasized translational research, developing personalized medicine initiatives that deliver new therapies to patients more quickly. Like Jeff Balser, Jameson has a dual role as dean of the medical school and chief of the hospital, though in Jameson's case he is VP of the entire Pennsylvania Health System. Balser's management of VUMC, the flagship hospital, is constrained by dealings with VHAN, the larger health-care network, while Jameson has absolute authority over business decisions because of the unified organization.[16]

As I've pointed out, the old model of a medical center owned and operated by the university makes protection of academic objectives that much easier. The wind, though, is blowing the other way, with more and more research universities preferring to partner with outside entities rather than run their own hospitals—which is why the right kind of affiliation is so important in supporting learning environments for physicians in training.

Organizational configuration is a key factor, but I don't want to give the impression that sustaining academic excellence is simply a matter of structural arrangements. The curricula of medical schools across the country are changing in response to all the pressures described in this chapter, and much thought is being given to preserving the quality of the profession while keeping an eye on costs and efficiency. One obvious development in the past two decades has been the digitalizing of many aspects of medicine, from electronic medical records to algorithms that offer diagnoses and suggest treatment protocols.

Many have greeted the computer models with hosannas, predicting a new era of medical perfection free of pesky human errors. Watson, the IBM computer, has been getting a daily diet of every new research paper published in journals across the world, meaning he (it?) "knows" more than any single human being ever could. But before we proclaim a new utopia, I will point out that a recent study found that an astonishing 80 percent of research experiments could not be replicated—so who really knows what Watson "knows"? When the data are flawed, the conclusions are flawed: "garbage in, garbage out."[17] Many experiments are influenced by confirmation bias, and many journals publish only positive results. We still have to teach medical minds to think, and think hard, about clinical and basic science problems rather than simply encouraging students to type a question into a search engine.[18]

Computers and technology are here to stay, and both, despite flaws, unquestionably contribute to medical education and health-care delivery. But another development in medical education, the incorporation of arts and humanities into the standard science curriculum, provides important balance—an attempt to preserve the human dimension of the field as it grows increasingly technocratic, bureaucratic, and fragmented. Studies have shown that medical students actually decline in empathy during the course of training, given the increasing emphasis on efficiency and cost-effectiveness rather than compassionate care and the doctor-patient relationship. Courses in ethics and the arts at Stanford, Harvard, Columbia, Penn State, and elsewhere aim to make students better physicians by enhancing insight into the moral and emotional dilemmas of modern medical practice. The literature of illness and disease allows students to imaginatively rehearse encounters with patients, and courses in the arts, training students in visual observation, improve their reading of radiologic images and other markers of disease.[19] Bioethics courses address end-of-life issues and the knotty contradictions between what is technically possible and what is morally right in an era of transplantation, gene editing, and designer drugs.

I am heartened by this development as medical schools respond to new realities, yet hold to fundamental values and train medical students in critical thinking and empathic connection—a case of universities doing what they do best. And, to return once again to my earlier point, I also believe that the right organizational structure can solve thorny problems. Hospital affiliation agreements that free a university from undue burdens while preserving governance authority and hence medical training are a structural response to the new world we're living in.

In addition to making advantageous agreements with health-care systems, what else can university presidents do to promote medical research, teaching, and clinical care in the face of encroaching corporate influence on medicine? The discovery of new knowledge—basic and translational research generating new models, treatments, procedures, and devices—has always been the gold standard of academic medicine. As such, research is likely to continue despite financial pressures and structural changes in the profession. However, teaching and clinical practice are more vulnerable to current trends; if these activities become "rote" and less scholarly, medical schools may end up resembling trade schools more than they do professional ones.

Teaching and clinical service are not mere add-ons to the enterprise of academic medicine; they are its heart and soul. A broader definition of scholarship formulated by Ernest Boyer in *Scholarship Reconsidered* (1990)[20] proposes, in addition to discovery, three other categories of scholarly activity: integration, application, and pedagogy. Clinician-educators in academic medicine are practicing these last three pursuits, in an environment where their activity is critical not only to the functioning of hospitals, but to the quality of the medical profession as newly minted MDs embark on their careers. This kind of "engaged scholarship," which I discuss at greater length in the next chapter, has been underrecognized in higher education generally. In the case of medicine, it's a particularly unfortunate oversight, because the teaching of young physicians and the care of patients have enormous practical implications for the well-being of society as a whole. University presidents can help preserve the mission of academic medicine by working to recognize and promote faculty engaged in teaching and clinical care, bringing deans and department heads into the discussion and building support in the medical community at large.

One school that is making efforts in that direction is the Virginia Commonwealth University School of Medicine, where promotion and tenure guidelines specifically reference Boyer in itemizing the kinds of activity that will be considered for promotion to full professor at the medical school.[21] This kind of explicit messaging, offering the possibility of reward and advancement, can change the culture and quality of a medical school, encouraging young faculty and safeguarding the traditional analytic, pedagogic, and clinical pursuits associated with academic centers of excellence.[22]

In short: We as university leaders can build consensus, champion quality, and support all the varied aspects of a medical school's scholarly mission, even while ceding primary control over hospital administration to external organizations. We can preserve what is best about academic medicine while ceasing to let the tail wag the dog.

6

Brave New World

Innovation and Scholarship

The idea is not to raze the ivory tower, where scholars of integrity, brilliance, and creativity are pursuing knowledge of both immediate and long-term importance. The idea is to let in some light and air rather than suffocate under the weight of tradition.

Thirty years ago when I was dean of the Weatherhead School of Management at Case Western Reserve University, I, along with my colleagues, spearheaded the development of a new doctoral program, the Executive Doctorate in Management (EDM), combining scholarship with a focus on problems of practice. We saw that the university could be a resource for the business community by offering a model of lifelong learning for people with a passion for knowledge and discovery. That this was a relatively new idea in the business school world only made it more appealing. Why play "me too" in relation to other schools when you could be the first to implement a new pathway to learning, competence, and creativity? The program, specifically for high-potential midlife professionals, was designed to address broad social, economic, and political processes affecting management decisions and allowed students to research issues applicable to their own organizations. By bringing practical experiences into the academy and bringing scholarly analysis into the workplace, the program represented an emerging "scholarship of engagement" that recognized the value of turning outward to the world to grapple with needs and problems in the public realm.

But when we proposed the program to the Faculty Senate, my colleagues and I encountered serious resistance from faculty members, who feared that a "doctorate in management" would essentially be an inferior PhD unworthy of the name. As dean, I navigated people's objections in a number of ways. First, I made it clear that I wasn't going to sign on to anything short of a doctorate. I took this hard line out of a strong conviction that we could offer executives advanced knowledge and skills that would prepare them to become better leaders and engaged citizens of the world. Because my own area of scholarship is business administration, I have always been interested in the intersection of theory and practice, and in my mind, nothing but a doctoral degree would meet the need of seasoned executives in search of new understandings and insights. Our already-existing PhD program, focused on scholarly research and teaching, was unsuitable for this demographic, and a new masters program, no matter how you framed it or what you called it, would not attract these senior managers, most of whom already had an MBA degree, or accomplish these specific goals.

In addition to drawing a firm line, I tried to shepherd faculty along to a new way of thinking. We collaborated on a "perpetual first draft," open to edits and revisions, and I took straw votes on a given idea without asking for a commitment—until, that is, I closed the discussion and said we had sufficient consensus to move on. I also put John Aram, the faculty member most adamantly opposed to the idea, in charge of developing the EDM, on the theory that critics could help us. I knew that John would set the highest possible standards of scholarly excellence in order to justify granting a degree at the doctoral level, and he did just that, giving the program a substance and heft that satisfied the skeptics.

But the process was slow. It took nearly nine years, 1986 to 1995, of talking and persuading (and of not backing down or giving up) to inaugurate the Executive Doctorate in Management in an academic environment where tradition was sacred and change was suspect. Things move faster when events dictate, and Hurricane Katrina in 2005 was, among many other things, a catalyst for change. As mentioned earlier, in the tense months after the storm, shared governance, along with the usual rules (and constraints), was suspended with the scattering of the faculty across the nation. Faced with the devastation around us, we who were working to reinvent Tulane came to the notion of public service as a core element in our mission. In 2006, twelve months after Katrina, enrollment in a program at the Center for Public Service became an integral part of the core curriculum.

Since then, numerous service-learning courses have been developed, often in partnership with community organizations, combining academic inquiry with a host of activities designed to meet the social challenges associated with neglect and poverty in an urban population.[1] For a decade now, "engaged scholarship" has been on the rise at Tulane, everything from community building in Ecuador (as I'll be describing later) to a study of the urban planning crisis in New Orleans post-Katrina to a program teaching debating techniques and classical rhetoric to middle and high school students all over the city.

These forms of scholarship, reaching out to communities near and far and connecting theory with practice, haven't achieved full recognition within the university, with some Tulane professors still questioning the scholarly value of engagement. In 2013, the Tulane Office of Academic Affairs together with an ad hoc faculty committee, formed to discuss community service and collaboration, issued a white paper, "Academic Review and Engagement at Tulane University," arguing for inclusion of engagement as one of the categories considered in the granting of promotion and tenure to faculty members, and citing research showing its pedagogical effectiveness. The scholarship of engagement must achieve the same recognition accorded the scholarship of discovery, that is, the creation of new knowledge, if it is to acquire legitimacy.

At both Weatherhead and Tulane, despite faculty members who were prone to circle the wagons and defend their territory, I acted on my belief in the kind of scholarship—practical, risk taking, innovative—that directly addresses problems in the real world. At the other end of the spectrum from domain-specific theoretical inquiry, such practical scholarship transcends disciplinary confines in order to do justice to the complexity of contemporary issues.

One way of framing the continuum between pure and applied scholarship is Pasteur's quadrant, developed by Donald Stokes, which assigns a given accomplishment in the STEM disciplines to one of four areas on a graph.[2] The sweet spot on the graph, where the y axis represents "fundamental understanding" and the x axis "considerations of use," is the upper right quadrant, indicating the intersection of knowledge and practical application—exactly what many university researchers are seeking.

A seminal document that strongly influenced me to appreciate practical as well as pure scholarship is *Scholarship Reconsidered* by Ernest Boyer, published in 1990.[3] Boyer offered a wider lens on the work of the academy, dividing scholarship into four types: discovery—original work that creates new knowledge; integration—the synthesis of knowledge across disciplines to create new insights and understandings; application—the exercise of knowledge through service directly related to scholarly inquiry and evaluated according to standards of excellence; and teaching—the practice of transmitting knowledge to the next generation, thereby inspiring and mentoring talented young people to create and innovate, and the systematic study and evaluation of such practice. Naturally, these divisions aren't rigid; innovative scholarship often has aspects of all four types.

Boyer's reframing has had important consequences within the academy, including a vocabulary for describing multiple scholarships and the development of new guidelines that acknowledge the legitimacy of scholarly activities other than discovery. You'll recall that Boyer's language found its way into the promotion and tenure guidelines of Virginia Commonwealth University School of Medicine, sign of a developing trend to broaden the definition of scholarship in professional schools. And though promotion and tenure guidelines traditionally focus on national and international preeminence as evidenced by publications, lectures, and meetings, engaged scholarship, which characteristically has a local or regional emphasis, generates a much wider impact than that would imply, creating models that can be widely replicated and establishing new standards shared by an interconnected world. Ultimately, Boyer's framework has the potential to make our colleges and universities more globally distinctive while fostering broader types of innovation and a more inclusive environment for a wide variety of disciplines and professorial interests.

Despite this potential, the more inclusive notion of scholarship is as yet largely unrealized. Discovery is still privileged within universities, and traditional metrics and evidence (top-tier publications, citations, federal research awards) continue to dominate promotion and tenure decisions. From my perspective, this narrow interpretation of scholarship is detrimental to a university's ability to best serve its students and society at large in a rapidly changing world.

Given my view, I will devote minimal space here to the already well-documented scholarship of discovery, a form of scholarship I highly value, in order to explore academic endeavors that have been neglected or undervalued. But to give credit where credit is due: a list of "greatest hits" from the research community might include the discovery of streptomycin, part of the wave of new antibiotics that ushered in a revolution in the treatment of formerly fatal infectious diseases (Rutgers University); retractable locking seatbelts that radically reduced driving fatalities (University of Minnesota); 47 percent faster weight gain in premature infants who are massaged, as compared to those left in an incubator (university research supported by the National Institutes of Health); the CRISPR gene-editing technique that holds potential for preventing and curing a number of diseases (coinvented at UC Berkeley and further developed at Harvard and MIT's Broad Institute); the lithium ion battery for smartphones and tablets (University of Texas at Austin); touch screens (University of Kentucky) and multiscrolling capability (University of Delaware); and Social Security (the result of social science research at the University of Wisconsin).

All these accomplishments underscore a central fact: the commitment to scientific and technological innovation has put the

United States at the forefront globally and yielded extraordinary contributions to human knowledge, social progress, and individual well-being. At the same time, I want to recognize the powerful importance of the humanities and arts, under siege in a society that privileges science and technology but another jewel in the crown of higher education. Discovery and innovation are not confined to the lab bench; scholarship in the liberal arts and the social and behavioral sciences has yielded new insights into gender, diversity, sexual orientation, and identity that have transformed our culture, contributing to political movements and policies that ensure greater social justice. Such scholarship has enriched our understanding of other cultures and eras and sharpened our aesthetic and moral perceptions. To repeat the old chestnut attributed to George Santayana: "Those who cannot remember the past are condemned to repeat it."

I also want to underscore another fundamental contribution of the liberal arts: the critical-thinking and problem-solving skills developed in humanities courses apply to every field—medicine, law, business, politics—and to every job a graduate will hold in the future. Such analytic abilities are also central to participation in a democratic society, where evaluating the source of a website, the truth of a campaign claim, or the benefits of a policy allows citizens to separate fact from fiction and to exercise their rights intelligently.

The cultivation of rational thought, the preservation of the past, and the pursuit of knowledge that contextualizes the present and illuminates the future remain vital missions of higher education (and for some institutions, the prime mission). Not to be too dire, a neglect of the liberal arts, rooted in the trivium and quadrivium of antiquity, could lead to another Dark Ages—and the need for another Renaissance, to recover lost knowledge and reconstitute a lost world.

The task of preserving and enhancing both STEM and the liberal arts is a central mission of institutions of higher education, but another task, equally important, is to embrace scholarship that is responsive to the times we live in and, directly or indirectly, engages with the world outside the ivory tower. Examples of such engagement with contemporary issues, occurring all across the sector, are numerous and varied; the forthcoming illustrations, drawn from the disparate realms of the social sciences, ecological studies, design thinking, and online pedagogy, will serve to indicate both the breadth and the depth of this emerging scholarship. I'll begin with endeavors in the social sciences that have had tremendous impact on how we act in the world, and how we frame and understand our choices.

In the realms of economics and psychology, "choices" is a key word. A century's worth of research on decision making has yielded multiple strategies for choosing the right option in situations of uncertainty, and especially financial uncertainty. One element of this research is its multidisciplinary aspect. The rational economic man pursuing "expected utility" on the basis of statistical evidence—so-called decision analysis—was the work of operations researchers from World War II, mathematicians, and game theorists, as well as economists. Countering this model of choice based on decision trees and Bayesian probabilities, two psychologists, Daniel Kahneman (winner of the Nobel Prize in Economic Sciences) and Amos Tversky, performed experiments in the 1970s showing that people fail to make decisions on the basis of reasoned assessment; instead, they are inclined to rely on rules of thumb and gut instincts, that is, on heuristics and biases.[4]

In a book entitled *Nudge*, University of Chicago economist Richard Thaler and coauthor Cass Sunstein built on these earlier psychological insights, developing a new model of the economic man: a creature of implicit biases, mental shortcuts, and irrational impulses, someone who requires cues and incentives—nudging—to make good choices.[5] Thaler and Sunstein coined the term "choice architecture" to describe ways of presenting information that steer people toward constructive behaviors. The field that emerged from the work of Thaler, Sunstein, and others is behavioral economics (though Thaler will be the first to tell you that there's more psychology and common sense than economics and mathematics in many of his proposals).

One policy initiative stemming from the work of Thaler and Sunstein is automatic enrollment in retirement savings plans. Based on an understanding of the human bias toward inertia—passivity as the default setting of the mind and preferable to the cost, however minimal, of opting out—automatic enrollment has resulted in major increases in participation. Recent applications of behavioral science include the "Save More Tomorrow" plan, which commits a percentage of future wages to pensions (future wages are more acceptable for that purpose than present take-home pay); the Affordable Care Act, which is to some degree a default enrollment plan; voter registration (Oregon has recently initiated automatic voter registration in the state); and free school meals for poor children (putting the meal on the table, as it were, rather than requiring low-income families to apply or enroll).[6]

Behavioral economics is also influencing policy on climate change. Ben Ho, a behavioral economist now at Vassar College, has developed an interest in how feelings of guilt, altruism, and satisfaction affect people's willingness to reduce their carbon footprint. People aware of others' energy consumption reduced their own if it was higher than average; frugal households continued to be frugal if they received a smiley face on their bill; people who could see their consumption via glowing orbs and smart meters were more inclined to change their behavior.

Other measures to incentivize new behaviors include using scare tactics to tap a visceral emotional reaction, for example, emphasizing climate effects close to home—disappearing ski slopes at Vail rather than sinking islands in the South Pacific—to jolt people into action. Another line of research has found that people cooperate in energy conservation when they feel that they are part of a group, and that they have an active role in solving the problem. Still another identifies multiple climate audiences, from deniers to alarmists, each requiring different persuasive language and arguments.

Most social scientists agree there is no single silver bullet—rather, as one researcher puts it, what's needed is "silver buckshot." The hope is that hitting many targets and working on many fronts will produce a groundswell of public opinion similar to the shift in perspective that radically reduced smoking in the United States. The idea is, we can break the carbon habit, too, with the proper choice architecture, incentives, and communication.[7] It's this kind of scholarship, connecting disparate disciplines and making results accessible to both fellow researchers and the lay public, that will generate solutions to the most pressing problems of our time.[8]

In a sense, universities are returning to their roots by championing scholarship of this kind. The Morrill Act of 1862 that established land-grant colleges in every state emphasized the teaching of "agriculture and the mechanic arts"; not long after, the Hatch Act of 1887 gave federal funds to each state school for an agriculture experiment station to study soil minerals and plant growth in order to improve food production. These stations, funded by combined federal and state dollars under the National Institute of Food and Agriculture, continue to turn research into action in areas that now include food security and safety, climate change, environmental sustainability, and bioenergy.

Ever since Katrina, Tulane has been at the forefront of a more collaborative and applied scholarship, committed to change-oriented scholarship that brings together faculty members, students, and local residents in projects addressing community needs. An illustration of this engaged, public scholarship is the work of Jordan Karubian, an assistant professor of ecology and evolutionary biology at Tulane, who combines traditional research with community building for the critical purpose of saving biodiversity on the planet.[9]

Among Karubian's many initiatives is a study, close to home, of the foraging ecology of the brown pelicans of the Gulf of Mexico after the Deepwater Horizon oil spill of 2010. Farther afield, in the Choco rainforest of Ecuador, Karubian has educated local residents as de facto biologists and conservation advocates and offered environmental tutorials to teachers in fifteen communities in Ecuador's Mache-Chindul Reserve, reaching five hundred children annually.[10] Similar efforts are underway in Milne Bay Province in Papua New Guinea, where local residents have been trained to oversee conservation of hyperdiverse grasslands and savannas threatened by population growth, climate change, agricultural development, and fossil fuel exploitation.

Karubian points out that such community engagement improves not only the quality of life in these regions, but the quality of the research that his lab conducts. He describes community partners who "excel in knowledge of the natural history and basic biology of our study organisms," and who thus help generate the hypotheses that Karubian's lab ends up testing with standardized data collection. Karubian has also emphasized that community engagement contributed directly to twenty-nine of his publications and provides evidence of "broader impacts" valued by federal funding sources and society at large. His effectiveness in creating positive change in these biodiverse societies has established his lab as a hub for solutions-based research.[11]

Karubian embodies what I consider to be a holistic scholar—one who excels in the traditional sense (papers on such things as fairy wren sexual dimorphism published in peer-reviewed journals) but also makes a broader impact by engaging with local residents, who under his tutelage have become computer literate and who design their own studies, publish in major scientific journals, and give international presentations, thereby seeding a conservation movement in these ecologically rich corners of the world. His lab is committed to pedagogy across the entire spectrum, from public school children in remote areas to university students from all over (the United Kingdom, the Netherlands, Germany, Australia, as well as from schools across the United States).

Karubian, a "hybrid" scholar whose efforts outside the realm of discovery are lauded but generally perceived as extrascholarly activity, is a rare bird (pun intended). In order for scholars like him to flourish and become the norm, the academy needs to recognize and reward engagement as scholarship. The scholarship of discovery—an article like Karubian's "Mating Behavior Drives Seed Dispersal in the Long-Wattled Umbrellabird *Cephalopterus penduliger*"—adds to the net sum of human knowledge, but Karubian's community building in remote areas has equal importance, strengthening the prospects that the natural world will continue to survive in all its variety and splendor.

I want to invoke here the idea of a paradigm shift that I mentioned at the outset of this book, in reference to Thomas Kuhn's *The Structure of Scientific Revolutions*: the notion that accumulating data force a rethinking of a prior model and generate a new template aligned with new facts. The next generation of scholars won't be satisfied with the traditional approach to scholarship. Schooled in a world of instant communication, crowdsourcing, big data, and an acute awareness of global problems, the students of today are unaccustomed to boundaries, disciplinary or otherwise. Already used to expressing their scholarship in nontraditional ways—online, using multimedia formats—they also are likely to have had experience with service learning and community engagement. They come to higher education with a hunger to apply their knowledge to the real world.

The Institute of Design at Stanford, known as the d.school, is an exemplar of this "real-world" scholarship that breaks the old mold. The d.school escapes the orthodoxies of academic departments and hierarchies because it doesn't grant degrees (though courses there earn credits) and because it is a deliberate, somewhat brash "mash-up of industry, academia and the big world beyond campus." Rather than focusing on design as aesthetics, David Kelley, the founder of the d.school and CEO of Ideo, a consulting firm, has proposed the concept of "design thinking" and developed a methodology combining creative and analytic approaches. The ethos is utilitarian, in the broad sense, proposing practical answers to multifaceted societal problems.[12]

Design thinking involves a resistance to obvious solutions, a tolerance of the uncertainty and ambiguity associated with complex ("hairball") problems, empathic engagement with people out in the world who are experiencing the problem, and the creation of prototypes that are tested in the field and recycled through various iterations until the best solution is reached. For example, one problem posed to a student team was how to make expensive infant incubators in rural hospitals in Nepal more affordable. The obvious answer would be to reduce the cost of the incubators through redesign and use of less expensive materials. But the team that traveled to Nepal saw the situation at eye level and realized what the problem really was. There were, in fact, functional, empty incubators at the hospital, but they were unreachable by babies born in far-off villages. The need was not cheaper incubators but effective transport from the villages to the hospital, so the team designed the "Embrace Warmer," a portable device that keeps premature babies warm during transport. It's now used in eleven countries.[13]

The core method of the d.school is an elevation of inductive process, using fieldwork and observation as a spur to identifying the right question and suggesting a range of answers. In one sense design thinking is a version of the traditional scholarship of discovery, open-ended investigation of a question via experiment. But in another sense, it's a shake-up of academic norms, in its cross-disciplinary approach, its turn outward to the "real world," and its rejection of received ideas.[14] Finding the problem, reframing the question, and coming up with a range of unexpected solutions based on experience is far from the orthodox (and often heavily theoretical) approach of professional graduate schools. Management theories in business, diagnostic algorithms in medicine, and precedents and logic in law are things to learn "inside the box"; design thinking steps away from the known and expected, and leads to outside-the-box innovation.

Teaching is often relegated to an afterthought in any consideration of serious scholarship, but the study of pedagogy (as opposed to the practice of it) is gaining in importance as universities and colleges explore innovations in online learning, seeking to control costs, improve productivity, reduce achievement gaps, and broaden access. William Bowen (who, sadly, died recently), president emeritus of Princeton University and founding chairman of ITHAKA, a nonprofit organization supporting the transformation of scholarship and teaching in an online environment, has written that the digital revolution is fact, and that a new generation embraces it. It's time, he says, to adjust to a new reality. Referring to recent research on hybrid learning (interactive online materials combined with once-a-week meetings), Bowen says, "The most important single result of our study: It calls into question the position of the skeptic who says, 'I don't want to try this because it will hurt my students.'"[15]

The study in question, carried out in 2012 at public university campuses (two in the SUNY system, two in the CUNY system, and three in the University of Maryland system), compared a treatment group taking a hybrid course in statistics, using online materials from Carnegie Mellon University, with students in traditional statistics classes. The results showed that hybrid learning occurred more quickly and saved staffing costs and classroom space. A later study (2014) tested the effectiveness of hybrid formats in seventeen math and biology courses at the University System of Maryland, with an additional ten case studies of smaller courses in the arts, literature, and psychology. Teachers used online materials in a variety of ways: to supplement textbooks, enhance presentations with video lectures, and strengthen critical-thinking skills. The results indicated that students from hybrid sections performed as well as or better than students in traditional sections, but were less happy with reduced face-to-face time with professors. Faculty (interestingly, since they weren't automatic enthusiasts at the beginning) were generally pleased with incorporated online materials.[16]

Bowen's conclusions are nuanced: he says more research is needed and that, to date, online learning might be better used in a statistics than a literature or international affairs course.[17] Bowen also suggests that it's important to study traditional as well as online modes of teaching and to analyze which settings and populations would most benefit. In the end, Bowen recommends a portfolio approach. Online learning is not a cure-all, and one size doesn't fit all.[18]

Kim Cassidy, president at Bryn Mawr, where another study of blended learning occurred, makes the further point that faculty need to see for themselves the advantages of online modalities if these initiatives are to take root. The study of a self-paced online math supplement to improve performance in difficult introductory STEM courses was not a controlled experiment because Cassidy didn't want to inhibit professors' personal adaptations by using a rigid experimental protocol. Bryn Mawr, while not able to make specific comparisons with face-to-face outcomes given the looseness of the study, reported results for blended-learning students, including Pell-eligible students, that were better than the historical mean of traditional sections.[19]

Traditional teaching continues to have a place—indeed, some would say, an indispensable place—in universities, but excellent pedagogy, as a practice rather than a research domain, is hard to quantify, somewhat intangible, and susceptible to a range of emotional distortion, everything from idealization to satire. It's associated with "hearts and minds," a phrase that's often discounted as empty rhetoric but in fact captures a profound truth about the college experience. Ways of thinking are established and passions ignited in those four years. In the realm of "scholarship," face-to-face, one-on-one teaching is often regarded as nonscholarly but here, too, the academy has to rethink its standards and priorities. Institutional preoccupations with rankings, revenue streams, and grants can draw faculty toward the activities that win them recognition, and away from teaching. But teaching clearly contributes to core institutional goals, as does mentoring of students and younger faculty. "Good citizenship"—committee work relating to accreditation, general education requirements, internal policies, and a host of administrative study groups—counts, or should count. The unbundling of faculty roles, with nontenured adjuncts assigned the citizenship/teaching jobs and research reserved for elite faculty, can undermine innovation and vitality throughout the institution. We will all benefit if the scholars at our institutions are not only allowed but challenged to put teaching on a par with research.

What stops us from expanding our notion of substantive and worthy work in the academy? I believe the chief cause is the socialization of the faculty to traditional norms involving legitimacy and academic rigor, creating anxiety about change of any kind. There's a mind-set of exclusion and exclusivity: jump through these particular hoops. What's needed, first, is a new set of metrics that are more appropriate to the aims of other forms of scholarship; rather than the traditional publications and citations, such things as qualitative analysis, digital media presence, and evidence of "real-world" impacts, including policy reports and policy changes, could be used to document the merit of other forms of knowledge making. Boyer's language of the "scholarships" has been available for over twenty-five years; it's time to genuinely operationalize this concept and change our processes of promotion and tenure. The idea is not to raze the ivory tower, where scholars of integrity, brilliance, and creativity are pursuing knowledge of both immediate and long-term importance; the idea is to let in some light and air rather than suffocate under the weight of tradition.

Which brings me to the subject of the next chapter: shared governance, and the weight of tradition.

7

Can We All Get Along?

The truth is, it isn't easy to make beautiful music together. Shared governance is a compelling idea, but in practice it often devolves into conflict and cacophony.

My first convocation address to Tulane back in 1998 was in large part about the issue of shared governance, that central and enduring conundrum of American colleges and universities. Actually, I made a joke about it. I described my brief time as president as the second-best job I'd ever had. What was the best? My six months of being president-elect—the wonderful honeymoon period when I was welcomed with open arms, intently listened to, and rarely disagreed with. With no responsibility and the freedom to say and do virtually anything, I could do no wrong.

As any university president knows, that isn't the way it works on a college campus. The thing about shared governance that makes it so hard is the sharing, and almost every decision a president makes—even if it comes after extensive discussion with the board and the faculty—has a reasonable probability of eliciting dissent from one or more of the university's stakeholders. In that same speech of nearly twenty years ago, while embracing the basic values of academic freedom and shared governance, I noted the importance of context and of adaptive change, urging a reexamination of how those values are implemented in the constantly evolving environment of higher education.

I also offered an image of how our community might achieve its highest potential, picking the Cleveland Orchestra, the pride of my previous hometown, as a symbol of what Tulane could become.

The orchestra, with its 104 musicians, its hundreds of staff members working in the background, its enthusiastic audience, and, of course, its conductor, could be viewed as a metaphor for the university, with the world-class musicians representing the faculty, the administrative staff creating the environment enabling a stellar performance, the students and alumni playing the loyal audience, and the president—standing on the podium, conductor's baton in hand—attempting to create unity out of a disparate assembly.

But the truth is, it isn't easy to make beautiful music together. Shared governance is a compelling idea, but in practice it often devolves into conflict and cacophony. Leaping ahead to my own experience at Tulane after Katrina decimated the campus, I was censured by the American Association of University Professors for terminating tenured professors during a suspension of normal operations and traditional governance during the emergency, when we were forced to close several departments under financial exigency. University presidents often have to walk a fine line between making decisions in an institution's best interests and honoring the democratic process of shared governance. The AAUP's censure illustrates a conflict that is always latently present between faculty and administration, which have differing objectives according to their roles and responsibilities.

When these conflicts burst out, a major factor is contingency—cultural upheaval, political shifts, and economic stresses, not to mention catastrophic events that no one can anticipate. As I've said often in this book, we are in one of those moments of external turmoil that puts unusual pressure on universities. Another factor in crises of authority is the personalities of those in leadership positions. And a third factor—the underlying common denominator of most derailments—is structural, involving the ways authority and accountability are distributed within universities.

The history of governance in our institutions of higher education sheds some light on the nature of this structure. From its beginnings in the colonial period, American higher education differed from the European template of a learned and revered professoriate as the locus of authority.[1] Founded in the Middle Ages and featuring master- and student-led guilds at the universities of Paris and

Bologna, European universities were primarily governed by faculty, with "rectors"—external representatives of church and state—subsidiary to the will of the professors. But in America, starting in the seventeenth century, lay boards with members coming from outside the university had dominant control, largely because in the early days faculty were transient tutors preparing for careers in the ministry, with little commitment to their teaching jobs.

Lay governance meant that the trustees in essence *were* the college or university, holding the power to hire and fire faculty and make ultimate institutional decisions.[2] Another feature dating to the seventeenth century was the necessity of recruiting a strong president, who at that time was invariably a learned clergyman with experience as a teacher. As the only educator on the lay board, the president accrued additional power, becoming head of the board and reporting to trustees. Though an external board and strong president remain fundamental attributes of American universities, social forces and market pressures have considerably altered trends in governance. In the first half of the nineteenth century, more power went to faculty, who had increased in number and were called upon to impose discipline on unruly students, with authority also going to alumni philanthropic associations that could help offset mounting financial deficits.[3]

Growing numbers of alumni on boards led to a division of labor, with narrow powers over curriculum and student affairs given to faculty while the public face of the institution, and all decisions relating to strategy and mission, belonged to the board. With the Morrill Acts of 1862 and 1890, which established the land-grant colleges, a similar division occurred at the great public universities, with trustees appointed by state governors exercising significant institutional authority and faculty retaining control of academic matters only. Given these developments, the president became a mediator between opposing factions—less the conductor with a baton than a peacemaker or consensus builder, and, in the end, the "decider."

From an organizational point of view, the three-way distribution of authority is problematic. Personally, I think the concept of shared governance is theoretically appealing but increasingly difficult to implement in a rapidly changing world where universities live and work in a fishbowl of attention and scrutiny. Among the difficulties of shared governance is the slow pace of change as proposals wend their way through committees and everyone has a say. Sometimes the "say" is significant—for example, when faculty raise legitimate concerns based on their deep experience—but sometimes dissent stems from self-interest, a clash of personalities, or competing goals held by various stakeholders. And the plans that issue from the drawn-out deliberative process tend to be watered-down compromises between opposing camps rather than vigorous or innovative strategies that inspire the whole community.

One reason for the widespread dysfunction in governance at this particular moment is the increasing divide between boards and faculty, as well as, in some cases, the administration. Given current fiscal realities and various stakeholder demands, a more corporate model has emerged, one that emphasizes fiscal responsibility and radical innovation. Boards with members drawn from the business sector and the political sphere are exerting more influence on institutional strategies and goals, with concomitant faculty unrest. Global and technological forces have also weakened faculty authority and commitment. Online learning, increasing disciplinary specialization, and a rise in the number of adjunct teachers have frayed the ties between faculty and university. And universities often fail to promote or compensate faculty who are "good citizens," serving on administrative committees and helping advance strategic goals. An us-versus-them mentality is not uncommon on college campuses, with distrust and incomprehension on both sides.

Meanwhile, presidents are looking for that magic baton that helps everyone sing in unison.

Before describing some case studies that demonstrate discord as well as a case (relatively rare, unfortunately) of harmony, I want to offer a few general observations on the main players in the governance triad. To begin with the role of faculty, the American Association of University Professors, the leading organization of college teachers in the country for the last one hundred years, has been a tireless advocate for faculty as a "locus of authority." Emphasizing the issue of autonomy in its 1915 "Declaration of Principles on Academic Freedom and Academic Tenure," the AAUP claimed that faculty were "not in any proper sense the employees" of the trustees who hired them, because of their particular areas of competence and because of their need for freedom of thought "without fear or favor." The AAUP mobilization was in part a response to a specific threat to academic freedom at a time of political suppression, with faculty being dismissed at institutions across the country for criticizing the potential entry of the United States into World War I.[4]

Later AAUP declarations asserted that faculty consent (either directly or through elected representatives) should be a prerequisite for any changes in educational policy, and urged that teachers be given ultimate authority over peer review, promotion, and selection of academic officers. In the last fifty years, the AAUP has promoted faculty participation in budgetary and departmental decisions, supported "dual-track bargaining" (a faculty union that negotiates salaries and a faculty senate engaged in traditional academic governance), and called for academic oversight of intercollegiate athletics.[5] At the same time, as mentioned earlier, a decline in institutional loyalty and an uptick in individual self-interest among faculty, particularly those in nontenured positions, call into question demands for more authority in matters of long-term strategy and goals without an equivalent measure of accountability on the part of the faculty.

Speaking now of boards: In my former life as a management professor with a research interest in corporate governance, I used to describe boards as one of four types: statutory (passive CEO and passive directors); underdeveloped (strong CEO, passive directors); underutilized (passive CEO, strong directors); and value creating (strong CEO, strong directors). From my experience in the academy, these classifications also apply to university board governance. The value-creating board is devoutly to be wished—a president with a clear vision, open mind, and commitment to transparency, and board members who are inquiring, creative, knowledgeable about their roles and responsibilities, and deeply committed to the institution. Many collapses of governance stem from dysfunctional pairings, with one weak partner and one strong, or, worst of all, two weak partners staggering under the burden of decision making. Another major distinction between boards is the difference between private self-perpetuating boards that appoint their own members, who tend to be parents or alumni with an emotional connection to the institution, and public boards where members are appointed by the state governor and consequently divide their loyalties between the institution and the politicians who backed them.[6]

As for the role of presidents, the characteristics of effective CEOs that I've described in writings on management apply as well to the university setting, despite the special requirements of shared governance. These traits are unsurprising to anyone versed in the literature of leadership: openness, transparency, confidence, the ability to communicate and listen, and the strength to take responsibility for ultimate decisions. Poor leadership is in essence the flip side: someone who lacks transparency and is defensive, captive to other interests, unable to communicate effectively and connect with people, rigidly resistant to opposing views, and incapable of decisive action.[7]

It would seem possible (if not necessarily easy) to arrive at good governance if everyone would just play his or her part. But because of the parties' differing objectives, the drawn-out process of gaining consensus, and unpredictable personality clashes, derailments are not infrequent. A case that has drawn headlines in recent years was the attempt by the Board of Visitors, that is, the trustees, at the University of Virginia to oust President Teresa Sullivan, a coup of sorts, which ended two weeks later with her reinstatement. The collapse of shared governance at UVA brought into focus long-standing problems with the board, the president, and the faculty.

The story, in brief, is this: The chair of the board, Rector Helen Dragas, initiated a campaign demanding Sullivan's resignation, setting off a full-throated protest from faculty, students, and alums. Dragas had expressed concern to another board member, Mark Kington, a hedge fund manager, about "big trends and long-term prospects for higher education delivery and funding," urging the introduction of online courses to compete with platforms being developed by schools like Harvard and Stanford. A month later Dragas received a letter signed by 450 faculty members complaining that salaries of $141,000 for full professors were far below average for the sector—a letter she interpreted as a "cry for help" given an unresponsive administration. Dragas, circumventing a Virginia law that required public announcement of any meeting of more than two visitors, began lobbying board members for Sullivan's ouster via one-on-one phone conversations, also briefing Virginia governor Bob McDonnell, who had appointed the university visitors, and approaching key donors and alumni as well. Within two months of initiating the campaign, Dragas and Kington presented Sullivan with a separation agreement. The next day, Sullivan consented to sign the agreement and resign, and two days after that, an email went out to the entire community announcing the resignation.

Then all hell broke loose. The UVA Faculty Senate reacted with shock, with the leader of the senate, law professor George Cohen, writing that faculty were "blindsided" by the decision. The salary letter seemed to have been more the airing of a grievance, not uncommon on campuses, than a complaint targeted at Teresa Sullivan, herself a scholar (a social scientist and demographer, whose work at the Universities of Texas and Michigan had been specifically about middle-class debt) and hence "one of them." Other segments of the community followed suit: program chairs, department heads, deans, students, families, and alumni all requested clarification from the board, invoking the principles of open debate and shared governance. Governor McDonnell wrote to the board that he did not intend to dictate the outcome, but barring action within a few days he would ask for the resignation of the entire board.

Two and a half weeks after Dragas and Kington presented Sullivan with the separation agreement, Sullivan was reinstated by a unanimous vote of the board. Though Dragas was reappointed by Mc-

Donnell for one more year, when she left the board in the summer of 2016, she said, "If I learned anything during my board service, it was that big decisions at public institutions need to be made in public."

That, surely, is one lesson, but what else can we learn from this tale? Some observers saw the matter as a conflict between wealthy business executives in love with the idea of "disruptive innovation" and advocates of public education, dedicated to the school's academic mission and cautious about change. Those skeptical about corporate influence blamed the Board of Visitors. Hunter Rawlings, head of the Association of American Universities, called UVA an "egregious" instance of boardroom intrigue.[8] Some blamed the president for being insufficiently inspirational, devoted to process rather than outcome, and not attuned to the bottom line—an "incrementalist" and "perseverer" rather than a dynamic visionary. Since her reinstatement Sullivan has formed a partnership with Coursera, introducing online courses[9]—one of Dragas's original objectives—but she has done so carefully and deliberately, cautioning that online platforms are still experimental.

This is a classic case of dysfunctional governance, with an overactive board that tried to intervene in day-to-day management (from determining the cost of historic building renovations to decisions on particular course offerings),[10] and a president who was perceived to be insufficiently attuned to the rising financial pressures affecting, among other things, the university hospital and research funding. Sullivan was also concerned about faculty buy-in and due process, resistant to raising tuition or expanding enrollment (two recommendations made by her predecessor John Casteen), and inclined to retrench and economize rather than imagine novel means of generating revenue.

An additional factor, specific to the University of Virginia, is its long history. Originally "Mr. Jefferson's University," an "academical village," as Jefferson described it, the school was steeped in tradition, governing itself without executive authority and relying solely on the Board of Visitors. Only early in the twentieth century did the university hire its first president, which meant some waning of the board's influence; yet even now a seat on the BOV remains one of the most prestigious gifts a governor can bestow on a Virginian.

In retrospect, the ingredients for a disaster were all in place: a board consisting of political appointees, mostly hedge fund managers and corporate executives rewarded by the governor for campaign contributions, and not one member with a background in education; a highly traditional culture (all male presidents, previously, and a board that continued to have considerable power); a push for innovation in a particular area, online courses, that trespassed on traditional academic purview; a school that, as one of the top five public universities in the country, was not in need of quick turnaround or "disruptive innovation"; and a president who was a woman, an outsider, a scholar (more aligned with the faculty than with the board), and an incrementalist rather than a change agent.[11]

Some might see the clash between Dragas and Sullivan as a strong trustee challenging a passive president. Clearly, Dragas had a bias for action, while Sullivan was more attuned to the usual pace of academic decision making. But I think the deeper issue here involves not personalities but the "when" and the "how" of effective action. UVA was not in crisis or in any urgent need of an immediate major transformation, so the board action was, at a minimum, ill-timed. The lack of transparency and communication also made it ill-conceived.

But the end of the story is ironic. The school wanted more flamboyance, dash, and bravado, and in the torrent of coverage about how the community came together to champion Teresa Sullivan, she became exactly that figure the board had been longing for—a national star, capable of commanding crowds and attracting dollars.

The orchestra analogy holds: each member is an individual, but if the ensemble is to succeed, all must play their roles with the knowledge that the sum is greater than the parts. When any member of the triad assumes a privileged status, the whole structure is likely to collapse. If UVA is a story of board overreach, involving conflicting personalities and agendas, the story of John

Silber at Boston University, president between 1971 and 1996 and chancellor between 1996 and 2003, is by and large the tale of one personality and one agenda. After Silber's death in 2012, a *Boston Globe* article on Silber's "passionate, opinionated legacy" described him as an elitist who repeatedly traded blows with liberal opponents. Welfare, feminism, and bilingual education were all targets of his disdain. To take a single example, he used to call the English Department at BU, a quarter of whom were women, "a damned matriarchy."

Today such sexist language would be met with immediate outrage on campuses where the talk now is of "safe spaces" and "trigger warnings," but even in a time of less political correctness, Silber operated outside the pale of most presidents. Many perceived him as a tyrant and bully, and historian-activist Howard Zinn twice led faculty votes in attempts to oust him. Nora Ephron called him "the meanest SOB on campus" in a 1977 *Esquire* profile. Silber took a leave of absence in 1990 to run for governor of Massachusetts; his unguarded (and barbed) remarks appealed to populist resentment of the political establishment, and he came within seventy-seven thousand votes of winning the governorship. In 2003, while still chancellor, he promoted Daniel Goldin, a former administrator at NASA, as BU's ninth president and then, in no-explanation, no-apology mode, dismissed him with a $1.3 million payout before Goldin ever took office.

A decline in faculty authority and an embittered atmosphere on campus during Silber's tenure as president did not preclude some major accomplishments. BU's endowment increased from $18.8 million to $430 million, its physical plant more than doubled, four Nobel laureates joined the faculty, and—perhaps the boldest stroke of all—Silber disbanded BU's football team, citing financial losses. Silber, acting on his own authority, certainly got things done, but the trade-off between efficacy and democratic process did not sit well with the larger community.[12]

In 2004, after Silber's departure, attempts to shore up shared governance, with president Robert Brown and provost David Campbell creating new procedures for faculty input, led to an improvement in campus morale. But with the economic downturn in 2008, last-minute layoffs at the College of General Studies, mainly of non-tenure-track faculty members, subverted the fragile rapprochement.

Some of the turbulence under Silber can be attributed to the times, when identity politics were coming to the fore and disrupting traditional (white, male) hierarchies on campus, which Silber took it upon himself to defend. Some is attributable to Silber's irascible temperament and improvisational style; he made an art of being impolitic. Today, a new round of socioeconomic and political upheaval has stirred things up again, and presidents often face faculty unrest. Between 2011 and 2013, faculties at more than a dozen universities held votes of no confidence, a move that used to be quite rare.

John Sexton, president emeritus at NYU since 2015, described in a *New Yorker* article as an "imperial president," illustrates what happens when a president fails to fully convince faculty of his vision at a time of rapid change.[13] Sexton was a take-charge leader who made a number of changes to the university, many of them hailed as accomplishments. He was a skilled fund-raiser, raising $3 billion in seven years, who also brought depth to the faculty, hiring 125 tenure-track professors, recruiting star scholars (and paying them top dollar), providing home loans to 214 professors and administrators, and doubling the number of full-time adjuncts.[14] Sexton also elevated NYU to number 41 on the *USNWR* rankings, up nineteen places from its former slot; increased the number of applicants by 45 percent; expanded financial aid (though he also raised tuition); planned a $6 billion construction project around Washington Square to enlarge the university's footprint; and created campuses in a number of foreign cities including Abu Dhabi and Shanghai.

Despite these achievements, faculty members have repeatedly objected to what they see as unilateral moves that violate shared governance. They protested Sexton's appointment by the board of trustees without their consultation (a move censured by the AAUP as exemplifying a trend in universities "to reduce faculty power"). They denounced his disbanding of a graduate student union he had originally championed (which led to a strike by the graduate students). They questioned his global expansion to Abu Dhabi as a corporate solution to the university's New York real estate problem. And they condemned the arrest of democratic activists by the United Arab Emirates (which Sexton supported as an appropriate defense against security threats).

It should also be said that John Sexton, previously a professor at NYU Law School and then its dean, is a warm and outgoing person and a good communicator, who was formerly well-liked by faculty.[15] (I know John well, and can personally attest to all his positive attributes.) But his personal style and his background weren't enough to quell uprisings on campus. When he decided to go after strategic objectives, increasing the endowment, enrollment, real estate holdings, and global presence, and to do it on his own, the faculty viewed him differently—hence the hailstorm of petitions, protests, and votes of no confidence.[16]

How does a president hold the reins, or the baton, in such a way that everyone gets along? A school where a continuously collegial atmosphere has engendered astounding success over a period of decades is Stanford, where the president, John Hennessy, who recently stepped down after sixteen years, seems to have found the magic formula that brings unity and consensus to all parties. On the eve of his retirement, Hennessy was described by members of the Faculty Senate in the most glowing of terms—a man with charm, kindness, empathy, candor, a sense of humor, ingenuity, dedication, passion, executive acumen, equanimity, directness, patience, pride in his faculty, and the ability to inspire others. Even if we take into account that farewells tend toward hyperbole, the outpouring of appreciation by one professor after another is remarkable.[17] (Full disclosure: I know John, and it's all true.)

Personal qualities of leaders are important, as is a background in academics. The fact that John Hennessy came up through the ranks—faculty member, chair, dean, provost, and president—made faculty feel he was "one of us" and brought him a store of goodwill. But John Sexton of NYU, also a likable person, also originally a faculty member, encountered bristling hostility from faculty at many points during his presidency.[18]

What Hennessy was able to do was create a structural organization that brought together faculty and administration and created a common sense of purpose, building trust and encouraging a free flow of information. The president and provost served as nonvoting members of the Faculty Senate, meeting with the group every other Thursday, with informal lunches and office visits in between. And their attendance (near-perfect) wasn't just a matter of dutifully showing up. This structure helped develop ongoing relationships and provided space for regular discussions, which—and here's where personality comes in—were characterized by faculty as candid, knowledgeable, fair, and open, engaging them in institutional goals in a setting that made them feel valued.

Collaboration, engagement, openness, and respect marked all of John Hennessy's relationships, both with his faculty and with the Board of Trustees, and the university has certainly benefited from his hand at the helm. Among his many achievements are a number of interdisciplinary programs, from the Stanford Neurosciences Institute to the Stanford Woods Institute for the Environment to the Hasso Plattner Institute of Design (the d.school), and a commitment to the visual and performing arts, including new performance spaces in a dedicated arts district. Other accomplishments include twenty-one Nobel Laureates (eleven since 2000); construction of new quads, facilities, a stadium, student residences, a new medical center, and a new science teaching and learning center; the Bing Overseas Studies Program; new joint majors in the humanities and computer science; a pioneering role in how to use online technologies to increase access to high-quality education; and successful $1 billion and $6.2 billion campaigns to support undergraduate education, multidisciplinary research, financial aid, graduate fellowships, and other critical needs.[19]

Neither John Sexton nor John Hennessy faced a dramatic crisis—one of those flashpoints that spark the possibility of radical transformation—yet they both oversaw positive and enduring changes during their tenures. I suspect that Sexton's rockier road had to do with when and how he bypassed shared governance. When? All the time. How? Briskly. Focused on his own agenda, he tended to go full speed ahead, never pausing to make the case to the community about the necessity or urgency of the steps he was taking. Hennessy, with his regular and consistent interactions with faculty and administration, was able to sense openings and possibilities, and convince everyone to come along with him, every step of the way.

My last example is personal, about what happened at Tulane when a crisis forced the temporary suspension of shared governance—an anomalous situation, but illuminating precisely because of that. After Katrina, as mentioned, we ended up with an experiment in "benevolent dictatorship," where I acted in what I believed to be the best interests of the institution—a brief period that brought out both the strengths and the weaknesses of governance-as-usual. With faculty scattered all across the country, we relied on the Faculty Advisory Committee, consisting of elected representatives and charged with authority in cases when the full University Senate could not meet. Their feedback was invaluable as we hammered together the Renewal Plan, and their consultation provided legitimacy to the process. Additionally, I assembled a group of former and current university presidents to vet our ideas and offer criticism. That group—Harvey Fineberg, who was provost at Harvard; Malcolm Gillis, former president of Rice; Bill Bowen, president emeritus of Princeton; Jim Duderstadt, former president of the University of Michigan; and others as well—also legitimized decisions made by me and a small group of administrators and trusted advisers.

During the formulation of the Renewal Plan, the board also played a critical role, developing a strategic planning committee to work with our leadership team. Every meeting drew full attendance by the board, including emeritus members who returned to help. It became clear, given the magnitude of our losses, that Tulane would have to abandon some hallowed traditions, alter structures, and end programs close to the hearts of our trustees, many of whom were alumni. Not once did parochial interests override the university's needs or well-being.

Before the plan was finalized, the full board had two retreats to discuss every facet of it. Our board meeting in December 2005, in preparation for our planned reopening on January 16, 2006, lasted two days and had an intensity and focus unlike anything I've seen from any board with which I've served. I asked board members to accept the proposal in its entirety because cherry-picking might have caused the entire plan to unravel. I thought it was very courageous of the board to agree to an up-or-down vote given the number of viewpoints board members represented. In the end, Tulane trustees overwhelmingly approved the plan. The board really shone during a time of darkness, focusing on the mission and character of a new Tulane University, holding panels on campus for students and faculty to answer any questions they might have, and defending the plan against critics.

The governance lessons, for me, are these: The board, which in this instance rose above self-interest for the good of the school, is critically important—which means the criteria for membership are also important. The faculty, as the lifeblood of the institution, need and deserve a voice; in this instance, given the lack of consultation in the conventional sense, there was the expected outcry over terminations and downsizing (as well as a censure from the AAUP). However, the Faculty Advisory Committee of elected representatives provided an avenue for participation and lent credence to decisions and actions made in the absence of the senate.

As for the role of the president, I believe that transparency is the key to successfully navigating both day-to-day business and unimaginable disasters. I wasn't always able to be as inclusive as John Hennessy, given the life-or-death moment we were in, but my chief aim was to keep everyone in the loop and fully informed. In the immediate aftermath of the storm, I held online town meetings where I took and answered questions; as soon as it was possible for me to travel, I held a series of in-person events with parents, students, and alumni in population centers around the country. And in December, as soon as the Renewal Plan had been accepted by the board, we held a news conference and published the full text of the plan online and in a special edition of the university magazine. My staff and I also made ourselves readily available to the media. Communication of the facts was crucial in allaying anxiety and fostering trust in the future of the university.

The building blocks of a strong system of self-governance require the right people in the right jobs. An active step institutions can take to improve their system of governance is to look hard at the criteria they use for choosing appointees. As we've seen from these examples, and I could cite many more, the character and background of people in leadership positions strongly influence the way work gets done and decisions get made. For board members, experience in higher education, or at least a solid grasp of what distinguishes, and ails, our sector, is extremely desirable. The influence of money isn't going to go away—the academy is chronically in need of donors and of business executives who understand financial strategy—but wealth shouldn't be the only prerequisite of a place on a board of trustees, and the particular interests of moneyed contributors should not affect the central mission.[20] In short, the two most important traits a board member can have are an understanding of university governance and a loyalty to the institution's mission that transcends any personal agenda.

Faculty participation in institutional goals can also help shape and modify financial ambitions. At Western Carolina University, part of the public system of higher education in North Carolina, trustees approved a $2 million gift from the Koch brothers over faculty objections about the potential influence of such a donation on the college's autonomy and academic integrity.[21] The resolution of the conflict involved a revision of the proposal, hammered out by the Faculty Senate, that included faculty oversight of the Kochs' Center for the Study of Free Enterprise to ensure compliance with AAUP guidelines on academic freedom; publication of the full agreement (prior Koch gifts have had nondisclosure clauses); prohibitions against using Koch money to influence legislation, elections, or political campaigns; and clear provisos for faculty's academic freedom—but also stipulations affirming the Kochs' right to terminate the agreement at any point. This last element has been described by Ralph Wilson, a researcher for UnKoch My Campus, as an implicit form of control, but the general consensus on campus is that the faculty do have, and will continue to have, a say about implementation of the program.[22]

Faculty need to be part of any discussion for two reasons: one, because they operate as a check on untrammeled trustee or presidential power; and two, because they will be more engaged and loyal to the institution if they consult on critical decisions affecting the entire community.[23] Ironically, the AAUP declaration of 1915, designed to protect the academic freedom of faculty members from undue influence or pressure, has at the same time freed them from accountability, weakening their engagement with important institutional decisions. Boards and presidents are the ones ultimately held responsible for the results of those decisions, while faculty demands, protests, and petitions escape such an accounting. The moral is, universities make strange bedfellows; abrasive encounters will occur even in the best-regulated environments.

Acknowledging this reality doesn't mean we can't try to make our environments more collegial and harmonious. My recommendations for improving governance are twofold. First, I would propose Tulane's joint University Senate (as opposed to separate governing bodies for faculty, staff, and administrators) as a working model that might help align everyone's objectives and promote consensus. The University Senate, as distinct from the Faculty Advisory Committee that met in its absence during Katrina, is a permanent self-perpetuating body that includes faculty representatives, staff, administrators, and student representatives from the undergraduate and graduate schools. The university president is chair of the senate, meeting regularly with the full assembly. The chief strength of this arrangement is that everyone is in the room at the same time: communication automatically improves when all constituencies are present and hearing the same thing. And the fact that the senate comprises representatives from the entire university circumvents a common problem with organizations specifically devoted to faculty, student, or staff issues, which are often closed off from broad concerns confronting the whole community.

If I were to tweak this model a little, I would invite board members, the only group *not* present on the University Senate, to attend periodically, and appoint one or two faculty representatives to the board. Ideally senate members would also act as envoys to their wider constituencies, bringing them news of current debates and returning to report their views. The point is to open up new channels of communication wherever possible and to encourage feedback, giving everyone an opportunity to be heard.

The tone of communications can also help generate consensus. When I chaired the senate at Tulane, I tried to keep the conversation genuine. I used humor to rein in the inevitable rambling speeches—I'd say, "Just wake me when you're done," a line that always drew laughs—and I enjoyed having a bully pulpit, with the freedom to speak honestly when I thought something was flat-out wrong. Relationships forged over many years made me comfortable enough to be myself, and people who knew me well seemed able to take both jokes and bluntness in the right spirit while feeling quite free and safe to criticize me.

I've often thought that mutual comprehension and familiarity are the two elements that make it all work. John Hennessy, who was so successful at Stanford, was promoted from within his institution, making his job that much easier because everyone already knew him and what he stood for. The same thing applies, to a lesser extent, to John Sexton; though his take-charge agenda stimulated significant faculty dissent, he may have been able to survive the opposition and make NYU stronger precisely because he was on some level "one of them." As a newcomer to Tulane, I had to build relationships over time. When I first arrived in New Orleans from Case Western Reserve, way up north in Ohio, people would sometimes say, "You're not from here," an expression that captures the Big Easy's skepticism about outsiders. But after two decades, I can honestly say I am "from here." The university has been a home to me, and Margie and I now live in an apartment with a view of the Mississippi from our windows.

The point being: what you need to get the job done will never be solely a matter of structural organization. You need people of quality in these governance roles—people who are willing to put the welfare of the institution above their self-interests and to serve as effective ambassadors and good-faith critics, and who are truly knowledgeable about the changing landscape of higher education. You also need strong relationships, and the time and the will to develop those relationships. If Katrina had happened in the second rather than the seventh year of my presidency, I don't think I would have had anywhere near the kind of support I got from my board, my staff, and indeed the faculty, which, I'm happy to say, never voted no confidence despite the AAUP censure.

Selecting a president is one of the most important junctures for an institution's future, and I devote chapter 10 to a fuller discussion of criteria for picking the best possible candidate, with stories of the good, the bad, and the so-so. But here, briefly, I'll say the obvious: personal characteristics matter a great deal. A common mistake of boards is to be misled by shiny résumés that list a dazzling history at top institutions. As I've noted, John Hennessy, one of the best university presidents in the United States, was a homegrown product, whose best attributes were his gift for listening to people, his sense of humor, and an incalculable but essential human touch.

To go back to my original joke about the "first-best job in the world," when I was president-elect and on top of the world, and everyone listened to me intently: what has served me best has been not the ability to command a room and impose my will, but the ability to listen well—listen *to* instead of being listened to. A university is first and foremost its people. Relationships can make or break it. Which is why integrity, respect, and loyalty are what I am looking for in myself, and always listening for.

8

The Ivory Tower

The idea of doing good "to," or "unto," or "for" someone,
implicit in many descriptions of public service, ultimately
reinforces the chasm between town and gown. To heal the
divide, a better preposition would be "with"—doing good
together, strategically and collaboratively, in a mutually
beneficial way.

On my first day as president of Tulane I sat at my desk and wrote
out ten things I hoped to accomplish before I stepped down.
Number one on that list: I wanted to connect Tulane to the city of
New Orleans. I brought that idea with me from my twenty-three
years in Cleveland at Case Western Reserve University, where I'd
witnessed the turnaround of a failing city through mutually beneficial partnerships between the university and the community.

When I first came to CWRU in the 1970s, white flight to the
suburbs had left the inner city vulnerable to the forces of decay:
blight, unemployment, racial strife, crime, failing schools, and a
dwindling tax base. The Cuyahoga River had become a symbol
of the city's decline; a dumping ground of industrial waste, it had
literally burst into flames, making Cleveland the punch line of
countless jokes and earning it the mocking title "The Mistake on
the Lake." But in the 1980s and '90s, Cleveland Tomorrow, a civic
organization representing the largest private companies in the city,
spearheaded attempts to revitalize the downtown area, resulting in
an array of impressive projects including the Rock & Roll Hall of
Fame, a new baseball stadium and arena, renovation of landmark
art deco movie houses, and major neighborhood housing projects.[1]

When I left in 1998, it seemed that the city was on the rise. But then the recovery seemed to stall, partly because of the 2008 recession, but also because the apparent comeback had never gotten to the roots of the problem. Redevelopment efforts had focused on visible symptoms of blight rather than on underlying causes like unemployment, inadequate health care, and failing schools. A new project starting in 2004, the Greater University Circle Initiative (GUCI), has been more successful at addressing the sources of urban decay, targeting an area at the eastern edge of the city with a dense concentration of cultural riches.[2] The initiative brings together "eds and meds" (CWRU, University Hospitals, and the Cleveland Clinic), landmark cultural institutions (including the art museum and symphony), and an array of local businesses and community organizations in order to attack the fundamental causes of urban decline and fuel socioeconomic progress.[3] A second prong of attack directs resources to failing public schools in the area, via the Cleveland Plan for K–12 education and the Transformation Alliance, a public-private partnership that has developed a diverse portfolio of schools including high-performing charters.[4]

As dean of the Weatherhead School of Management at CWRU, I'd had some success in the 1980s in connecting the school with local businesses as part of the Cleveland Tomorrow initiative, which convinced me that community engagement was mutually beneficial to both parties. But I didn't really have the vocabulary for what I'd been observing—the concepts of "scholarship of engagement," "civic engagement," and "anchor institution" weren't as well articulated as they are now. On my arrival in New Orleans, I put off active efforts to engage with the city, even though it was number one on my top ten list. As I've noted before, I wasn't "from there" and thought the city would, quite rightly, consider me an interloper if I waded in as a rank newcomer. When Katrina occurred, seven years later, I'd built relationships not only inside but outside the university, and I felt a sense of belonging. I also felt, for reasons both moral and practical, that Tulane absolutely had to step up. If the university didn't start rebuilding the community, who would? At the same time, we were dependent on the city for our own recovery, a case of mutual, even symbiotic, connection.

The crisis forged an immediate relationship between town and gown, but, as I'll explain in more detail later, it still took Tulane many years to fully arrive as an anchor institution. You can't simply announce it; you have to work on it, and for a long time. I think of anchoring as a process with three distinct stages. First, an "opportunistic" phase that grabs hold of whatever opportunities happen to present themselves. Second, a more purposeful attempt to build coalitions and develop collaborative policies. Finally, in the best scenario, a full strategy of intentional engagement, with institutional support for public scholarship and alliances that reflect community agendas, represent local leaders, and have a measurable impact on society.[5]

Obstacles to engagement are many. As we've seen in the chapters on scholarship and governance, any shift toward public concerns tends to raise anxieties inside the ivory tower, leading to fights over resources, reputation, and mission. Universities focused on keeping their campuses safe often have a fortress mentality, defending their perimeter from what they perceive as external threats. Meanwhile, the community is inclined to see the university as lord of the manor, with large (and tax-exempt) real estate holdings and the habit of displacing residents through gentrification or new construction. When universities do offer help to their neighbors, it tends to be in a fragmentary and sometimes patronizing way.

This chapter looks at universities that have reached beyond the walls of the ivory tower to communities living in their shadow, with a focus on urban institutions that have achieved the status of anchors through a purposeful strategy of engagement.[6] Such engagement has practical outcomes for both school and city, but beyond the conventional metrics of improvement, it also has a moral dimension. To quote St. Augustine: "Since you cannot do good to all, you are to pay special attention to those who, by accidents of time, or place, or circumstance, are brought into closer connection with you." The one thing I might rephrase is "do good to all." The idea of doing good "to," or "unto," or "for" someone, implicit in many descriptions of public service, ultimately reinforces the chasm between town and gown. To heal the divide, a better preposition would be "with"—doing good together, strategically and collaboratively, in a mutually beneficial way.[7]

The history of anchoring, as with so many features of American colleges, begins with the state university system established by the Morrill Acts of 1862 and 1890. As land-grant colleges, public universities had a mandate to educate students in practical spheres such as the agricultural and mechanic arts in order to prepare them for socially useful careers. These schools were specifically tied to place: thirty thousand acres of federal land within a state's borders for each member of Congress a state had as of the census of 1860. As public institutions they were meant to engage with their communities, improve the "industrial classes," and strengthen the nation. In the course of time, higher education's mission grew to include research, medicine, athletics, and a host of other endeavors, but social responsibility and economic development have consistently remained part of the ethos of public universities.

In fact, the original Morrill Act of 1862 placed economic purpose at the heart of American higher education, setting specific benchmarks for productivity that stimulated "free farm" agriculture in the American West and US exports of agricultural products overseas. Though eighteenth- and early nineteenth-century schools in the United States largely copied the European system, which was devoted to educating church, military, and professional elites, the Morrill Acts changed that mission in favor of utilitarian and economic ends.[8] Private universities also began to embrace this philosophy of practical and engaged learning, more and more so in recent years because their pool of human talent and sizable economic impact offered enormous potential for improving urban communities under stress.

The seed of anchoring was implicit in the Morrill Acts and to some extent even earlier, in colonial colleges founded on the notion of service, but the concept gained increasing traction in the 1990s, as US cities spiraled into decline and urban universities were forced to confront the problems on their doorsteps. At the Aspen Institute Roundtable on Comprehensive Community Initiatives in 2001, an "anchor institution"—the first time the phrase appeared in print—was defined as a "fixed asset" of a city that could help revitalize the core.[9] The spatial relationship was the prime mover of engagement. City universities located next door to failing neighborhoods began to create shared public spaces and to engage with the community in order to improve their own environments, building secure and inviting campuses that would make recruitment of students and faculty easier. Their self-interest was enlightened, incorporating elements of social responsibility and moral purpose and also fundamentally linked with the mission of education. As students became actively involved in community service, it became clear that engaged learning—encountering what was new and different—was a potent and life-changing experience.

As noted, anchoring isn't simply a matter of intent, and many institutions that aspire to that status are in a phase of growth and development, but I want to stress how positive this movement is. Anchor institutions are potentially economic, social, and educational powerhouses, with the capacity to solve some of our most pressing problems as a nation, city by city, region by region.

I'm going to begin with the University of Pennsylvania, which has been a proponent of community outreach since the 1990s. Located in the middle of West Philadelphia, a blighted area with a high crime rate, Penn had a distant and sometimes hostile relationship with its next-door neighborhoods. Within a few years of Judith Rodin's arrival as president in 1994, two murders—a graduate student and a researcher killed on their way home from their labs—plus a spate of violent robberies created a sense of urgency about the safety of the campus. Rodin's response was not to put up walls or emphasize police presence, but to build bridges to the community. Through safety initiatives and urban redevelopment, she was able to create thriving public spaces shared by both the university and West Philadelphia, and launched the West Philadelphia Initiatives to generate educational, economic, and housing opportunities. Rodin's revitalization efforts also included a new hospital complex in the city's old convention center, the launch of Penn-assisted public schools, and, together with other anchor institutions, the development of Keystone Innovation Zones near the university.

The Netter Center for Community Partnerships, started two years before Rodin's presidency, has since developed health clinics, urban gardens, local businesses, service-learning courses, and model public schools.[10] Ira Harkavy, the director of the Netter Center, has remained a continuing force for community engagement over three decades, developing an Anchor Institutions Toolkit to apply in areas of youth development, education, health, and service learning.[11] One example of Penn's partnerships, in the area of community health, is the Dr. Bernett L. Johnson Jr. Sayre Health Center, named for an African American dermatologist who was an award-winning teacher and mentor at Penn Medical School. The clinic, located at Sayre High School, is a full-service primary care facility that provides clinical services to the residents of West Philadelphia and educational opportunities to both high school students and students in social work, nursing, dental, and medical programs at Penn.[12]

Another example is the Penn Alexander School, K–8, one of the university's "University-Assisted Community Schools." Penn donated the land, managed building construction, provided $800,000 of funding, and helped develop the curriculum. Harkavy has championed quality public schools like Penn Alexander not only for their evident educational benefits but as "social glue"— hubs for community activism, where parents and organizers can meet and collaborate to solve local problems. Penn Alexander has also had a notable economic effect on the neighborhood, increasing homeownership, median income, and population.[13]

Many of the gains made during Rodin's ten-year tenure came after years of working on neighborhood revitalization. Because of trust earned over time, community members were more inclined to support new construction and new programs, and splintered community organizations were more willing to collaborate on joint ventures. In addition to her efforts in the community, Rodin maintained Penn's standing as a major research university, doubling its funding and tripling the size of the endowment; increased applicants and selectivity; created a unified organization, Penn Medicine, comprising the university's medical school and hospital—a structural arrangement, as you'll recall from chapter 5, that has successfully preserved the mission of academic medicine despite radical changes in health care; and elevated the university in the *USNWR* rankings (despite its flaws) from sixteenth in 1994 to fourth in 2002.[14] Most remarkable of all, she achieved these academic successes, requiring considerable resources and a focus on internal goals, while continuing outreach and retaining the goodwill of the community.

Another outstanding example of anchoring, also in West Philadelphia, is Drexel University. Under the leadership of President John Fry, who has said that his aim is to make Drexel the most civically engaged university in the United States, the school has become an engine of economic growth, urban redevelopment, and community engagement. Originally a management consultant specializing in colleges and universities, Fry was executive vice president and chief operating officer at Penn under Judith Rodin and later president of Franklin & Marshall College in Lancaster, Pennsylvania, where he oversaw one of the largest "brownfield" reclamation projects in the nation, creating green spaces and an eds-and-meds corridor in place of a landfill, an abandoned factory, and a defunct rail yard.[15]

Fry's current initiatives are also rooted in his immediate locale, focusing on educational, health and wellness, housing, commercial, and cultural enterprises in the neighborhoods of Mantua and Powelton adjacent to the Drexel campus. The Dornsife Center for Neighborhood Partnerships and the Innovation Neighborhood, along with the Lindy Center for Civic Engagement, have created opportunities for student volunteerism, service and experiential learning, and social entrepreneurship. Schuylkill Yards, a $3.5 billion twenty-year project to build parks, residences, businesses, and shops in a decaying industrial area between the Drexel campus and Amtrak's 30th Street Station will connect the impoverished neighborhoods near Drexel to the revitalized University City District created by Penn. It will also support local businesses through procurement, employ a local diverse workforce, offer workforce development programs to neighborhood residents, and invest in neighborhood schools in Mantua, West Powelton, and Powelton Village.[16]

Fry has been lauded for his efforts, but he has his critics, too, who protest what they see as gentrification, consumerism, and the loss of a familiar community. This criticism is not uncommon for anchor institutions committed to partnering with their communities. Fry's counterargument, combining a sense of moral responsibility with an understanding of enlightened self-interest, is his belief in the potential of change to "lift all boats" through inclusion-driven growth.[17] In 2016, he was named chairman of the Greater Philadelphia Chamber of Commerce and, in a speech to fourteen hundred business leaders, spoke of a "crisis of opportunity" and the prospect of making Philadelphia a hub of innovation and a center of investment—a case, he said, of "doing well by doing good," a phrase often attributed (appropriately enough) to Ben Franklin, Philadelphia's favorite son.[18] His vision of Drexel as an anchor institution highlights shared economic growth in tandem with increased social cohesion and communal goodwill.[19]

Goodwill was precisely what James Harris III, the new president of Widener University, was seeking when, in 2002, he first encountered the distrust poisoning relations between the university and the city of Chester, Pennsylvania. On his arrival, senior administrators immediately showed him architectural plans for a fence around the campus; meanwhile, the mayor of Chester was describing Widener as "a dragon that eats up land" that would otherwise have provided the city with tax dollars. The facts of

Chester were not unlike those of Cleveland or West Philadelphia: depopulation, loss of manufacturing, increasing poverty and crime, and troubled schools. In addition to these forbidding conditions, geography also conspired to isolate Widener from the city. Interstate 95 separated the university from downtown Chester, acting as a wall keeping town and gown apart and allowing suspicion to grow in the space between them.[20]

What Harris did in the face of this polarization was to establish a strategic planning committee, the first in the school's history, that created a new vision for the university as a "metropolitan college."[21] This language signaled a major change of mission and identity, immediately triggering anxieties about recruitment. Traditionally Widener had been a private tuition-driven institution, drawing most of its students from suburban Philadelphia. The objection was that it would now be perceived as an urban commuter school, and Widener couldn't successfully compete with such schools, which tended to have deeper pockets for research and scholarship. But the biggest opposition to engaging with the city was around issues of governance. During the eighteen months of transition, despite town hall and campus meetings designed to encourage participation and garner feedback, many faculty members protested their exclusion from any role in drafting the new mission statement and the strategic plan, also complaining of administrative intrusion on curricular matters.

Despite a rocky period of upheaval and dissent, Widener in the last ten years has become the anchor institution Harris envisioned. Animated by a strong sense of social justice, Harris—the son of a factory worker and the first in his family to go to college—harnessed the university's strengths in order to improve the entire community.[22] To use Harris's own terms, the school has been a "facilitator," using a standing Civic Engagement Committee to support faculty involved in community research and service learning, and to foster university and community partnerships with schools, business and civic leaders, and faith-based organizations. It has been a "leader," creating a Social Work Counseling Services initiative to provide direct services to local residents, and opening the Chester Community Physical Therapy Clinic to provide services and wellness education to low-income patients. And it has been a "convener," launching the Widener Partnership Charter School, the first university-sponsored charter school in Pennsylvania,[23] and bringing together the presidents of an array of other local institutions, including a historically black college, a community college, a faith-based institution, a satellite campus of a large public university, and an elite liberal arts school, to form the Chester Higher Education Council—a case of local anchor institutions pulling together to create a place-based approach to the problem of inferior public schools.[24]

Syracuse University is another school that, despite difficulties, radically transformed its identity under the leadership of Nancy Cantor, president from 2004 to 2013. From earlier appointments as provost of the University of Michigan, where Cantor fought to uphold affirmative action, and as chancellor at the University of Illinois at Urbana-Champaign, where she tried to ban the school's racist Native American mascot,[25] Cantor brought with her a passion for social justice that fit well with Syracuse's history of abolitionism in the nineteenth century and women's liberation a hundred years later. Over the years she has often quoted Wayne Gretzky—"go where the puck is going, not where it's been" (a favorite mantra in business circles)—and critiqued the arrogance of the ivory tower, saying of academics, including herself, "we're not good at humility." She has argued that universities are a "public good" and that being a neighbor is not just a geographical but a moral term.

Most of all, she crafted a compelling narrative to describe the school's transformation. Recognizing that the site of Syracuse on University Hill, high above the city and separated from it by Interstate 81, was an obstacle to engagement, she wrote, "We had to jump that highway, physically and psychologically." The first bridges to the community were spatial. The school took over a windowless furniture warehouse downtown and converted it to

The Warehouse, renovating the building as a home for the School of Architecture's UPSTATE Center for design, research, and real estate, as well as for programs in journalism and the arts. Then the university and the city collaborated with a range of community groups, government agencies, businesses, nonprofits, and arts organizations to create The Corridor, a mile-and-a-half-long district that encourages interaction in an inviting public space, served by a newly created bus route that carries 17,000 passengers (up from 250) every month.[26]

Cantor also built trusting relationships with community leaders, including an activist minister, presidents of tenant associations, owners of neighborhood grocery stores, and many others. In the end, forty-five local organizations came together with Syracuse in a joint venture, the Near West Side Initiative, devoted to the city neighborhood that had suffered the worst of the area's industrial decline after World War II. Cantor quotes "the wisest grandmother on the West Side," who said to her, "Nancy, ask *us*. We put our heads down here at night."[27] Instead of a command-and-control system, the initiative adopted a collaborative model, helping generate both social glue and economic strength in a blighted section of Syracuse.[28]

Over the course of Cantor's tenure, the university poured tens of millions of dollars into urban development, encouraged professors to focus their research on the city, and gave free tuition to local high school graduates. Cantor also doubled the applicant pool, increased undergraduate enrollment by 20 percent, raised minority representation from 18.5 to 32 percent, increased the number of Pell Grant recipients from 20 to 28 percent, reduced merit scholarships, and tripled the money spent on need-based aid.[29]

But some faculty members—Cantor calls them "a small group of (very loud) traditionalists"—have questioned the school's shift to community engagement, pointing to markers of declining reputation and selectivity: a spike in the acceptance rate from the mid-50s to 60 percent,[30] GPAs and SAT scores for incoming freshmen that are lower than those at peer institutions, a fall in the

U.S. News & World Report rankings from 40 to 62, Syracuse's withdrawal from the prestigious Association of American Universities, less money going to academics and more to administration and diversity initiatives, and potential problems recruiting topflight faculty. The details of the squabble are somewhat disheartening. One professor said inclusion might be an admirable goal "but it is going to have an impact on our reputation," and another said, "Our primary mission is not managing cities."

The basic facts of the matter have been disputed as well, with a debate on the metrics that affected Syracuse's withdrawal from the AAU. Cantor suggested that the organization had narrowed its membership criteria, focusing exclusively on federal grants for medical and scientific research when other projects are worthy too. The AAU maintained it hadn't changed its criteria and compared a school only to peer schools to make its judgments.[31] The argument about metrics and the related issues of reputation and mission are critical as the sector adapts to rapidly changing demographics and worsening societal tensions. To make the case for universities as anchor institutions requires crafting metrics appropriate to the scholarship of engagement. Cantor urges a redefinition of what constitutes exciting scholarly work, and her Scholarship in Action campaign at Syracuse is an effort to cultivate, recognize, and reward scholarship of benefit to the community.[32]

What happened at Syracuse illustrates both the potential and the peril of mission change. The truth is, Syracuse's value and impact should be measured by mission success, student outcomes, and access, as well as by contribution to knowledge and community—not by whether it is in the AAU. Excellence in research, teaching, and engagement are not mutually exclusive, and there are many great public and private universities (Notre Dame and Dartmouth, for example) that are not in the AAU. I also think it is safe to assert that Syracuse's departure from the AAU was not related to its commitment to community and social justice. Even if you buy the notion of "Syracuse's Slide,"[33] to quote the title of an article from the *Chronicle of Higher Education* in October 2011, the game might be worth the candle. Prestige isn't the only thing that matters, and rankings are always suspect in any case.

I think it's a mistake to use Syracuse as a cautionary tale to inhibit other schools from fully engaging with their cities and communities. Diversity, as noted in chapter 2, is costly but beneficial, and collaborating with neighbors for the public good has a moral dimension. At the same time, I believe that discovery, teaching, excellence, and selectivity aren't necessarily going to diminish if you take on the role of anchor institution. That certainly wasn't true at the University of Pennsylvania and hasn't been the case at Tulane. But, as both Widener and Syracuse suggest, it would be wise to engage in a long-term process when embarking on mission change, including efforts to foster and reward engaged scholarship, in order to lessen opposition from faculty and make for a smoother transition to a new order. An eloquent expression of purpose yoked to a clear strategic plan can further unify factions and also inspire students. Twenty-first-century students expect to engage with the world—and, given their youthful idealism, they fully expect to solve all its problems, given half a chance.

Penn, Drexel, Widener, and Syracuse, all private tuition, have expanded their traditional mission of research and teaching to include community engagement. Public universities and colleges, on the other hand, are place-based institutions whose core mission is to serve their local populations.[34] Miami Dade College (MDC), one such school, has almost single-handedly rebuilt downtown Miami through innovative strategies that have strengthened the city both economically and culturally.[35]

Miami Dade has been led for the past twenty-plus years by Eduardo Padrón, who arrived in the United States as a refugee from Cuba in 1961 and graduated from MDC, earning his PhD in economics from the University of Florida. In 2016, Padrón received the Medal of Freedom for his contributions to community engagement, social justice, and diversity. During Padrón's presidency, Miami Dade has developed into the largest institution of higher education in America, with an enrollment of more than

165,000 students. The school is notable not only for its size but for its diversity, graduating more Hispanic, African American, and low-income students than any other institution in the United States.[36] The university has also invested in local and minority entrepreneurs through procurement and contracts, expanded employment in the region, and improved quality of life in Miami and beyond through the educational and medical services it provides.

A central mission of MDC is to build community strength and bridge differences through arts programs that offer performances in public spaces. Back in the 1970s, Miami Dade produced a concert series called Lunchtime Lively Arts, with downtown office workers gathering at dance performances and jazz concerts in public spaces at midday. Today it's called Jazz at Wolfson and is one of the longest-running jazz series in the country. Books by the Bay was established in 1984 by an independent bookseller and a few local librarians in collaboration with Padrón, who believed a book expo would help transform the campus's downtown area. That first year, twenty-five thousand people showed up at the fair, ignoring the Miami of "cocaine cowboys, racial strife, and paradise lost" reported in newspaper headlines.[37] The event has grown into the eight-day Miami Book Fair International, recognized as the nation's finest literary festival and featuring authors like Mario Vargas Llosa, Garrison Keillor, and Allen Ginsberg.

The book fair enhances social cohesion, binding people together as participants in a collective cultural experience. Miami Dade's Center for Literature and Theatre has a similar function; it offers book readings, writing workshops, literacy classes, and cultural events, as well as administers the book fair and Teatro Prometeo, MDC's Spanish-language theater initiative. The New Orleans Rebirth Brass Band, performing in Miami's African American Overtown neighborhood as part of the center's culturally specific concert series, was, Padrón writes, "a communion of sorts, the horns seemingly blowing down the separation between strangers."[38] Padrón considers such experiences a birthright, as essential as the right to health and education. In a country that is increasingly devoid of common beliefs and rituals, anchor institutions that provide access to literature, visual art, and theatrical performance help people unite in awareness and feeling.

To return to Tulane and our efforts, founded in disaster, to forge a strong identity as an anchor institution in New Orleans: those efforts have included all the ingredients—spatial, relational, socioeconomic, cultural—that have been in play, to varying degrees, at Penn, Drexel, Widener, Syracuse, and Miami Dade. As with all these schools, the specifics of place were the first determinants of engagement. Our uptown campus is on high ground, situated on the "sliver by the river," the natural levee built up along the crescent curve of the Mississippi by centuries of flooding. The urban core of low-income and minority residents live mainly in "the bowl," areas below sea level sandwiched between the Mississippi on one side and Lake Pontchartrain on the other.

One of our earliest aims after Katrina was to provide opportunities for students and faculty to come into direct contact with residents in the bowl through the Center for Public Service and service-learning courses that Tulane instituted after Katrina. In 2006, Tulane became the first and only major research university to integrate public service into the core curriculum. The university also partnered with socially innovative programs like Grow Dat Youth Farm, a youth development and leadership program that provides fresh food to food deserts in New Orleans, with students and faculty serving as collaborators and advisers.[39] It also developed a number of academic and cocurricular programs that focus on social innovation and entrepreneurship and design thinking. These and other changes had a transformative impact on Tulane, including its culture and key academic metrics.

Another way of building bridges to the community has been to relocate parts of the university in the heart of New Orleans. After sixty years on the uptown campus, the School of Social Work moved into a new building in the downtown medical district near Tulane Medical Center, close to the population students serve in their field placements. The School of Architecture has made a similar move, locating a Tulane City Center satellite in Central

City, bringing design students into contact with the daily life of the urban residents they are attempting to design for.

Tulane is leaving its uptown perch, just as Drexel is building its way to University City, and just as Syracuse came down from its hill and Penn and Widener crossed their interstates. Almost invariably there is a spatial chasm between a university, with its enclosed spaces and clustered buildings, and the town it inhabits. Of course spatial divisions aren't the only thing to conquer. Racial and class differences are tearing our country apart, and "jumping the gap" is more than a geographic move. Despite Tulane's efforts to build both literal and figurative bridges, I still felt we weren't achieving sufficient scale to really change things.

In the latest phase of our evolution as an anchor institution, we turned to a model of collective impact, based on the idea that no one organization can solve today's most complex problems alone. Through this collective and aligned approach, local organizations from diverse sectors, such as youth services, economic and workforce development, city government, K–12 and postsecondary education, juvenile justice, and philanthropy, band together with each other and with young people in urban neighborhoods to address a core issue affecting the city: youth disconnection. Often referred to as "opportunity youth," this is a population of young people ages sixteen to twenty-four who are disconnected from school and work. In New Orleans, this population is 87 percent African American, two-thirds have a high school diploma or equivalent, and nearly half live in or come from households with income below the poverty line. This group is subject to the full range of social injustices—racial discrimination, failing schools, unemployment, family collapse, incarceration, violence, poverty—that affect our city, and indeed all cities. If we can help create conditions that will empower these young people to change their futures, then we can change the future, period.

That belief has fueled EMPLOY, Employment and Mobility Pathways Linked for Opportunity Youth, with backbone support (staff, communications, policy, and data) from Tulane's Cowen Institute.[40] More than twenty-five organizations, including Tulane,

Delgado Community College, Baptist Community Ministries, the City of New Orleans, the New Orleans Business Alliance, the Urban League, JPMorgan Chase Foundation, and others, along with youth leaders, coordinate policies and practices, such as data sharing and training for service providers, to address youth disconnection. Take the case of a young man who is seeking a college degree or certificate but is also homeless: he needs several types of organizations to help him on his way, and EMPLOY members can coordinate these services to prevent duplication. The idea is to build an ecosystem that supports continuous reconnection, enabling independence and self-sustainability.

Serving as a backbone organization for a community-wide cross-sector collaborative comes with inherent challenges, especially if the issue that needs solving is as complex as youth disconnection. Maintaining trust and buy-in will always be a key part of this work, but EMPLOY's growth and collaborative governance structure demonstrates how the role of Tulane as an anchor institution has evolved as well.

Some question the local and regional emphasis of anchor institutions, particularly in light of pressing national and world problems that deserve a university's attention. We in higher education often say, "Act locally, think globally," but how does one translate to the other? A program at Tulane, the Disaster Resilience Leadership Academy, underscores the intimate connections that often exist between the world up close and the world at large. Founded in the aftermath of Katrina, the academy publishes data and insights from Katrina and the BP oil spill as well as reporting in real time on contemporary disasters, from Hurricane Sandy to the earthquake in Haiti to Hurricane Matthew. Though it began as a homegrown entity, DRLA has developed global reach, with scholars from all over the world using it as a resource to study trauma, leadership, and crisis management.[41] What begins at home has ripple effects far, far away.

Across the sector, institutions are rethinking their role in their local communities. The examples here can provide a template for developing community engagement and evolving into an anchor institution that lifts local populations and revives inner cities and depressed regions. My own experience suggests how much a crisis can precipitate this development by banishing hesitation, quelling opposition, and presenting a stark moral imperative. But the more usual course requires internal motivation followed by unwavering conviction, the kind that Rodin, Fry, Harris, Cantor, and Padrón showed in expanding their institutional mission. To one degree or another, they have all experienced an evolution from intermittent engagement with the community to anchoring as a strategic goal, making it part of the institution's identity and putting personnel and resources into forging that identity.

Such an evolution depends on collaborating first at the grass-roots level with individual programs and partners; then building collaborative networks based on a shared purpose; and finally moving toward collective action through larger umbrella organizations that coordinate an array of services and policies. The key to success is not only collaboration but, as Cantor argues, humility. Finding trusted leaders in the community, not assuming that we in the academy have all the answers to all the questions (some of which are not even the community's questions), offering support and services without marking out our own turf or taking all the credit—these are the ways to make things happen. To repeat: humility, and also mutual respect in the interest of mutual benefit. Enlightened self-interest between equal partners promotes the kind of feedback loop I observed long ago at the Weatherhead School of Management, when partnering with local businesses proved invaluable to the businesses and equally invaluable to the school.

Any change in institutional direction or commitment, as we've seen often in these pages, is likely to result in governance struggles and fights over resources. One way to combat opposing forces is a powerful narrative using vivid language that arouses support for and enthusiasm about change. Another way to smooth the transition is to lay the groundwork and build strong relationships with stakeholders—community leaders, first and foremost, but also board members, faculty, students, parents, donors.

Some argue for a model, the opposite of anchoring, that features placelessness, virtual education, and the "University of Everywhere." However, the public goods that emerge from our anchor institutions—understanding difference, conquering income inequality and injustice, improving the environment, enriching quality of life—are crucial to our democratic society. Higher education is having an identity crisis, and one way of resolving it is to "disaggregate" a university's services and put them online. But I believe in, and hope I've demonstrated, the tremendous power of the university—existing in a given place and at a given moment—to construct a creative ecosystem based on physical presence, direct contact, mutual benefit, and joint purpose. I believe in our cities and towns, and in the role of anchor institutions in keeping them alive and vital.[42] We need to respond to the imperative to "go where the puck is going" and adapt to new realities rather than ossifying and becoming a relic of the past.

Which brings me to the next topic—branding, mission, and the ultimate institutional question, "Who am I?"

9

Who Are We?

It's easy to become a slave to external forces.
It's hard to find one's own soul.

Back in 2006 when parents and prospective students resumed visiting the campus in the aftermath of Katrina, I posed the question "Why Tulane?" Out of four thousand schools across the country, why come here?

My answer to the question was a description of Tulane's unique features. First, we were the only major research university in the United States to make public service an integral component of the core curriculum. Second, we were one of a select group of research universities to focus on undergraduate education as its highest priority. Third, we had created a single portal for all entering freshmen in order to build a shared ethos, sense of purpose, and flexibility in course selection before they committed to choosing an ultimate field of study. We were more than the sum of our parts: all three features, taken together, set us apart from the myriad schools that students could choose from. And of course, there was New Orleans, and there was Katrina. I told them, "If it's not in your DNA to help rebuild the city of New Orleans and the world, don't come."

The admissions office was apoplectic: their view was, never say "don't come" to prospective applicants. The aim of admissions offices everywhere is to increase the number of applicants in order to reject a good percentage of them, hence earning points for selectivity in the college rankings. But in 2006, our place in the rankings paled in comparison to the existential question we faced.

Our survival as an institution depended on clarifying, to ourselves and everyone else, who we were and what we aspired to be.

I've often said that we in higher education are good at adding things and bad at subtracting things. Subtraction has benefits: distinctive schools define themselves not only by what they do, but by what they don't do. As mentioned before, Tulane's Renewal Plan required painful and difficult decisions—cuts to programs, termination of faculty, and consolidation of the men's and women's colleges into a single entity. This process of elimination, though impelled by fiscal necessity, was also, more profoundly, the sign of an identity crisis that ultimately led to transformation of our mission. I'm reminded of the story—too good to skip, though it's probably apocryphal—about how Michelangelo came to sculpt the *David*: he looked at the block of marble and carved away everything that wasn't the *David*. The will to sharpen our definition, removing excess and cutting to the core, grew out of our unusual circumstances, but looking back, it was a moment when we became a better and more distinctive school.

We did it by committing ourselves, heart and soul, to a new vision. Our mission of engagement and public service, combined with our commitment to scholarship and learning, shaped decisions about everything from resources to curriculum; it influenced campus culture, inspiring the enthusiasm and dedication of the entire community; and it strengthened our identity, allowing us to find the students who belonged here and allowing those students to find us. The school is still confirming that identity, every day, by its choices and its actions in the world.

To parse these terms further: Mission is a definition of ultimate purpose, an institution's "who I am" and "why I exist." Vision proposes future aims, "what I aspire to be." Identity is the distinctive "self," the unique character arising from the mission and vision statements and from the day-by-day activities of the institution. These aspects of university life transcend administrative functions, financial strategies, and ad campaigns. Though all these are important in sustaining the strength of a school, a mission is more than a marketing strategy, and institutional identity can't be reduced to a catchphrase or logo, however much signs and symbols attract an audience. What an institution stands for and aspires to is expressed by the shared values created by the entire community, in their work and their relationships. We in higher education talk frequently about accountability, and we've come to rely on the metrics cited by the media, state and federal agencies, and national pundits to tell us how we're doing. But the result, often enough, is that the metrics, some of them spurious, end up driving our actions instead of the other way round. It's easy to become a slave to external forces. It's hard to find one's own soul.

Rather than cede control of the narrative to others who are not always well-informed about the complexities of higher education, it would be good to take responsibility for ourselves—for the promises we make and the progress we seek.[1] It would be good to take back our own story, speak our own truth, and affirm our own identity.

One mode of self-definition relates to a school's fundamental educational objectives, that is, the granting of a certain level of degree. This kind of mission differentiation found one of its most effective champions in Clark Kerr, who, as president of UCLA at the time, was the chief architect of the Master Plan of 1960, a comprehensive restructuring of the higher education system in the state of California. The Master Plan created a three-tiered "layer cake" of schools: ten University of California research institutions granting doctoral and professional degrees; twenty-three California State universities, which grant BA and master's degrees; and the California Community Colleges system, 113 open-access low-cost institutions that grant associate degrees with guaranteed transfer to an upper-level school for completion of the BA degree.[2] Simon Marginson, director of the Centre for Global Higher Education, describes the California Master Plan as "at one and the same time steeply hierarchical, open and democratic—emblematic of the American approach to higher education."[3]

The Master Plan, designed to enhance both excellence and access, provided a coherent and cost-effective structure that allotted clear objectives and responsibilities to each of the three tiers and minimized duplication and waste. The UC system has become a template for higher education plans across the nation, but other states have had less success in building a comprehensive network of schools and finding public dollars to support system-wide success.[4] California itself has seen erosion of its original plan in the decades since its inception: Proposition 13, passed in 1978, limited property taxes in the state, reducing a reliable source of funds for higher education, and the state slashed the higher education budget after the 2008 recession. A trend toward "mission creep," with community colleges offering BA degrees, the four-year schools offering some doctoral degrees, and the flagship research universities accepting more full-tuition out-of-state students, seems motivated in part by the need to offset state budget cuts.

It should be said that, despite economic stresses, the UC system remains one of the strongest in the country. The originality of the California Master Plan lies in its assignment of differentiated missions with flow among the three segments, creating an organic whole that serves the state's young people and fuels economic impact across the state, from small communities to large cities.

The lesson we can draw is that differentiation is to be preserved wherever possible in the interests of keeping the entire sector strong and accountable, excellent and democratic. One of the beauties of American higher education is its multiplicity, with varied missions animating an array of widely different institutions and with students sorting themselves out as they find their own fit. Those varied missions are central to the health of the entire sector. If we could imagine the enterprise of higher education across the United States as an ecosystem with many parts, then the entire "body" would function more effectively if each institution operated with a defined objective and served a defined demographic. It is the range of distinctive possibilities that makes postsecondary education an accessible (and sometimes affordable) option, as well as an engine of social growth, scientific innovation, and cultural enrichment. And this differentiation of mission needs to be preserved against regulatory forces, federal, state, and regional, that attempt to impose one-size-fits-all rules on all institutions.

The California Plan represents the structural differentiation of schools, but within that overall system, institutions of all kinds seek to establish their own unique character, primarily by emphasizing location, novel pedagogy, or religious affiliation. To begin with place: the most basic answer to the identity question is an X on the map. Place is a defining characteristic of a school, and as we saw in the previous chapter, an unwavering dedication to a specific locale can create unique value and meaning. But some institutions, especially state schools lacking the distinction of a flagship or land-grant university, have difficulty using their location to advantage and thus defining themselves within the larger ecosystem.

This "lesser-than" status seemed to be the fate of Portland State University, which for most of its history was overshadowed by the University of Oregon in Eugene and Oregon State University in Corvallis. What it had that the others didn't was Portland, but it took a while to come around to that recognition. Starting out in 1946 as an extension campus for World War II veterans returning to college on the GI Bill, PSU didn't achieve degree-granting status for another fifteen years—and it wasn't until 1990 that the school found its true identity under the leadership of Judith Ramaley.

Faced with the immediate challenge of Measure 5, a tax proposition that forced severe budget cuts to education, as well as a Governor's Commission report suggesting a special mission for the university, Ramaley decided she would use the budget cuts as an opportunity to strip away excess and reshape the school. She said in an interview many years after the fact, "What intrigued me at the time was, how do universities and communities actually connect with each other and how does that inform the lives of each." Her first act as president was to commission a new seal for the university bearing the motto "Let Knowledge Serve the City," signaling her intention to make PSU a modern urban university. Throughout her seven-year tenure, Ramaley stressed her commitment to cooperation and teamwork, vowing to take her direction from the needs of the community.[5]

In the course of the last two decades, PSU has sharpened its identity and been recognized for its community engagement by the Carnegie Foundation, the Peace Corps, the Corporation for National and Community Service, and the Association for the Advancement of Sustainability in Higher Education. Among its many partnerships with the city of Portland is a Sustainable Neighborhoods Initiative focusing on community needs: affordable housing in gentrifying neighborhoods, employment of local residents, urban agriculture, waste recycling, watershed restoration, transportation studies, and green infrastructure.[6] Portland State is now recognized as an anchor institution for the city, contributing over $1.4 billion to the local economy, educating Oregon leaders and innovators, and pursuing a vision of equity and inclusion in its initiatives both on and off campus.

In addition to building the school's capacities as an anchor, Ramaley redesigned the general education curriculum, which has evolved into the current University Studies program of mentored courses on critical thinking, writing and speaking skills, and thematically clustered content areas. She also deftly handled governance issues, appointing a faculty member as the president's "faculty advisor," encouraging broad participation in university planning, curriculum development, and community partnerships, and including a recognition of community outreach in promotion and tenure decisions.

The story of PSU is similar to others in this book, especially those of Penn, Drexel, Syracuse, and Widener, which all traveled similar roads to achieve anchor status.[7] Like them, Portland State evolved because of a leader's conviction, but more than those other anchor institutions, which were more widely recognized to begin with, PSU dramatically elevated its standing, both in the state of Oregon and nationwide, by committing itself to community needs.

Not only in the case of anchoring but in the areas of diversity and financial sustainability, the schools that are most distinctive are driven by powerful ideas and ideals. To pick just a few examples out of the many schools named in earlier chapters: Xavier University in New Orleans has consistently achieved its aim of educating African American students as future doctors and pharmacists; Stanford, true to its founders' goal of producing useful citizens, has developed a productive feedback loop with Silicon Valley; Trinity Washington University, once a struggling Catholic women's school, has become a leader in educating lower-income students of both genders, from many backgrounds; and Vassar, a former Seven Sisters school, has become a model for diversifying student enrollment. Advice that focuses on marketing and rebranding ultimately misses the mark. It wasn't "messaging" that changed these schools; it was hewing to a particular vision and telling a story with substance.

"Why do we exist?" and "What do we want to create" are what Daniel Seymour, author of a recent book on the mission of higher education, refers to as "visioning questions," critical to a sense of purpose and an atmosphere of striving and hope.[8] He also describes the "Wite-Out Test": when vision statements of schools in a given category (community college, four-year college, research university, and so on) were placed side by side with the names blanked out, they sounded so alike that it was impossible to distinguish which was which. Even some of the institutions I've just cited as distinctive fail to put across their message strongly in their mission and vision statements—which suggests that what you do may be more important to your success than what you say. People know Syracuse, for example, as the school that has championed the city, even though its vision statement—"Syracuse University aspires to be a pre-eminent and inclusive student-focused research university, preparing engaged citizens, scholars, and leaders for participation in a changing global society"—could apply to any number of schools.

Leaders often look to the right and the left to see how their institution compares to peers and competitors, often with an interest in emulating others, and the general drift in mission and vision statements is toward sameness. Our organizational, administrative, and pedagogical practices also tend to be much alike, across the board. Jon McGee of Saint John's University in Minnesota puts it this way: "If, say, 98 percent of our organizational DNA is shared with peers or competitors, then the two percentage points of difference had better make a real difference. They must be known, valued . . . and cultivated." He warns against a "sustained slippage toward weakness" and recommends resisting the lure of being "pretty good" at everything.[9] Better, by far, to focus energy and attention on core issues—those specific differences that make you "you."

One school that achieves such mission specificity is Berea College, which combines a dedication to place—its Appalachian roots and Kentucky history—with a strong commitment to a distinctive set of values. Its emphasis on access, diversity, and service dates back to its origins as a one-room school started in 1855 by Reverend John Fee, an abolitionist, with the first teachers recruited from Oberlin College, an antislavery institution that served as a model for what Fee named Berea College, after the biblical town that was receptive to the gospel. Instead of the usual mission statement, Berea's website offers a lengthy description of its history, its motto ("God made of one blood all the peoples of the earth"), and its "8 Commitments" that emphasize racial and gender equality, service to the "neglected region" of Appalachia, manual labor, nonsectarian Christian values including love, peace, and justice, and a foundation in the liberal arts.[10] Its booklet *Berea by the Numbers* (2012–14) begins with "$0—The amount of money 1,623 Berea College students paid for tuition."

The college's dedication to its original mission is demonstrated not only by free tuition for those in need, but also by a long list of noteworthy accomplishments, including high enrollments for African American students and low-income white students from Appalachia, and a devotion to the region—environmental activism (recycling, conservation, reforestation), indigenous crafts workshops, archiving of Appalachian history, and farming on college land. Academic achievements include Watson Fellowships, speech and debate awards, and high retention, graduation, and employment rates that attest to the belief in the liberal arts as the foundation for career success. Berea has been named a "Best Value" college by many publications—"The best education money can't buy"—and among the best liberal arts schools in the country.[11]

Berea is yet another exemplar of the power of place and history to define a school. St. John's College in Annapolis, Maryland, with a sister campus in Santa Fe, New Mexico, represents another pathway, achieving distinction through novel pedagogy. Known as a "great books" school, St. John's requires a rigid program of study based on classic texts including (and this is just a sampling) Homer, the Bible, Dante, Shakespeare, Jane Austen, Dostoyevsky, Bach, Mozart, Marx, Heidegger, and Einstein, as well as four years of math, four years of foreign languages, three years of laboratory science, and two years of music. But it's not simply the prescribed curriculum that makes St. John's what it is; it's the method of teaching, which is unwaveringly Socratic and marked by open dialogue. The teachers are tutors, facilitating discussion but providing no definitive answers or interpretations. They are resolutely *not* specialized and are routinely asked to depart from their own prior areas of expertise, with physicists teaching Aeschylus, art historians teaching Euclid. The school promotes a deeply collaborative approach, without departmental guidelines, and, indeed, without departments.

The mission, strenuously intellectual, is to restore the liberal arts to a society that has become increasingly fragmented and career oriented.[12] The students come from the elite, are few in number (eight hundred students on two campuses), and can afford the steep price of their off-the-beaten-track education. Some consider the entire project too quirky to figure seriously in the landscape of higher education, but by presenting such a radically different model—no electives, no departments, no talk of preexisting "aptitudes" or "interests," no excuses for not participating—St.

John's offers insight into basic processes of inquiry and thinking. A former board member writes, "Is it for everyone? No. But it is one of our age's failings—a liability of thoughtless 'democratization'—to assume that if something isn't good for everyone, it is good for no one."[13]

St. John's is a little like Reed College, which refused to play the rankings game because it basically didn't need to. Both are niche schools, though St. John's is tiny compared to Reed, which is merely small. St. John's has periodic enrollment and resource difficulties, but it doesn't play to the marketplace any more than Reed does. It is what it is.

Hampshire College in Amherst, Massachusetts, another bastion of alternative education, has also had enrollment difficulties and has also held true to its pedagogical mission. Hampshire is nothing if not quirky. For years it was known as the "Frisbee school," because an enterprising student fulfilled all the requirements for graduation through intensive study of (yes) the Frisbee.[14] On occasion there have been sheep at the entrance gate (a farming project) and dogs wandering on the lawn (an experiment to breed dogs to guard livestock). But Hampshire's pedagogic program to develop creativity, independence, and entrepreneurial ability has remained at the core of its mission since its inception in 1970.[15]

The school particularly deserves mention because of its policy of test-blind admissions, which targets students who have the intellectual initiative to pursue self-directed study without grades or exams, as well as opening the door to minority and low-income students given the built-in bias of many entrance exams. You'll recall from chapter 2 that in 2015, the first year the policy was implemented, both applicants and yield increased, including more disadvantaged students, and the average GPA of 3.5 was the same as that of earlier classes. However, in 2016, enrollment fell sixty-two students short of the goal, a serious deficit given that Hampshire is a relatively young school with a small endowment, and thus heavily tuition-dependent.[16] But the school has stuck to its unorthodox enrollment strategy as a reflection of its mission of social justice, innovation, entrepreneurship, and sustainability. At the inauguration of the test-blind policy in 2014, Jonathan Lash, president of Hampshire, explained the school's rationale: "We have made the decision to reduce the size of the student body and seek those students who most want, and will most benefit from, our unique and demanding academic approach." While acknowledging the financial pressures on many colleges, he stressed the ultimate importance of values and purpose: "Mission, after all, is the central institutional reason for being."[17]

Pedagogic distinctiveness is not confined to idiosyncratic liberal arts schools. A large school that for many decades pursued a unique approach to education is Northeastern University, which, for many of those years, was dismissed as a trade school because of its emphasis on experiential learning. Its cooperative education (co-op) model was launched in 1909 with eight engineering students and four Boston employers as an earn-to-learn program. Currently, nine thousand students and three thousand employers in thirty-five states and eighty countries are engaged in the co-op experience, with 92 percent of students participating in at least one, and 76 percent in two or more six-month employment stints during the course of their undergraduate education. Co-ops are tuition-free but earn eighteen semester hours of "experiential learning credit" per six-month employment; students are paid a fair wage but do not receive company benefits. Co-ops cannot be undertaken alongside academic courses, and though they are not required for graduation, some form of service learning or research is a requirement.[18]

It seems that the world has finally caught up with a model that is more than a century old. Northeastern's co-ops offer actual experience in the workplace, in fields chosen by the student according to his or her interests, helping young people find their career path and, a key point, get jobs. Ninety percent of Northeastern graduates are employed full time or enrolled in graduate school in the year following graduation, with 89 percent of those employed doing work related to their major and 50 percent receiving a job offer from a previous co-op employer.[19] In a moment when the worth of a college education is being discussed and contested, Northeastern has succeeded with a mission that stresses vocation and practical skills. For the fall of 2016, the school received a record 51,014 applicants and was one of only 15 out of 499 schools to receive a "positive outlook" by Moody's Investors Service.

We've looked at schools that derive meaning from their location and others that embrace a particular pedagogy. A third organizing principle is religion, a phenomenon that goes back to the beginning of higher education in this country. In the colonial era, colleges were founded specifically to train ministers; in the nineteenth century, Protestant and Catholic denominations opened colleges all across the nation. Broadly speaking, many of these colleges, while still ostensibly Quaker or Methodist, Dominican or Jesuit, have grown more secular over time, expanding their enrollments to include students of many different faiths and backgrounds and emphasizing missions that are virtually indistinguishable from those of schools without religious roots. But there are exceptions, and among them I would count Notre Dame, which still has the values and tenets of its origins in the Congregation of Holy Cross.

Notre Dame's mission statement is notable for its length and specificity, emphasizing the intersection of Catholic thought "with all the forms of knowledge found in the arts, sciences, professions, and every other area of human scholarship and creativity"; stressing the contribution of Catholic intellectuals to its educational aims; encouraging "a way of living consonant with a Christian community and manifest in prayer, liturgy and service"; maintaining that faith and reason are not alien to each other; and also proposing, "There is, however, a special obligation and opportunity, specifically as a Catholic university, to pursue the religious dimensions of all human learning." The mission statement ends with an affirmation of the spirit of Jesus Christ as a source of grace.[20]

The university, top ranked by *USNWR* (number 18 among national universities, number 6 in accounting, number 11 in management, number 40 in engineering),[21] with strong international study and research programs, provides the educational opportunities of other elite institutions but with a commitment to religious belief that shapes the entire school. Notre Dame's very high retention and graduation rates, putting it among the top schools in the country, reflect a strong campus culture and community ethos, and its First Year of Studies program, a portal for all incoming freshmen, helps unify the community through a shared intellectual and ethical foundation. The school has the oldest marching band and the oldest college magazine in the country, as well as the largest Catholic university press in the world—not to mention its outstanding athletics, from the days of the Fighting Irish and Knute Rockne to its current standing as the university with the second most Academic All-Americans among Division I schools.

Catholic identity is central to the university's mission. Over 80 percent of the student body is Catholic, and many buildings on campus—a replica of the Grotto at Lourdes, individual chapels in each of the twenty-nine single-sex residence halls, and, most famously, the Main Building with its Golden Dome topped by a statue of the Virgin Mary—provide places for prayer, meditation, and the saying of masses. A recently constructed building housing the Center for Social Concerns and the Institute for Church Life exemplifies the school's cohesive philosophy, combining the values of service, social justice, and a spiritual life centered on the church.

A number of Catholic universities—Georgetown, Boston College, John Carroll, and others—define themselves by their religious values, but these tenets are not as powerfully ingrained in the culture of the school as at Notre Dame. The effort to be inclusive, attracting students of different faiths and cultures, may have a diluting effect: for example, Notre Dame's enrollment is 80 percent Catholic, Georgetown's only 40 percent, with a resultant difference in ambience and character. In some cases the attempt to appeal to non-Catholic students may be motivated by marketing concerns and anxiety about enrollment, especially for tuition-dependent private institutions.

Loyola University in New Orleans is one school that saw a dramatic shortfall in enrollment in 2013—250 fewer than the expected incoming class of 875, representing a budgetary loss of $7.5 million. The decline in the number of freshmen, partly the effect of a long-term inability to rebuild enrollment after Katrina, was likely also due to the university's abrupt reduction in financial aid, a move meant to increase tuition. Starting with the recession of 2008, wealthy families have proved increasingly resistant to high tuition prices, particularly at institutions perceived as nonelite. Given that the full price tag at Loyola in 2013–14 was $48,700, the drop in yield may have represented pushback from consumers.[22]

In response to its financial crisis Loyola has cut programs, offered employee buyouts, and embarked on an aggressive fund-raising campaign, but it has also looked for ways to increase enrollment to former levels. Father Wildes, the president, in an effort to be more inclusive in his approach, has recently invited faculty committees to propose solutions to curricular and recruitment problems. Project Magis, started in 2015, has led to new degrees in computer science and food studies, an expanded theater arts program, and the restoration of a degree for adult learners in response to the interests of potential students. Outreach is an essential part of the initiative, with professors, students, and recent alumni contacting applicants via emails and texts to offer advice and information. The net result: 800 high school seniors have sent in tuition deposits for 2017, up from 615 in 2016 and Loyola's highest number since 2012, even as the price tag has increased to $52,158 a year. Still, only time will tell whether the curriculum changes, successful as they appear to be at the moment, will add sufficient value in the minds of prospective students and their families to justify the cost of a degree.[23]

What a school costs is part of its basic description and "Best Value" schools are a recognized category, with their own lists and rankings. Best value, in essence, means "best bang for the buck," but sometimes "the buck" is the more important element. There are schools whose core mission is to be affordable and hence accessible to many—what in business would be called a "commodity" as opposed to a "value-add."[24] Many community colleges that offer a lower-cost option could be described as commodities, offering stripped-down services to an ever-growing number of low-income students, while at the opposite end of the spectrum are the most prestigious private universities (think Harvard) and flagship publics (think Berkeley), where amenities are abundant, admission is selective, and price is no object.

Borrowing from the business sector, we could classify schools further, as aspirational, mainstream, niche, or peripheral, terms used to describe the selling of everything from cars to beer. Let's acknowledge at the outset that investing in a college education is vastly different from buying a car, but the marketing language is still instructive when we consider how prospective students and their families might look at the choices in front of them. An aspirational brand is the luxury model with high distinctiveness and high price—the brand everyone aspires to become. Again, think Harvard, and also think "Harvard envy."[25] The widespread hunger to enhance prestige in order to compete with the Ivies can lead to mission creep and the multiplying of strategic aims, which often has the consequence of blurring, rather than sharpening, a school's identity. Another cause of mission creep is the failure of society to arrange for the collective provision of many services—things like child care, food pantries, counseling services, medical care, and financial and legal consults—which then fall to universities, diverting person-hours and resources from a focused educational mission to other activities.

Mainstream brands are the next tier down, with the name recognition and the revenue streams to shape markets and preferences. Not to stretch the analogy too far, but any of the flagship state schools and many private research universities—schools with sufficient resources to develop innovative institutes and global initiatives—would fit the "mainstream" category. Then there are the niche brands, the St. Johns, Reeds, and many other small liberal arts schools, with high distinction and high price, which are successful even with low enrollments. The most problematic category, be it cars, beer, or schools, is the "peripheral" class, which suffers not from Harvard envy per se (that would be too far a reach) but from a general "me too" strategy, trying to imitate more elite schools. However, in order to survive, such schools tend to have a much lower price, which can't be nudged upward because of a perceived lack of value and distinctiveness.[26] Of course marketing and mission are not one and the same thing; the topics of branding and pricing come up only because a weak or vague mission will almost inevitably lead to existential risk to the institution.

Throughout most of this chapter, I have been arguing that substance and quality, not advertising or branding, are the critical determinants of institutional vitality and viability. Still, language counts. Though rhetoric on a website can be misleading or vague, with everyone sounding more or less the same, the wording of a mission statement, if carefully chosen, can be an important guide to institutional objectives.

In a roundup of colleges and universities in New Orleans in 2016, presidents and chancellors offered campus forecasts about the likely future of their institutions. Almost everyone—participants from Dillard, LSU, the University of New Orleans—remarked on the financial pressures they were under, and how they expected to increase revenue, but Father Wildes, interestingly, spoke solely of Loyola's identity: its cultivation of a learning-centered community, its commitment to educational excellence, its devotion to students' discovery of their career and a life of service, and its roots in Jesuit tradition.[27] Loyola's mission statement includes the phrase "Inspired by Ignatius of Loyola's vision of finding God in all things," before continuing with language about its liberal arts and professional studies programs. Its vision statement again refers to St. Ignatius: "By thinking critically and acting justly, students are to embody the Ignatian ideals of faith, truth, justice, and service." Though the school's new courses and majors were developed to entice applicants, these curriculum changes are similar to those at other institutions and may not, in the end, distinguish Loyola sufficiently from its competitors. The reaffirmation of existential purpose—reaching back to the teachings of St. Ignatius of Loyola and recovering the conviction and dedication that would elevate the university's distinctiveness and academic reputation—could be a more effective way to move out of the middle range of schools and confirm the value of a Loyola degree.[28]

Another school that has reasserted its foundational purpose is Paul Quinn, mentioned earlier as a historically black college founded by the African Methodist Episcopal Church in the nineteenth century, which has begun accepting Latino students to expand its enrollment and increase its financial sustainability. What sounds like a departure from its African American roots is actually, in its newest incarnation, a return to core values. Michael Sorrell, the president, revisiting the school's original vision, outlines four ethical principles in the college handbook—the Four Ls of Quinnite Leadership: "Leave places better than you found them; Lead from wherever you are; Live a life that matters; and Love something greater than yourself." The handbook includes a statement affirming the Apostle's Creed and articles of belief drawn from Methodist doctrine, including "we believe that creation occurred in six literal days."[29]

Paul Quinn's mission statement includes no language about reconciling faith and reason, religion and science, in the manner of the great Catholic universities. The religious foundations have in practice become a set of expectations for "greatness," fostered and encouraged by caring support from Sorrell and the entire school; Quinnite character, combining faith-based principles and aspirations for success, is the essence of "Quinnite nation." Partnering with businesses in Dallas, Paul Quinn is the first small urban college to become one of the nation's designated "work colleges," with the aim of ensuring that students graduate with no more than ten thousand dollars of debt and find jobs in a technological and corporate economy. It's not unlike Berea College in its religious origins, its respect for labor, and its dedication to "doing well by doing good," but it operates in a city environment rather than rural Appalachia. Zeroing in on the values of work and service, the school strives to build character, develop skills, create a sense of meaning and purpose, and help young people rise from poverty to more fulfilled, secure lives.[30]

Returning to foundational meanings is one way to strengthen a core identity, but sometimes institutions find it necessary to recraft the mission statement in order to articulate a new sense of purpose. Fort Lewis College in Colorado, chiefly known as Colorado's only public four-year liberal arts college, rewrote its mission statement in 2016, shifting from a sole emphasis on the liberal arts to incorporate practical concerns about employment, reflecting the changed environment in higher education generally. The old and new statements sound similar, but the few changes are loaded with significance.

The earlier statement: "Fort Lewis College offers accessible, high quality, baccalaureate liberal arts education to a diverse student population, preparing citizens for the common good in an increasingly complex world."

The new statement: "Fort Lewis College provides an integrated and formative liberal arts and professional education to a diverse student population, preparing global citizens to work in and contribute to a complex world."

To get from one statement to the other required eight months of intensive discussion with all stakeholders (faculty, staff, professional associates, alumni, trustees, and groups in the community), with much of the discussion focusing on whether to retain mention of the liberal arts. Word choice was important: the addition of "professional education," "global citizens" and "work" all adjusted the mission of the school in important ways, without abandoning the prior commitment to the humanities. The mission statement guided the articulation of a further set of "core values," including education, diversity, community, high expectations, stewardship, and relevance.

Perhaps as important as the statements of mission and values was the process of creating them. Respectful consideration was given to students and faculty as well as to administrators, trustees, and local residents, reinforcing the school's sense of communal purpose. Fort Lewis lived its creed in the very act of stating it.[31]

Words matter, but deeds matter just as much, if not more. It's not only the articulation of purpose but the enactment of it, through shared governance, committed scholarship, community engagement, and open dialogue, that creates the distinctive spirit and character of an institution. Mission and vision statements provide guidance, not as rules to be obeyed, but as a reminder of enduring values and goals—who you are and what you strive to become. It's the job of leadership to inspire the community to be its best, and truest, self—which brings us to the final chapter, "Presidential Leadership: Character and Context."

10

Presidential Leadership
Character and Context

Now more than ever, when the paradigm has shifted
and a new world is emerging, we need people in charge
who can do the job. But we have trouble finding them.
How can we search out and vet the right people to lead
complex organizations through a period of constant
and rapid change?

Since stepping down from the presidency of Tulane, I've been
teaching an undergraduate course at the university called The
Mythology and Reality of Leadership. Class discussions cover all
types of leadership, including adaptive, transformational, team,
servant, and authentic, and assignments include self-assessments
and development of a personal leadership plan. But it's not only
the students who are engaged in self-assessment; the course has
also been an opportunity to reflect on my own experience with
leadership. Although leadership has been a theme throughout this
book, in this final chapter I want to offer a comprehensive view
of what it takes to lead and how we can select the right people for
the job of university or college president.

If higher education is to have a bright future, it will need leaders with the experience, skills, and knowledge to guide our institutions with clarity and courage in rapidly changing times. As in
prior chapters, I'll be looking at presidential successes and failures
in order to elucidate what it is we're looking for when we search
for the next cohort of leaders. Unfortunately, we seem to have

trouble finding the right leaders; we even have trouble recognizing them when they're standing right in front of us. In fact, the number of failed and mediocre presidencies has increased over time. A critical step to ensure the future health of the sector will be to systematize and strengthen the process of presidential succession, an area where guesswork and mistakes are all too common, especially when all the stakeholders have their eyes set on an outside candidate. I will be discussing the nuts and bolts of presidential succession further on in this chapter but will note, for now, that a self-aware process is likely to yield better results than choices driven by hopes and illusions.

One reason presidencies fail is the sheer difficulty of the job. Preparing the materials for The Mythology and Reality of Leadership and reflecting on my own history helped me crystallize some observations about the multiple challenges of being a university or college president. The role is exceptionally demanding because of the diversity of disciplines and functions under a president's purview, along with the responsibility of managing a significant budget and pool of human talent. A second challenge is that no single measure of organizational success is commonly accepted by all of the university's stakeholders (i.e., students, faculty, staff, trustees, parents, alumni, the community, and the list goes on); in fact, many of these stakeholders have competing interests. Managing conflict is a central task in the system of shared governance in which a president works—a system that often slows decision making and leads to suboptimal outcomes. Another challenge is the "fishbowl" environment of academic institutions; because of social media and twenty-four-hour news cycles, higher education has major visibility in the public eye. Meanwhile, the problems facing a university or college are often a microcosm of the complex and contentious issues, including dwindling financial resources and rising income inequality, that are occurring more widely in society. Finally, the primary focus of a university president is young people from the ages of eighteen to twenty-two—a serious responsibility given that most are living away from home for the first time, and many are likely to encounter developmental issues or experiment with risks of various kinds.

All these difficulties have grown even more acute in a tumultuous era of mounting pressures both inside and outside the academy. At the same time, without question, assuming the role of president is a great privilege, offering the opportunity to shape young lives and contribute in myriad ways to the advancement of society as a whole. Because the position is both arduous and influential, we need principled, courageous, creative leaders who will secure the future of our colleges and universities and sustain our nation's preeminent position in the world.

To return, for a moment, to my own experiences leading organizations, I would say that I came to Tulane as an "unfiltered" leader[1]—a dark horse, of sorts, with a background in business administration and without the standard résumé, that is, degrees in the nonprofessional fields from the most prestigious institutions and prior experience as a provost in between a deanship and a presidency. "Filtered" leaders, socialized to an academic setting and with all the right credentials, often follow the expected path and check all the required boxes, yet ultimately may not succeed in an emerging landscape of higher education characterized by change and innovation.

I've always had a dual perspective, one foot in and one foot out of the academy, and not only because of my somewhat atypical résumé. My history, as I've noted, includes undiagnosed dyslexia during my schooling, as well as the fact that my sister and I were the first in our family to graduate from college—a biographical feature, as it turns out, of many of the university presidents documented in this book. I've also had extensive experience in the corporate and broader nonprofit worlds, which has given me the opportunity to interact with extraordinary leaders from various walks of life. And partly because of my learning difference, partly because of formative experiences as a student athlete and in the army, I've always learned better by doing things out in the world, in concert with other people, rather than alone with a book or sitting in a classroom. All these experiences have made me less a typical academic, and slightly more "unfiltered," than the usual university president.

In the late 1990s the Tulane board was looking for someone who was entrepreneurial, used to working in an environment with scarce resources but high expectations, and with a demonstrated ability to significantly advance an organization's quality, distinctiveness, and reputation. I had spent the previous twenty-three years at Case Western Reserve University, first as a professor and then, for the last fourteen years, as dean of the Weatherhead School of Management. I'd also had significant corporate board experience during that time. The other finalist for the presidency was a humanist and provost at an Ivy League university. Happily for me, the board determined that I was a match for Tulane's needs, challenges, and opportunities—and thus began my sixteen-year tenure as Tulane's president.

Traditionally, in searching for leaders in higher education we have focused on "filtered" candidates—outstanding academics with administrative experience, especially at elite schools, mostly in the humanities, sciences, and engineering, and much less so in the professional school ranks—in the belief that they will make the most effective presidents. That belief isn't always justified, as many who look the part don't always play the part very well. An "unfiltered" candidate can bring the promise of fresh perspectives and innovative strategies—though as we'll see in the forthcoming examples, those from outside the academy can also disappoint.[2]

Let me take a moment here to speak of demographics: those features that define a person by age, gender, socioeconomic class, race, and ethnicity. According to a recent report by the American Council on Education, the typical university president of 2016 was a sixty-two-year-old white male with a doctoral degree. That cohort—of which, until recently, I was a member—is about to retire in large numbers, with more than half of current presidents planning to step down within the next five years. Now is the chance to look for candidates who represent the diversity of our students, 57 percent of whom are women and many of whom are nonwhite (40 percent at four-year public institutions). Though statistics can never fully define an individual, consideration should be given to personal data that shape attitudes and perceptions. As I mentioned earlier, five decades ago my own demographic was "first in the family to go to college," and it seems significant to me that many of the presidents described in this book share the same background. We represented a wave of graduates who went on to academic careers and in many cases leadership positions. Today, leaders who represent rising segments of our society are likely to bring experiences and perspectives crucial to sustaining the relevance and vitality of our institutions of higher education at a time of intense upheaval.[3]

Given changes in the social fabric and the concomitant need to move beyond the status quo, I doubt that the traditional candidate will automatically be the best choice for the future. If the past can't be our guide, how then can we find and evaluate the right people to lead organizations of immense complexity through what will almost certainly be turbulent times in the coming years?

A good candidate should have a realistic grasp of the future of higher education and of how a particular institution, including its culture, challenges, and aspirations, fits into this landscape. Meanwhile, a university should identify the relevant experiences, skills, and competencies best suited to its particular needs at a particular moment in time, with an awareness, as well, of the advantages an "outsider" candidate can bring. From an institutional point of view, organizational fit, proper vetting and due diligence, seamless transitions, and clarity of expectations can make all the difference between a successful presidency and a failed or mediocre one. One thing I have learned for certain: no organization can achieve or sustain success without a leader who has the character, vision, and behavioral skills to match the task, as well as the instincts and experience to understand and respond to the complex context of the leadership position.

I want to focus for a moment on the process of leading and what I see as the essential nature of that process. In my view, the fundamental job of a leader is to effect change, whether transformational (as in Tulane's do-or-die moment after Katrina) or incremental (for example, the long process of consensus building that Norman Francis undertook at Xavier University). The vagaries of institutional life, including financial setbacks, athletics scandals, faculty unrest—indeed, all the topics already discussed in this book—continually offer the possibility (and sometimes the necessity) of significant reinvention and modification. Even in periods of relative stability, a leader needs to seek new ways of doing things in order to sustain institutional growth and anticipate the future. It is only by continually adjusting to changing circumstances and persistently seeking innovative paths that presidents ensure the evolution of the institutions they oversee. But in the absence of a crisis that necessitates immediate action, the president has to build a compelling case for change step-by-step, appealing to the institution's mission and core values in order to create a sense of necessity and urgency.

It seems to me that certain talents and attributes are vital to achieving meaningful and enduring institutional change. Storytelling skills that inspire others to share in a common vision and interpersonal skills that ease friction and conflict are critical in bringing a community together. Also essential: integrity, because sticking to your values is the only way to set an example, elicit respect, and elevate the ethos of an institution; courage, because not everyone (and sometimes, it seems, not anyone) will like you; perseverance, because any change—from the most dramatic to the most mundane—always demands, in the end, long-term commitment; and political and administrative acumen, in order to map out a strategy, facilitate negotiations, and (the sine qua non of progress) raise funds.

From my perspective, the most successful higher education leaders seem to have a near-perfect blend of vision and practicality, humility and persistence, and credibility and resilience. They also tend to have a high level of emotional intelligence. An example of this blend of talents is Steve Sample, who as president of the University of Southern California transformed USC from a good school, dismissed by some as the "University for Spoiled Children" and the "University of Second Choice," to a premier research university and anchor institution.

Sample came to the school as an academic insider. A PhD in electrical engineering, he rose through a series of administrative posts to become president of SUNY Buffalo at the age of forty-one, elevating that school by emphasizing undergraduate education, building research capacity, and strengthening service to the community—achievements that led to membership in the prestigious Association of American Universities.

But Sample was also an atypical president in many respects. He was fascinated by the humanities and science as well as engineering and read widely outside of his discipline. He had a creative, restless mind and was an inspired innovator; while in his twenties, as a young professor at Purdue, he invented the touch pad now used in microwaves and other appliances worldwide. An *LA Times* magazine Man-of-the-Year article devoted to his presidency at USC described him as a Mr. Fix-It, who sometimes brainstormed while lying on the floor, coming up with new ideas in a playful experimental way.[4]

One such experiment was mailing five-dollar bills to random alumni with a self-addressed return envelope in the hope of ratcheting up donations. Though it didn't pan out (most alums kept their five dollars), Sample took a good-humored view: "It was not a good idea. But a lot of other ideas have worked. And the good news is that we have doubled alumni giving since I got here."[5] People refer often to his charisma and sense of humor, his magical salesmanship leading to enormous gifts to the university, his understanding of the academic environment, and his gift for innovative problem solving. He had flaws, or at least some people thought so. Staff saw his temper flare in private, and some noted the performance aspect of his presidency, a "charm offensive" he could turn on at will to get the results he sought. But by general consensus, he was a leader in the genius mold.

Sample won that consensus not only because of who he was but because of what he did. In 1992, a year after he arrived at USC, the Los Angeles riots erupted right on the school's doorstep. During the crisis he stayed on campus, sleeping on the floor of his office and going down to the dining hall to eat with fearful students. He resisted calls to "do a Pepperdine"—another Los Angeles school that had decamped to Malibu after the Watts riots of 1965—and instead set about creating close ties with the immediate neighborhood, concentrating USC's service programs in south Los Angeles. Under his leadership, USC redefined its location by developing an arts and cultural corridor that runs from the university to downtown. Morton Schapiro, then president of Williams College, said, "Steve has managed to relocate USC from the ghetto of South-Central Los Angeles to the edge of vibrant downtown L.A.—without moving an inch."[6]

The 1992 crisis at USC went beyond the Rodney King riots. It was also the year of a significant tuition shortfall and, a blow to Trojan fans, a dismal football record. A little more than a year later, a damaging earthquake hit Los Angeles. Sample saw the serial setbacks as an opportunity to transform the school, picking four goals—strengthen undergraduate education, expand interdisciplinary research and teaching, extend global reach, and emphasize anchoring and community engagement—articulated concisely in fifteen pages. The clarity and brevity of the strategic plan created unity of purpose and a campus-wide commitment to original thinking and unconventional approaches.

Sample had no wish to make the University of Southern California a copycat school, a "Harvard of the West" or "Stanford of the South." He expressed the hope that in the future USC would continue to "keep asking our signature question and keep finding answers to it: What can we do better than anybody else in the world?" In a sense Sample did everything well: he increased the number and quality of applicants, attracted top-tier faculty, founded an association of Pacific Rim universities, and strengthened the communities around USC (fifteen thousand undergraduates volunteering in the neighborhoods, three hundred social outreach programs). But he also kept finding new ways to define and underscore USC's unique value.

A chief way, as noted earlier, was through fund-raising, hence the USC School of Cinematic Arts (supported by the Lucasfilm Foundation), the Robert Zemeckis Center for Digital Arts, the Thornton School of Music, the Annenberg Center on Communication Leadership & Policy, the Keck School of Medicine, the Alfred E. Mann Institute for Biomedical Engineering[7] . . . the list goes on. Many of Sample's efforts—for example, in cinema, television, and videogames—focused on industries specific to Los Angeles. The proliferation of well-funded programs has led to a new level of intellectual achievement, including superb faculty (among them a Nobel Prize winner), an increase in productive research, and cutting-edge interdisciplinary studies.

Sample had a mix of qualities—formality and playfulness, toughness and compassion, charm and diligence—that defies categorization. As an exemplar of the blended model of leadership, he was a problem-solver and skilled administrator and, at the same time, an inventor, tinkerer, Pied Piper. And he had "situational aptitude": for nineteen years, he was able to master contingency, including a diagnosis of Parkinson's halfway through his tenure.

Steve Sample is not alone among university presidents; we've seen others like him in the course of this book, individuals with the capacity to rise to the occasion, nurture a vision, and effect meaningful and substantive change according to the contexts in which they found themselves. But examples can't tell us precisely how to find others who will be as effective, and no one has a crystal ball to reveal the occasions and contexts a leader might be required to face in the future. There remains an element of alchemy to successful leadership, and finding an effective leader can feel like a fishing expedition, hoping you'll catch a big one.

In a thoughtful analysis of the presidential selection process, Stephen Trachtenberg and his coauthors examine presidencies "derailed," focusing on leaders terminated before the end of their first contract.[8] Trachtenberg lists traits of ineffective leaders—

incompetence, rigidity, intemperance, callousness, corruption, insularity, and evil (yes, evil)—and of effective leaders with exactly the opposite characteristics. But the trait model has its limits as a description of what makes a good leader; there are skills and experiences, whether acquired inside or outside the academy, that equip someone for the task, beyond the kind of person he or she happens to be. Insofar as traits are a useful predictor of performance, what's important is not just personality (withdrawn or gregarious, warm or cool) but those deeper aspects of self that I would describe as "character," connoting the virtues of honesty, humility, self-confidence, drive, maturity, creativity, transparency, and self-control that Trachtenberg mentions.

However, even the most upright candidates can fail. Some people with all the skills to be highly successful deans or provosts fail because they may simply have risen to the level of their incompetence (think Peter Principle).[9] Negative traits sometimes emerge in the course of holding office, where a sense of entitlement and an illusion of omnipotence may grow inside the bubble of authority. And sometimes people simply don't agree on the issue of character, and the same action can be seen as decisive or autocratic, realistic or callous, depending on viewpoint.

Beyond the traits and temperament of the individual at the helm, the larger context—the culture of academics generally and the tone of a given campus in particular—can contribute to a derailment. Perhaps the most crucial element in selecting a leader is, as I've mentioned, the "fit" between a candidate and an institution's values, mission, academic and financial profile, and general ambiance. Which brings us back to the topic of "filtered" insiders, those with the sterling résumés and academic experience, and "unfiltered" outsiders, who bring new perspectives and change agendas. Many derailments involve poor organizational fit.

One such derailment occurred in 2016 at Mount St. Mary's University in Maryland, where Simon Newman, the new president, departed before the end of his first year in office after a faculty vote requesting his resignation. The Mount, the second oldest Catholic university in the nation, had problems similar to Loyola's in New Orleans. As a less elite but highly expensive school with a liberal arts orientation and a mission focused on religious values, the institution saw drops in enrollment and resultant fiscal shortfalls. Backed by the board of trustees, Newman, formerly an executive in the financial industry, came in with a change agenda designed to boost enrollment, shore up finances, and raise national profile.

Newman made an immediate and ultimately fatal misstep: he developed a questionnaire for freshmen that probed mental health issues, disabilities, and financial stresses, with answers linked to students' IDs, in order to cull between twenty and twenty-five students from the freshman class in order to improve the school's retention rate. The survey promised "no wrong answers" but was actually a covert instrument to dismiss students likely to be low-performing. Subsequently, Newman fired two professors who had criticized him and demoted the provost who had served as adviser to the school paper that had published information about the questionnaire.[10] No students left the school on the basis of the survey, but Newman's response to faculty objections—saying of students that "you have to drown the bunnies, put a Glock to their heads"—magnified both the incident and the attendant outrage.[11]

Newman's ploy instantly attracted media attention, including a call for his resignation by the *Washington Post*. Faculty were infuriated not only by the treatment of students, but by Newman's peremptory firing of the two faculty members and his unilateral plans for curricular reform. Though some professors supported Newman's intentions to pare down the core curriculum, ramp up programs that offered students marketable degrees, and add high-demand courses in technological areas, many others objected to the de-emphasizing of the liberal arts, the subversion of the school's Catholic mission,[12] and the callous disregard of shared governance.

An impolitic hard-charging corporate executive, supported by a board hoping for innovation and improved fiscal health, collides with academic norms about which he knows nothing: Newman's presidency, a governance clash compounded by an ethical lapse, was a marriage of opposites doomed to end in divorce. I believe that Mount St. Mary's did the right thing. The rapid removal of a president who had failed to gain the trust of the community and had elicited such negative national coverage was essential to the future of the school. When you've made a bad bet, dragging on in the hopes of a magical metamorphosis only makes things worse.

The future of the school looks significantly brighter under the current leadership of interim president Timothy E. Trainor, a retired brigadier general in the US Army and previously dean and chief academic officer of the US Military Academy at West Point. Though bringing an outside perspective, his academic experience has made him a much better fit for Mount St. Mary than his predecessor; as one faculty member says of Trainor, "he gets it—he understands governance." He is highly visible on campus, eating lunch with students whenever he can, and he has collaborated with faculty on the college's strategic plan, encouraging conversation and working to bring the community together.

Some on campus speak respectfully of Newman's campaign to modernize the school, a program he dubbed Mount 2.0 that included new majors in cybersecurity and other burgeoning fields, as well as investment in athletics—changes that have, in fact, been realized since his departure. But with Trainor as president, the school has seen a number of substantial improvements—expanded enrollment, increased retention of first-year students from first to second semester, a new center for student engagement to support at-risk freshmen, a surge in donor contributions—as well as a rise in school spirit and a renewed sense of possibility. Thane Naberhaus, a faculty member reinstated after having been fired by Newman, attributes the changed atmosphere to Trainor: "The amazing thing is what a difference a single person can make."[13]

How risky was it for the board of Mount St. Mary's to select an outsider like Newman? Back in the 1990s when I was dean at the Weatherhead School, I wrote an essay in praise of mavericks, though admittedly I was speaking of lower-ranked executives and not CEOs.[14] Those who come at a problem from outside often bring fresh air and new ideas, and their disdain for the status quo can be a healthy corrective to institutions mired in tradition and resistant to change. A nonconforming, independent perspective can energize and inspire an entire institution—Steve Jobs had a wide streak of maverick in him—but the itch to shake things up, particularly without regard for details and consequences, also comes with the risk of significant, even spectacular, failure.

Pinning institutional hopes on traits like "independent-minded" or "innovative" is risky because the desired qualities may be illusory or, as in the case of Simon Newman, may lead to unintended and unwelcome consequences. How can an institution negotiate between the Scylla and the Charybdis of the selection process— the danger of picking the person with the expected résumé, who, though acquainted with university norms, may fit all too well with academic culture and settle into a mediocre and uninspired tenure; and the opposite danger, of picking a maverick brought in from the worlds of business or government as a breath of fresh air, whose failure to understand the academy may lead to destructive clashes or hasty termination?

Approaches that focus on the process of selection—the "how" as well as the "who"—can significantly reduce the risk of a wrong choice and better the chances of a right one. To avoid the risk of derailment, one suggestion I would make is a more rigorous and open vetting of candidates before a final selection is made. In recent years consultants and boards have increasingly opted for highly secretive and confidential search processes for fear of losing potentially great candidates. From my perspective, this approach is not in the best long-term interests of either candidates or institutions. If someone isn't already a sitting president, there's little risk to engaging in the process; if someone is, then transparency might inhibit needless job shopping. For institutions, a secretive process often leads to governance battles and community dissension.

I personally favor longer and more extensive and transparent selection processes of the kind I myself experienced back in 1997, when I was a candidate at Tulane. When the list had been pared down to two or three finalists, I was invited to a lengthy visit on campus, meeting with everyone from students to board members. The vetting process felt like a kind of beauty contest—a combination talent show and dress rehearsal. I had the opportunity to get the feel of the place; the place had the opportunity to look me over and sense what kind of a person I was. The "feel" is a predictor (not perfect, but still a predictor) of fit, which is in itself a predictor of success. I also believe that a candidate's extended exposure on campus creates a communal sense of ownership and buy-in, thereby improving the chances of a successful presidency. Such open vetting also lessens the chance that board members will be too involved in pushing a private agenda on the one hand, or too disengaged to help guide a transition on the other.

Board behavior is often the chief culprit when a poor choice is made, and Trachtenberg in *Presidencies Derailed* devotes considerable space to board antics that can lead to a derailment, including internal schisms, flawed search processes, breaches of confidence, conflicts of interest, micromanagement, and weak oversight. Both activism and negligence affect the performance of boards. One or more very vocal trustees can promote a candidate and override other members; they can conduct a search without solid data about the institution's strengths and weaknesses and the appropriate fit of prospective candidates; and they can think of themselves chiefly as cheerleaders and check writers rather than exercising their fiduciary responsibility to conduct the search and help formulate the strategic plan.[15] They can also fall in love with a résumé or someone who impresses in interview and subsequently fail to conduct the proper due diligence in screening candidates. To reiterate, a more self-aware and systemic approach to presidential succession is needed to avoid such damaging behaviors.

The University of Iowa's Board of Regents represents a case of dysfunctional board activism in the face of declining state support of the university and a reluctance to continue hiking tuition. When the board asked the search committee, which included three regents, to present them with a slate of varied candidates, the ultimate aim (not publicly stated) was to find someone from the business world who would discover new revenue sources and contain costs. Bruce Rastetter, president of the board who also served on the search committee, championed Bruce Harreld over three other qualified candidates with strong academic experience. Harreld had a background in agribusiness similar to Rastetter's, as well as the corporate turnaround experience the regents sought.

The board's secretive campaign to get Harreld selected ignored the results of their own public process, which led to a sanction by the American Association of University Professors for violation of standards of shared governance and good common sense. One faculty member pointed out that "universities are one of the few areas of American culture—really Western culture—where market logic doesn't trump everything else," referencing the famed Iowa Writers' Workshop, which doesn't generate much revenue but has immeasurable cultural value.

The wish to borrow expertise from the business sector can lead to a poor fit between leader and institution, as was the case with Simon Newman, and as many predict may be the case with Bruce Harreld, who has held contentious town meetings with faculty, staff, and students and has been widely criticized for his blunt manner, his lack of sensitivity to gender issues, and his financial focus at the expense of a broad vision for the university. Unfortunately, and sadly from my perspective, there is a growing tendency among colleges and universities to hire presidents from outside their own organizations. In the corporate world, such a practice would be generally seen as a failure of succession planning by the board and CEO. As we've just observed, outside candidates have a greater degree of risk associated with them, especially when the searches are highly confidential, making their transitions even more difficult in a job that is already fraught with challenges.

Of course it's possible to find talented and capable individuals who come from outside the academy. Mitch Daniels, former governor of Indiana and, as mentioned, now president at Purdue, and Janet Napolitano, former secretary of homeland security and now president of the University of California system, come to mind. But fit remains a crucial consideration. Lack of prior experience in running a complex organization, a job that requires consensus building rather than simply top-down management, is a significant deficit for any new university president. Adding to any candidate's potential for failure is a procedural issue: not only who is hired, but *how* they are hired. If the process is confidential and nontransparent, as at Iowa, the person chosen, however skilled in fiscal and curricular turnarounds, won't have sufficient support from the entire community to succeed in the highly collaborative environment of academia.

One way to help a newly selected president become an effective leader is to organize a transition process that passes the baton in a seamless manner. At the University of Dayton, the board of trustees did not simply choose the new president and wish him all the best; they asked the new inductee to work with the retiring president for many months in advance of taking office and clearly communicated their own goals for the institution. Certainly Eric Spina, the new president, came with the kind of résumé—dean of engineering and then provost and vice chancellor at Syracuse—that made him an excellent prospect. But to ensure his full readiness for a presidency, Dayton lent a helping hand.

This sort of planned orderly transition is rare, largely because trustees fail to meet their responsibilities by not being thoughtful about presidential transition.[16] Transitions occur more smoothly when sufficient time is built into the process, with thorough analysis of trends rather than hasty interventions and with performance reviews in the course of the first two years, both to evaluate a new president's effectiveness and to support his improvement. The clear statement of expectations and feedback, with the president and trustees jointly agreeing on a set of goals and the strategies to achieve them, encourages success and at the same time establishes measures of accountability.

A smooth transition is often hard to achieve after a long-serving and effective president steps down, particularly when the successor may have a dissimilar style and different aims. Boards can help ease the way by promoting continuity with the previous era while also supporting the continuous evolution of the institution. You'll recall John Fry's outstanding success at Franklin & Marshall, with a brownfield reclamation project and building campaign that changed the face of Lancaster, Pennsylvania. In the course of that campaign, he built a $50 million life science and philosophy center, renovated a center for business, government, and public policy, refurbished four student residences, and built a fifth, New College House. The College Houses all have common rooms that serve as intimate settings where professors, speakers, and students mingle and converse.

The succeeding president, Dan Porterfield, sings the praises of John Fry for providing these "third spaces" in the residences, where the life of the classroom and residential life merge. In contrast to Fry, Porterfield is a "filtered" leader in the classic mold: a Rhodes Scholar and English professor with a BA from Georgetown and a PhD from CUNY. The chair of the board of trustees, Susan Washburn, also an admirer of Fry, is equally appreciative of what Porterfield brings to the table, describing the two men as "the right match for the right time." She sees Porterfield's focus on diversity initiatives, need-based financial aid, and curricular initiatives as building on what Fry did. "John gets juiced from looking at space and seeing the potential for it. Dan Porterfield gets juiced by the potential of students." That narrative of continuous growth, emanating from the board, has lent coherence to the institution's evolution from one presidency to the next.[17]

In addition to board guidance, oversight, and messaging, mentoring can be extremely helpful to a newcomer, especially one unacquainted with the rules and norms of academic institutions, but even those who just come from a different kind of school or prior administrative post. Counselors and collegial advisers are necessary even (or especially) when they are critics. In my own history, you'll remember that while dean at Weatherhead, I made my chief adversary head of the committee to develop a plan for the executive doctoral program, because his skeptical views were likely to make the plan stronger. When I first came to Tulane I rounded up an ad hoc advisory board of presidents and provosts in my first two years in office, figures I greatly admired, who helped me get acclimated to my new job, and later I found an equally outstanding group of advisers during the crisis of Katrina.[18] Lawrence Schall, president of Oglethorpe University in Atlanta, Georgia, looking back to the beginning of his tenure in 2005, describes how he squeaked through a major financial and accreditation crisis with the help of a few trustees and one colleague whom he knew slightly. He says that a more structured and continuous program of support, education, and mentoring would have helped him immeasurably as a rookie president.[19]

There's one more way of assuring a smooth transition: hire from within, which I believe can be an effective move when done right, within a well-managed system of presidential succession. Among the Ivies, Harvard, Yale, and Princeton are known for promoting from inside their institutions, as is Stanford. USC, too: the current president, C. L. Max Nikias, served as provost under Steve Sample. All these schools obviously have no need of a transformation wrought by a maverick outsider bringing in fresh ideas. The downside of elevating talent within the organization is the danger of ossification and complacency at a time of intense and unpredictable change, which is why a self-aware process is helpful in preventing mistakes. I wouldn't worry too much about the elite of the elite—they're doing fine—but everyone else would do well to think about organizational fit, vetting, transitions, and expectations in order to maximize their prospects for both continuity and growth. I also suggest, as I've indicated throughout this chapter, that university boards take succession planning much more seriously, because in the end it is the "who" that determines whether an organization will be successful or not.

All these strategies for ensuring a high-quality pick and helping a rookie adjust to the job could, if instituted widely, improve the chances of "catching a good one" at many institutions facing vacancies. A candidate's prior administrative experience also improves the odds of a successful presidency, because the fundamentals—developing a vision, planning a coherent strategy, being a fund-raiser (and friend-raiser!), focusing on performance, and attracting high-quality colleagues and staff members—don't change. What does change are the external forces that affect an institution. Currently, the forces affecting higher education are gathering into a storm. Now, more than ever, we need a varied cast of characters who bring with them the background and experience to understand the diverse students we aim to educate. Now, more than ever, we need "blended" leaders who not only observe the fundamentals of good management but also think outside the box; who have the flexibility, intelligence, sensitivity, creativity, and strength—the "situational aptitude"—to master the vicissitudes to come. We're back, again, to the "right stuff," all the traits that play a role in successful leadership.

But more than all these characteristics (and who can argue with that "leaderly" list?), a university president needs the ability to learn on the job. With a given trait, you either have it or you don't. But leadership, as we've seen again and again, isn't simply a collection of qualities; it's a dynamic process of absorbing experience, experimenting, and persisting. Steve Sample brought a visionary brilliance to the task, but he also said of his arrival at USC, "I came . . . as a student—someone who wanted and needed to listen and learn about this particular institution which I had been called to lead." You have to be willing to learn the environment and then, once you've learned it, keep pace with ceaseless changes in that environment. Along with change as a way of life comes a perpetual learning curve.

As president emeritus, Sample offered some reflections on the theme of mutability and tradition in higher education, noting that this is a period of rapid and sweeping change, including interdisciplinary, engaged, and interconnected learning, education at a distance, and the commercialization of university research—all of which he found healthy and even necessary. But he also noted that universities are "in the people-building business," and that the values of moral discernment and the love of truth and beauty are unchanging.[20]

The ability to find a balance between preservation and innovation, between an inside and an outside perspective, is what we should look for in our leaders. Along with an adherence to processes that work, a "what-if, why-not" zest, and an ability to learn by doing, emotional intelligence is another essential skill. Patricia McGuire, president of Trinity Washington University and winner of the Hesburgh Award, describes people skills—psychological sensitivity and the ability to understand symbolic gestures, silences, and body language—as the core of a successful presidency. She says search committees need to help develop a president's ability to read people well and thus motivate them to move collectively toward the school's goals and vision.[21]

Before I conclude, I want to take a moment for personal reflection. Looking back on my own experience as president of Tulane, I think of the moments of personal pride, especially the post-Katrina accomplishments when we pulled victory from the jaws of defeat and reinvented the institution's mission and identity. I am proud of our commitment to community engagement, social innovation and entrepreneurship, residential living, and the reenvisioning of several of our academic schools and programs. Primarily because of Katrina, we ended up ahead of the curve on the development of multiple forms of engaged scholarship and experiential learning, renewing our dedication to educating the next generation of leaders and engaged citizens of the world.

I also think of those moments when it wasn't possible to reach an ideal outcome: the difficulties we had achieving diversity, solving the puzzle of athletics, and realizing the full potential of our academic medical center. I can't leave this review of what it takes to lead without mentioning all that a leader can't control: time, chance, uncertainty—the slings and arrows of outrageous fortune. Katrina was a sling-and-arrow that, ironically, turned out to be propitious, but sometimes there is no salvaging an opportunity from unfortunate events. When the world presents you with intractable facts and insoluble conundrums, realism, pragmatism, and good judgment are, in my view, the most effective—indeed, the only possible—response.

To succeed as a leader, you need, most of all, an unrelenting will to improve what you inherited. And to do that, you basically need it all: acquired skills and inborn traits, realism and idealism, experience and innocence, creativity and caution. It is very hard to write about leadership without falling into paradoxes and clichés. For my last stab at a definition, I'm going to end with an emphasis on mission: a leader is one who clarifies and executes an institution's vision and goals through changing circumstances and in differing contexts, by inspiring and motivating others to achieve things they may have not thought possible—not only the particular mission of a particular institution, but the overarching mission that characterizes higher education generally. Though diverse in their identities, all universities and colleges exist to develop the potential of the young, to improve society, to sustain our cultural past and present, and to create a meaningful future. All universities and colleges depend on individuals coming together to achieve these ends. To put it another way, a university is founded on "human capital," the official term we use to say something powerful and true: a university is its people and the relationships among them, joined in common purpose, in pursuit of shared meaning, elevated by a culture that promotes our deepest values—untrammeled inquiry, open dialogue, and the productive collision of differing viewpoints: "out of many, one." Our colleges and universities are living monuments to freedom and progress and the bearers of our collective hopes. As the future unfolds, the leaders we seek will have the integrity to guard this vision, the creative force to nourish it, and the human touch to sustain it.

Notes

1. On Impact

1. Ronald Brownstein, "Are College Degrees Inherited?" *Atlantic*, April 11, 2014, http://www.theatlantic.com/education/archive/2014/04/are-college-degrees-inherited/360532/.
2. *The Teen Brain: Still under Construction*, National Institute of Mental Health, https://learnzillion.com/resources/83632.
3. *Building a Stronger New Orleans: The Economic Impact of Tulane University*, June 2015, http://www2.tulane.edu/economic-impact/upload/Tulane-Report-June-15-15.pdf.
4. In April 2016, Tulane City Center was renamed for donors as the Albert Jr. and Tina Small City Center; however, I will continue to refer to it as Tulane City Center, or TCC, throughout this book, as that was the name it had during my tenure at the university.

   "Tulane Design Center Renamed for Donor, and Other Education News," *Advocate*, April 16, 2016, http://www.theadvocate.com/new_orleans/news/education/article_37f89a6e-0027-5ab8-a5a1-5d9e15cf0643.html.
5. In a survey of Tulane alumni, nearly half of those responding rated *US-NWR* rankings as "impressive news" about the university. The university, like many others, noted that alumni contributions affected rank, and the development office's requests for donations include specific mention of improving the *USNWR* ranking.
6. Sometimes Busby's office used LinkedIn data on nonrespondents, though LinkedIn is uninformative about salaries. Her general sense was that some

graduates from Tulane took high-impact jobs in the nonprofit sector—for example, in Teach For America—and later leapfrogged to higher-paying employment, but she didn't have the data to confirm this. The Statewide Longitudinal Data System collects longitudinal information on students in the United States starting in preschool through entry into the workforce, though FERPA, the Family Educational Rights and Privacy Act, places legal constraints on access to and use of these data.

7. Academic investigations of impact suffer from some of the same problems as Busby's Office of Assessment: it's very difficult to track graduates over time. A rare longitudinal study has attempted to draw a causal connection between undergraduate service learning and long-term impact in terms of service activities, jobs, attitudes, and beliefs. In 2001, an East Coast Catholic liberal arts college conducted a phone survey of 481 alumni who had graduated between 1992 and 1999, 48 of whom were identified as having taken a service-learning course as undergraduates. In that small subset, clear positive effects emerge, extending at least one to six years after graduation: positive attitudes toward social responsibility, personal political participation, and continued service involvement through volunteer work or employment. L. Mickey Fenzel and Mark Peyrot, "Comparing College Community Participation and Future Service Behaviors and Attitudes," *Michigan Journal of Service Learning* 12 (Fall 2005), http://quod.lib.umich .edu/m/mjcsl/3239521.0012.102?rgn=main;view=fulltext.

8. I am indebted to Tom Burish, provost of Notre Dame, for his succinct framing of the problem with *USNWR*'s metrics, which fail to answer fundamental questions about educational quality. Additional evidence of the pervasive absurdity of the rankings enterprise: One criterion of quality used by *USNWR* is "percentage of alumni who give." The only way to improve that statistic is, obviously, to increase the number of alumni donations, which many schools do by begging for as little as five dollars in their phonathons, explicitly mentioning the bump in rank that giving might produce. In a somewhat bolder move, one West Coast college took the creative alternative of decreasing the number of living alumni: they reclassified alumni who hadn't given money in five years as dead.

Nicholas Thompson, "Playing with Numbers: How *US News* Mismeasures Higher Education and What We Can Do about It," *Washington Monthly*, September 2000, https://www.unz.org/Pub/WashingtonMonthly -2000sep-00016.

9. Malcolm Gladwell, "The Order of Things: What College Rankings Really Tell Us," *New Yorker*, Dept. of Education, February 14, 2011, http://www .newyorker.com/magazine/2011/02/14/the-order-of-things. In his otherwise perceptive critique of the rankings, Gladwell mentions Tulane's lack of "efficacy"—an actual graduation rate of 73 percent in 2009 when its

expected rate was 87 percent, given the qualifications of its students. "That shortfall," he says, "suggests that something is amiss at Tulane." What was in fact amiss was the long-term consequences of Katrina.

10. Doug Lederman, "'Manipulating,' Er, Influencing 'U.S. News,'" *Inside Higher Ed*, June 3, 2009, https://www.insidehighered.com/news/2009/06/03/rankings.

11. The Admission page on the Reed College website explains the school's position on rankings: https://www.reed.edu/apply/college-rankings.html.

   An article in the *Atlantic* by a former president of Reed examines the issue of rankings for universities and colleges across the United States. Colin Driver, "Is There Life after Rankings?" *Atlantic*, November 2005, http://www.theatlantic.com/magazine/archive/2005/11/is-there-life-after-rankings/304308/.

12. Brand-new rankings come out every year, many of them focused on graduates' salaries (possibly in response to the recession of 2008 and a growing interest in bang for the buck among students and their families). *Money* magazine's 2015 rankings are better than most, offering a nuanced assessment of return on investment (ROI) at seven hundred four-year colleges and universities and explaining in detail the choice and weighting of metrics. *Money*'s index incorporates statistics specifically relating to students from low-income families, rating schools higher when this subset performs better than expected on such things as student loan default rates and graduation rate.

   "How MONEY Ranked Colleges: An In-Depth Look at Our Methodology," July 13, 2015, http://time.com/money/3952002/best-colleges-money-methodology/.

13. Another finding of the Gallup-Purdue Index was that completion of college in four years correlated strongly with superior quality of life for graduates, and consequently should be an objective, or at least an aspiration, of university presidents everywhere.

14. These schools constitute the Committee on Institutional Cooperation (CIC).

15. Bruce A. Weinberg, Jason Owen-Smith, Rebecca F. Rosen, Lou Schwartz, Barbara McFadden Allen, Roy E. Weiss, and Julia Lane, "Science Funding and Short-Term Economic Activity," *Science* 344, no. 6179 (April 4, 2011): 41–43, https://www.ncbi.nlm.nih.gov/pmc/articles/PMC4112082/.

16. XU Quick Facts 2015, http://www.xula.edu/mediarelations/quickfacts.html.

17. "Key Events in Black Higher Education," *Journal of Blacks in Higher Education*, https://www.jbhe.com/chronology/.

18. Nikkole Hannah-Jones, "A Prescription for More Black Doctors," *New York Times*, September 13, 2015, https://www.nytimes.com/2015/09/13/magazine/a-prescription-for-more-black-doctors.html.

19. David Starr Jordan, "Ours Is the Humbler Task," *Stanford Daily* 118, no. 58 (January 16, 1951), http://stanforddailyarchive.com/cgi-bin/stanford ?a=d&d=stanford19510116-01.2.31.

20. Andrea M. Hamilton, "Scholar Examines Links between Stanford, Silicon Valley," *Stanford Report*, April 6, 2003, http://news.stanford.edu /news/2003/april16/historysusv-416.html.

21. Farhad Manjoo, "Udacity Says It Can Teach Tech Skills to Millions, and Fast," *New York Times*, September 16, 2015, http://www.nytimes.com/2015/09/17 /technology/udacity-says-it-can-teach-tech-skills-to-millions.html?_r=0.

22. Beth McMurtrie, "Inside Startup U: How Stanford Develops Entrepreneurial Students," *Chronicle of Higher Education*, October 25, 2015, http://www .chronicle.com/article/Inside-Startup-U-How/233899. Recent recruitment of students with an interest in the humanities has raised its pool of applicants in that area from "well below" average to the university average.

23. David Leonhardt, "California's Upward Mobility Machine," *New York Times*, September 17, 2015, http://www.nytimes.com/2015/09/17/upshot /californias-university-system-an-upward-mobility-machine.html?emc=etal.

24. "Well known for its academic excellence, Amherst has long been committed to enrolling the most talented students from Massachusetts and beyond. In 1999, the college became the first in the nation to eliminate loans for low-income students, and in July 2007, Amherst announced that it would replace all loans with scholarships in financial aid packages beginning in the 2008–09 academic year. The college also extended need-blind admission to international students, making it easier for residents of other nations to live and work in the Pioneer Valley. These initiatives have helped Amherst continue to attract promising students from a wide range of backgrounds, adding to the robust and dynamic intellectual community that is Western Massachusetts."

    "Amherst College: Small College, Large Impact," https://www.amherst .edu/system/files/media/Amherst_small_college_large_impact.pdf.

    For more on Joe Paul Case, see Amherst College website, "Q & A on Paying for College," interview by Peter Rooney, May 22, 2012, https://www .amherst.edu/news/news_releases/2012/05.2012/node/397989.

2. Door Wide Open

1. The rate at which African American students were completing applications was more than 20 percentage points below the rate of other minorities (all nonblack minority applicants other than Asians) and even further below the completion rate of white students.

2. Laura Pappano, "Colleges Discover the Rural Student," *New York Times*, January 31, 2017, https://www.nytimes.com/2017/01/31/education/edlife /colleges-discover-rural-student.html.

3. Also gender. Women's liberation was an effective movement on many fronts, including the acceptance of women into previously all-male schools like Yale, Harvard, Brown, and others. But gender issues remain on campuses, where women face discrimination in STEM and other fields, and where sexual harassment and assault remain serious problems.

4. In *Regents of the University of California v. Bakke* (1978), the Supreme Court struck down the use of racial quotas as an infringement on the equal rights of nonminority students but maintained the constitutionality of using race as one factor, among others, in admissions decisions. Two later cases in Michigan, *Gratz v. Bollinger* and *Grutter v. Bollinger* (2003), essentially confirmed the judgment in *Bakke*.

5. In matching theory, this would be described as an "overmatch" (low-achieving student, top-tier college), and the reverse (high-achieving student and second-tier school) as an "undermatch." During oral arguments before the Supreme Court, Justice Antonin Scalia said that minority students with deficient academic credentials may be better off at "a less advanced school, a slower-track school where they do well . . . Most of the black scientists in this country don't come from schools like the University of Texas," he said. "They come from lesser schools where they do not feel that they're being pushed ahead in classes that are too fast for them." Adam Liptak, "Supreme Court Justices' Comments Don't Bode Well for Affirmative Action," *New York Times*, December 9, 2015, http://www.nytimes.com/2015/12/10/us/politics/supreme-court-to-revisit -case-that-may-alter-affirmative-action.html.

Richard Sander is the chief author of a paper attacking affirmative action for purported "overmatching" effects, focusing on black students at elite law schools. http://www2.law.ucla.edu/sander/Systemic/final/SanderFINAL.pdf.

He has also coauthored a book on the subject: Richard Sander and Stuart Taylor, Jr., *Mismatch: How Affirmative Action Hurts Students It's Intended to Help, and Why Universities Won't Admit It* (New York: Basic Books, 2012).

6. The amicus brief filed with the Supreme Court decisively countered the "mismatch" theory along many dimensions. http://gking.harvard.edu/files /gking/files/fisher_amicus_final_8-13-12_0.pdf.

7. William G. Bowen, Matthew M. Chingos, and Michael S. McPherson, *Crossing the Finish Line: Completing College at America's Public Universities* (Princeton, NJ: Princeton University Press, 2011).

8. Carole Carmichael, "The Transformative Power of Higher Education—for All," *Seattle Times*, January 2, 2016, http://www.seattletimes.com/opinion/the-transformative-power-of-higher-education-for-all/?utm_source=email&utm_medium=email&utm_campaign=article_title.

9. Deborah Son Hololen, *Do Differences Make a Difference? The Effects of Diversity on Learning, Intergroup Outcomes, and Civic Engagement*, Princeton University, Trustee Ad Hoc Committee on Diversity, September 2013, https://www.princeton.edu/reports/2013/diversity/report/PU-report-diversity-outcomes.pdf.

10. Kedra Ishop, enrollment manager at the University of Michigan, describes the effort as "a courtship": the university increased the number of minority students in the 2015 freshman class by almost 20 percent, the highest percentage since 2005, mainly by outreach efforts: personal calls to encourage students to attend, increased tuition scholarships, reducing the size of the freshman class, and admitting no one off the waiting list (which favors higher-income, often white and Asian, students).

    Anemona Hartocollis, "As Justices Weigh Affirmative Action, Michigan Offers an Alternative," *New York Times*, January 4, 2016, https://www.nytimes.com/2016/01/05/us/affirmative-action-supreme-court-michigan.html?_r=0.

    In the University of California system, African American enrollment has dropped by 50 percent at Berkeley and UCLA, the flagship schools, although it has increased at second-tier institutions within the system. Daniel Fisher, citing the contested "mismatch" theory, suggests that this distribution may be a good consequence of California's affirmative action ban, resulting in "overall" integration and placement of black students in schools matched to their skills.

    Daniel Fisher, "Poor Students are the Real Victims of College Discrimination," *Forbes*, May 2, 2012, http://www.forbes.com/sites/danielfisher/2012/05/02/poor-students-are-the-real-victims-of-college-discrimination/#28a767992007.

11. According to Daniel Fisher, poor students very often don't apply, and when they do, they're widely overlooked by admissions offices in favor of "more interesting" applicants whose résumés include expensive international programs and fancy extracurriculars. Fisher also refers to research from Sander, the mismatch theorist, suggesting that black students in the top quintile of socioeconomic status have a 48 percent chance of applying to an elite school, as opposed to a 4 percent chance if they're in the bottom fifth of household income; that is, the African American students who get in to selective schools are more likely than not to be middle-class.

    Fisher, "Poor Students Are the Real Victims of College Discrimination."

12. https://www.questbridge.org/high-school-students/national-college -match/who-should-apply. According to their home page from 2014: "Annually, approximately 30,000 low-income students score over 1300 on the combined math and verbal SAT scores, and another 42,000 score over 1220. Moreover, over a third of top low-income performers don't take the SAT."

https://people.emich.edu/redwar14/Questbridge/Old/homepage.html.

13. Israel's race-neutral class-based affirmative action policy, featuring "structural determinants of disadvantage" like poor neighborhoods and schools, increased geographic diversity and the number of new immigrants and lower-income students at four of its most selective universities, but led to fewer admissions of Jews of Asian or African origin and Arabs, all groups on the lowest rungs of Israeli society. A comparative study using US data from the Beginning Postsecondary Students Longitudinal Study, which charts information for six years starting freshman year, showed that the share of minority students at 115 elite American colleges would decline by almost a third under socioeconomic affirmative action.

Sigal Alon, "What Israel Tells Us about Affirmative Action and Race," *New York Times*, December 16, 2015, http://www.nytimes.com/2015/12/16 /opinion/what-israel-tells-us-about-affirmative-action-and-race.html?_r=0.

14. Kerry Hannon, "At Vassar, a Focus on Diversity and Affordability in Higher Education," *New York Times*, June 22, 2016, https://www.nytimes.com /2016/06/23/education/at-vassar-a-focus-on-diversity-and-affordability -in-higher-education.html?_r=0.

"Vassar College, #100 in 2017 Best Colleges in America," https://colleges .niche.com/vassar-college/diversity/.

15. "How Should Colleges Ensure Diversity?" *PBS Newshour*, April 23, 2014. Gwen Ifill talking to Roger Clegg, Center for Equal Opportunity, and Dennis Parker, ACLU Racial Justice Program, http://www.pbs.org/newshour /bb/colleges-ensure-diversity/.

16. John Eligon, "After Racist Episodes, Blunt Discussion on Campus," *New York Times*, February 3, 2016, http://www.nytimes.com/2016/02/07/education /edlife/university-of-missouri-struggles-to-bridge-its-racial-divide .html?emc=eta1.

17. In the aftermath of the "demands," the exchange of letters between President Martin and the Amherst Uprising is notable for its civility. "President Martin's Statement on Campus Protests," November 15, 2015, https://www.amherst.edu/amherst-story/president/statements /node/620480. Elaine Jeon and Jingwen Zhang, "Amherst Uprising Clarifies Long-Term Goals," December 2, 2015, http://amherststudent.amherst .edu/?q=article/2015/12/02/amherst-uprising-clarifies-long-term-goals.

18. Jess Bidgood, "Amherst College Drops 'Lord Jeff' as Mascot," *New York Times*, January 27, 2016, https://www.nytimes.com/2016/01/27/us/amherst -college-drops-lord-jeff-as-mascot.html. The mascot controversy carried over into blog posts from the wider community. Some Amherst alumni wrote that it would be better for students to learn from history rather than erase it and suggested that Lord Amherst should be judged in the context of his times.

At Oberlin, a small liberal arts school founded in 1833 with the mission of including women and African Americans, a similar protest issued in fifteen pages of "demands, not suggestions," including, among other things, specific faculty firings, new non-Western-centric courses, safe places, renamed buildings, and a grading system designed by students. The president of Oberlin, Marvin Krislov, said no to the black students' demands—"I will not respond directly to any document that explicitly rejects the notion of collaborative engagement"—and defended accused faculty and staff as dedicated and valued members of the community. At the same time, he acknowledged the pain expressed and vowed commitment to dismantling "systemic barriers" persisting at the college. Krislov's balance between expectation and empathy was on the whole very similar to President Martin's temperate handling of the crisis at Amherst. One alumnus, Thomas Shephard, representing the view of many Oberlin graduates who wrote comments, applauded Krislov for his patience in trying to separate "legitimate demands from juvenile outbursts." It's an irony that schools like these, with reputations as liberal bastions of open-minded discourse, have become battlegrounds of extremist rhetoric and angry confrontation.

Martin Krislov, "Response to Student Demands," January 20, 2016, https://oncampus.oberlin.edu/source/articles/2016/01/20/response-student -demands.

19. Bill Maher (who is, of course, famous for being "politically incorrect") said that suggesting Yale lacks cultural sensitivity is like saying Pier 1 doesn't have enough wicker, and asked, "Shouldn't 'microaggressions' evoke 'microanger'?"

Real Time with Bill Maher, HBO, January 22, 2016.

Jonathan Holloway quoted by Jelani Cobb, "What Divides Us?: An Interview with Yale College Dean Jonathan Holloway," *New Yorker*, November 15, 2015, http://www.newyorker.com/news/news-desk/what-divides-us -an-interview-with-yale-college-dean-jonathan-holloway.

20. Frank Bruni, "The Lie about College Diversity," *New York Times*, December 12, 2015, http://www.nytimes.com/2015/12/13/opinion/sunday /the-lie-about-college-diversity.html?_r=0.

21. Tremaine points out, "The disconnect between secondary and postsecondary institutions lies at the heart of the problem: Many high-poverty public high

schools lack the resources to prepare students for college reading and writing requirements; many colleges and universities, meanwhile, are unaccustomed to extending meaningful academic opportunities beyond their campuses. In this way, low-income high schoolers are very often confronted by both the weakest bridge between high school and college and the widest gulf to cross."

Stephen Tremaine, "The Promise of Early College," *Education Week*, August 9, 2010, http://www.edweek.org/ew/articles/2010/08/11 /37tremaine.h29.html.

22. "Bard Early College in New Orleans," http://www.bard.edu/ecno/about/.

23. The College Track mission statement can be found on its website: https:// collegetrack.org/. Caroline Hoxby has been a leading researcher on the recruitment of low-income students from nonmetropolitan areas.

http://www.npr.org/2015/03/16/393339590/why-many-smart-low -income-students-dont-apply-to-elite-schools.

Francisco Guajardo, "A Rural School District Rattles the Ivy Cage," *Daily Yonder: Keep It Rural*, February 12, 2013, http://www.dailyyonder .com/what-gets-rural-students-ivy-league/2013/02/12/5647/.

24. FinAid: The SmartStudent Guide to Financial Aid, "College Partnerships and Articulation Agreements," http://www.finaid.org/otheraid/partnerships .phtml.

Details vary state to state: some, like Connecticut and Mississippi, have statewide articulation agreements, while other states have a number of such agreements between particular community colleges and state campuses. For example, Ferris State University in Michigan has an articulation agreement with more than two dozen community colleges, in line with its mission of providing wider access to a bachelor's degree. Many such agreements, like the one between Framingham State University and Mass Bay Community College in Massachusetts, allow students to earn their bachelor's degrees at the satellite community college campus rather than traveling to, or residing at, the state campus.

25. Some schools are offering service-learning courses in the first two years— courses proven to enhance achievement and knowledge acquisition—in order to inspire students to continue their educations and pursue their career goals. At California State University Channel Islands in Camarillo, California, in conjunction with Ventura County Community College and Moorpark College (also a community college), chemistry majors used a pesticide "sniffer" to identify toxic chemicals at various sites, mapped the structure of the molecules they found, and submitted their findings to the National Center for Pesticide Information. English composition students studied the Palos Verdes blue butterfly, housed at the Moorpark College campus zoo, and wrote copy for a brochure used by the zoo to

advertise the endangered status of the butterfly. According to various studies, service learning enhances student achievement and knowledge acquisition. In addition, students in the pilot programs have reported increased interest in furthering their education and career goals.

Michelle R. Davis, "Collaborations between Universities and Community Colleges Offer New Educational Opportunities for Students," *Public Purpose*, June / July / August 2009, http://www.aascu.org/uploadedFiles /AASCU/Content/Root/MediaAndPublications/PublicPurposeMagazines /Issue/09_060708commcolleges.pdf.

26. Here is how Karishma Singh, a Posse Scholar from Bright Star Secondary Charter Academy in Los Angeles, describes the Dynamic Assessment Process: "I walked into a room filled with a hundred seniors competing for the same scholarship as me. They were so enthusiastic! Only fifty students were to be selected from the bunch and I knew I had to stand out. We addressed controversial topics such as our opinions on the death penalty and gay rights. We were challenged to speak to students we'd never met before to see how well we interact with strangers, and to see if we could hold an intellectual conversation with our peers. We built a straw house with one hand behind our backs to see if we work well as a team. We were given a topic and we had to create a skit in five minutes to see if we were able to listen to other people's opinions." As a semifinalist for admission to Kalamazoo, one of Posse's partner schools, Karishma participated in a "human bingo game" and was chosen to sing an impromptu song, also engaging in conversations much like those in the first round of interviews. The on-the-spot questions and interactive activities reveal hidden potential not always captured in a standard résumé.

"Posse Scholar Shares Her Story. BSSCA Senior Karishma Shares Her Story of Receiving the Posse Scholarship," June 26, 2015, http://www.bright starschools.org/District/news/1487-Posse-Scholar-Shares-Her-Story.html.

27. To widen the net of opportunity even further, the foundation has established Posse Access, a database available to admissions offices at Posse partner schools that lists the names of Posse candidates who didn't win scholarships but are nonetheless outstanding leaders and motivated learners. Posse Access allows partner schools to see the spillover list of candidates who didn't make the final cut, but Posse doesn't offer it to everybody (because why would any school partner with them if they gave their vetted and culled list away for free?).

28. To name a few individuals, Posse Scholar Opeyemi "Ope" Awe, a senior at Grinnell, is president of the Student Government Association; Cheska Mauban was the commencement speaker at Babson College; Charlie Draughter at Tulane won a social justice internship in Costa Rica with plans to attend

Georgetown Law School after graduating; and Bucknell University Scholar Ahmed Elnaiem, who is Phi Beta Kappa, has been engaged in research at the NIH studying cancer survivorship among elderly patients and worked in a Doctors Without Borders clinic near Sudan, his home country, with plans to attend medical school. These examples date from 2015, during the writing of this book, but new Posse Scholars are continuing to achieve in similar fashion. https://www.possefoundation.org/our-scholars.

29. Scott Jaschik, "'Dimensional' Admissions, *Inside Higher Ed*, September 25, 2014, https://www.insidehighered.com/news/2014/09/25/bennington -introduces-new-option-applicants.

30. Sarah Garland, "Vermont College Giving Some High Schools Power to Fill Seats," *Hechinger Report*, September 11, 2011, http://hechingerreport .org/small-vermont-college-giving-some-high-schools-power-to-fill-seats/.

"Pipelines into Partnership," US Department of Education, http://www2 .ed.gov/documents/college-completion/pipelines-into-partnership.doc.

31. Critics suggest a more cynical motive: more applicants and fewer accep-tances translate into greater selectivity on the *U.S. News & World Report* rankings, and the average SAT scores of such schools, another metric used by *USNWR*, tends to rise, because of the high scores of those who do submit them. (*USNWR* ranks test-optional schools if a certain percentage of their applicants submit SAT scores.)

32. Sarah Lawrence is also, it should be noted, the most expensive liberal arts school in the nation. According to its president, Karen Lawrence (who will step down in 2017), the high price tag is because of its hands-on, faculty-rich, "artisanal" intellectual and creative environment. But the steep price of admission undoubtedly also tipped the scale in favor of a return to rankings that purport to identify the quality of colleges, putting it in the luxury class of selective, expensive, and worth it.

Karen R. Lawrence, Commencement Address, Sarah Lawrence Col-lege, 2009, https://www.sarahlawrence.edu/news-events/commencement /archives/2009/karen-lawrence.html.

33. Scott Jaschik, "'Test-Blind' Admissions," *Higher Education*, June 19, 2014, https://www.insidehighered.com/news/2014/06/19/hampshire-becomes -only-competitive-college-country-wont-look-sat-act-scores.

34. "Turning the Tide: Inspiring Concern for Others and the Common Good through College Admissions," Harvard Graduate School of Edu-cation, https://mcc.gse.harvard.edu/files/gse-mcc/files/20160120_mcc_ttt _report_interactive.pdf?m=1453303517.

35. Donald J. Farish, "Stop Blaming Colleges for Higher Education's Unaf-fordability," *Chronicle of Higher Education*, March 23, 2016, http://chronicle .com/article/Stop-Blaming-Colleges-for/235799.

36. Ry Rivard, "Killing Off a Success," *Inside Higher Ed*, January 27, 2014, https://www.insidehighered.com/news/2014/01/27/uva-backs-away-loan-free-offer-its-poorest-students.

37. NPR staff, "When Money Trumps Need in College Admissions," National Public Radio, *Morning Edition*, April 24, 2014, http://www.npr.org/2014/04/24/306167197/when-money-trumps-need-in-college-admissions.

38. Hope Baptiste and Claire Cusack, "Carolina Covenant Celebrates a Decade of Student Access and Success," Office of Advancement, University of North Carolina at Chapel Hill, http://www.unc.edu/campus-updates/carolina-covenant-celebrates-a-decade-of-student-access-and-success/.

39. Edward B. Fiske, "How Carolina Scrapped Loans for Top Students in Need—and Became a Policy Leader," *Hechinger Report*, April 12, 2016, http://hechingerreport.org/carolina-scrapped-loans-top-students-need-became-policy-leader/.

   One in seven of the class of 2019 is a Covenant Scholar; the graduation rate for Covenant Scholars was 80.2 percent in 2011. Shirley Ort, director of scholarships and student aid and the first and only director of the Covenant program, has helped ensure its success by providing informal supports, including faculty and peer mentors, a dedicated counseling staff, "etiquette dinners," and funds for study abroad and summer internships.

40. As mentioned, Vassar's efforts to recruit low-income students and increase racial diversity have been largely successful.

41. Jon Marcus, "How One College Bucked a Trend to Take More Poor and Nonwhite Applicants," *Hechinger Report*, December 18, 2015, http://hechingerreport.org/how-one-top-college-bucked-a-trend-to-take-more-poor-and-nonwhite-applicants/.

42. Melba Newsome, "The Debt-Free College Degree," *Bloomberg Businessweek*, September 6, 2012, https://www.bloomberg.com/news/articles/2012-09-06/the-debt-free-college-degree.

   Another example is Amherst. Like Davidson, it is devoted to the mission of diversity, willing to dip into its endowment to make good on its commitment, and finding donors who are inspired by their goal.

43. Robert Gray, "Diana Natalicio, President, University of Texas at El Paso," *El Paso, Inc.*, February 10, 2013, http://www.elpasoinc.com/news/q_and_a/article_8bca594e-73a5-11e2-929b-001a4bcf6878.html.

3. Keeping the Ship Afloat

1. Kellie Woodhouse, "Widening Wealth Gap," *Inside Higher Ed*, May 21, 2015, https://www.insidehighered.com/news/2015/05/21/rich-universities-get-richer-are-poor-students-being-left-behind.

2. Institutions of higher education in the United States also exhibit significant regional distinctiveness: most private colleges trace their origins to a specific group of founders—a church or a particular demographic (women, African Americans, musicians, and so on)—and public institutions derive their identity from state charters. These widely various local histories tend to create a "snowflake phenomenon" of unique entities and tribal attachments. One size definitely doesn't fit all. Carol T. Christ, "The Sweet Briar Opportunity," *American Scholar*, September 7, 2015, https://theamericanscholar.org/the-sweet-briar-opportunity/.

3. Jeff Deen and Tom Detler, *The Financially Sustainable University*, Bain & Company and Sterling Partners, 2012, http://www.bain.com/Images/BAIN_BRIEF_The_financially_sustainable_university.pdf.

    The failure of the high-tuition, high-aid model is described in Josh Freedman, "How Not to Help the Poor: The Lesson of Soaring College Prices," *Atlantic*, July 10, 2013, http://www.theatlantic.com/business/archive/2013/07/how-not-to-help-the-poor-the-lesson-of-soaring-college-prices/277658/.

4. Ry Rivard, "Great Expectations, Bleaker Results," *Inside Higher Ed*, August 20, 2014, https://www.insidehighered.com/news/2014/08/20/consultants-best-case-scenarios-rarely-reality.

5. *Efficiency and Effectiveness Initiatives: What Business Leaders Should Know about Higher Education's Million-Dollar Consulting Engagements*, Education Advisory Board (EAB), Business Affairs Forum, http://www.scstatehouse.gov/citizensinterestpage/HigherEdEE&AReviewCommittee/October302014Meeting/Efficiency-And-Effectiveness-Initiatives.pdf.

    Some savings do result: to take a single example, Cornell University's Administrative Streamlining Program saved $85 million by setting up an online procurement system and renegotiating deals on bulk paper and toner.

    Kevin Kiley, "Where Universities Can Be Cut," *Inside Higher Ed*, September 16, 2011, https://www.insidehighered.com/news/2011/09/16/unc_berkeley_cornell_experience_show_where_administrative_cuts_can_be_made.

    The Education Advisory Board's overview of reports issued by consulting firms like Bain & Company showed that only redesign of the procurement process generates any appreciable savings for a college or university—which means that reducing administrative bloat is less of a panacea than people think. (See also Rivard, "Great Expectations, Bleaker Results.")

6. Kiley, "Where Universities Can Be Cut."

7. Deen and Detler, *The Financially Sustainable University*.

8. Davis Jenkins and Olga Rodriguez, "Access and Success with Less: Improving Productivity in Broad-Access Post-secondary Institutions," *Future of Children* 23, no. 1 (Spring 2013): 196, https://www.princeton.edu/futureofchildren/publications/docs/23_01_09.pdf.

9. Teresa Watanabe, "As UC Berkeley Tries to Close Its Deficit, Administrators Feel the Ire of Traditional Faculty Allies," *LA Times,* May 11, 2016, http://www.latimes.com/local/education/la-me-berkeley-deficit-20160421 -story.html.

10. Christopher Mele, "Nicholas Dirks Resigns as Chancellor of University of California, Berkeley," *New York Times,* August 16, 2016, https://www .nytimes.com/2016/08/17/us/nicholas-dirks-resigns-as-chancellor-of -university-of-california-berkeley.html?_r=0.

11. Which is not to say there wasn't significant pushback from those who felt the brunt of the cuts; as the UC-Berkeley case suggests, outcry is inevitable when you do things that affect a school's core activities and human capital.

12. Susan Svrluga, "Alumnae Vowed to Save Sweet Briar from Closing Last Year. And They Did," *Washington Post,* March 3, 2016, https://www.wash ingtonpost.com/news/grade-point/wp/2016/03/03/alumnae-vowed-to-save -sweet-briar-from-closing-last-year-and-they-did/?utm_term=.2a261c3c1be1.

13. "Closing Liberal Arts Colleges: Are They Worth Saving?" CBN News, *The Christian Perspective,* April 23, 2015, http://www1.cbn.com/cbnnews /us/2015/April/Closing-Liberal-Arts-Colleges-Are-They-Worth-Saving.

14. President McGuire, "If Higher Education Can't Do Social Change Well, Who Will?" Trinity Washington University website, March 15, 2016, http://www .trinitydc.edu/media/2016/03/15/pres-mcguire-remarks-tiaa-hesburgh-award/.

    It's worthy of note that McGuire has been president for twenty-plus years; length of a presidency may be one factor leading to major innovation and contributions. It generally takes significant time to build relationships, rally a community, and push through a period of uncertain transition to a successful outcome.

15. Samara Freemark, "The Reinvention of Paul Quinn College," *American RadioWorks,* August 20, 2015, http://www.americanradioworks.org /segments/reinvention-paul-quinn-college/.

16. Karen Woodhouse, "Moody's Predicts College Closures to Triple by 2017," *Inside Higher Ed,* September 28, 2015, www.insidehighered.com /news/2015/09/28/moodys-predicts-college-closures-triple-2017.

    Mark Suster, "In 15 Years from Now Half of US Universities May Be in Bankruptcy. My Surprise Discussion with @ClayChristensen," *Business Insider,* March 3, 2013, http://www.businessinsider.com/in-15-years-from -now-half-of-us-universities-may-be-in-bankruptcy-my-surprise-discussion -with-claychristensen-2013-3.

17. James C. Hearn, Jarrett B. Warshaw, and Erin B. Ciarimboli, *Strategic Change and Innovation in Independent Colleges: Nine Mission-Driven Campuses,* A report for the Council of Independent Colleges, https://www.cic .edu/r/r/Documents/CIC-Hearn-Report-2016.pdf.

18. A related effort to go beyond religious affiliation to a more inclusive mission has occurred at Valparaiso University near Chicago, a Lutheran school, which has recruited a large number of international students and created continuing education health science programs for employees of the University of Chicago Health System.

   Hearn et al., *Strategic Change.*

19. Bethany College in Lindsborg, Kansas, has emphasized its original mission, stressing the institution's Swedish heritage, Lutheran roots, and Great Plains regional identity, and enrollment has grown by more than a third in eight years' time.

   Hearn et al., *Strategic Change.*

20. Valparaiso University has created an "obsessively transparent" strategic planning process that includes the entire campus; President Mark Heckler says, "I've got students here who want to talk to me about the strategic plan," and the provost, Mark Biermann, points to a clear process in place for faculty to take "an idea they have while driving home from work to a program with students enrolled in the fall of 2017."

   Hearn et al., *Strategic Change.*

21. Julie Bosman, "Chicago State, a Lifeline for Poor Blacks, Is Under Threat Itself," *New York Times*, April 9, 2016, http://www.nytimes.com/2016/04/10/us /chicago-state-a-lifeline-for-poor-blacks-is-under-threat-itself.html?_r=0.

22. Christopher Newfield, professor of literature and American studies at UC Santa Barbara, author of *Unmaking the Public University: The Forty-Year Assault on the Middle Class*, says, "All the states are now trying to educate the students of other states so they can charge them three times more." Quoted in Michelle Goldberg, "This Is What Happens When You Slash Funding for Public Universities," *Nation*, May 19, 2015, http://www .thenation.com/article/gentrification-higher-ed/.

23. Michael W. Crow and William B. Dabars, *Designing the New American University* (Baltimore: Johns Hopkins University Press, 2015), p. 19.

24. ASU gives away 14 percent of its tuition income in financial aid. The university, not immune to the marketplace competition affecting everyone, has also doubled its enrollment of out-of-staters, who pay more than double the in-state tuition.

   Goldberg, "This Is What Happens When You Slash Funding."

25. "Reshaping Arizona State, and the Public Model," *New York Times*, April 10, 2105, https://www.nytimes.com/2015/04/12/education/edlife /12edl-12talk.html?_r=0.

26. Earlier in his career, as director of the Office of Management and the Budget under George W. Bush, Daniels was known as the "Blade" for his slashing budget cuts.

Jason Gray, "Mitch Daniels 2016: 8 Facts about Political Background of Potential GOP Presidential Hopeful," *Newsmax*, May 26, 2015, http://www.newsmax.com/FastFeatures/Mitch-Daniels-2016 -GOP-hopeful-background/2015/05/26/id/646833/.

27. Kevin Kiley, "Purdue's Outsider," *Inside Higher Ed*, April 2, 2013, https://www.insidehighered.com/news/2013/04/02/purdues-mitch -daniels-challenging-higher-education-leadership.

28. There has been an inevitable downside of freezing tuition: in-state students are, ironically, getting squeezed out by the need to offset the cost of the freeze, because their rate is so much lower than that of out-of-state students. In the last few years, in-state enrollment has declined, with an increase in seats given to nonresident and international students, who pay 29K and 31K, respectively, vs. in-state tuition of 10K. The upside is, everyone is aboard with cost-saving tactics, from selling off unused campus vehicles to consolidating purchasing to cutting administrative costs. And the consensus on campus is likely to be invaluable as Daniels continues to forge an affordable model, with an eye to strengthening the Indiana economy with a Purdue-educated workforce.

Joseph Paul, "Purdue University Tuition Freezes Squeeze Out In-State Students," *IndyStar*, August 3, 2015, http://www.indystar.com/story/news /education/2015/08/01/purdue-university-tuition-freezes-squeeze-out --state-students/31007167/.

29. http://www.northeastern.edu/hrm/benefits/healthy-you/index.html.

30. Tina Rosenberg, "How Colleges Can Again Be Levelers of Society," *New York Times*, May 3, 2016, http://www.nytimes.com/2016/05/03/opinion /how-colleges-can-again-be-levelers-of-society.html.

31. Ibid.

4. The Tail Wags the Dog, Part I: Athletics

1. John Gerdy, "UAB Football Debate: A Local Decision with National Implications," blog post, March 2, 2015, https://www.johngerdy.com /blog-overview/uab-football-debate-local-decision-national-implications ?rq=Expecting%20academic%20institutions%20to%20.

2. Though Harvard president Charles Eliot denounced football, describing its chief evils as brutality and cheating—both, sadly, profitable—the university still went ahead and built Harvard Stadium in 1903 with alumni contributions, paying the team's first head coach double the average salary of a full professor.

Christopher Klein, "How Teddy Roosevelt Saved Football," *History in the Headlines*, September 6, 2012, http://www.history.com/news/how -teddy-roosevelt-saved-football.

Katie Zezima, "How Teddy Roosevelt Helped Save Football," *Washington Post*, May 29, 2014, http://www.washingtonpost.com/blogs/the-fix/wp/2014/05/29/teddy-roosevelt-helped-save-football-with-a-white-house-meeting-in-1905/.

3. Taylor Branch, "The Shame of College Sports," *Atlantic*, October 2011, http://www.theatlantic.com/magazine/archive/2011/10/the-shame-of-college-sports/308643/?single_page=true.

A portion of the TV revenue went to a thousand or so NCAA member schools without big sports programs, which had the benefit of spreading the wealth even though the NCAA held the purse strings.

4. In 1991, to counter the perception of professionalism and commercialization, university presidents took over NCAA's governance from the athletic directors who had formerly run it. Some critics suggest that university presidents are highly unlikely to be reformers of athletic excess. Ronald A. Smith, in his book *Pay for Play*, calls them "cheerleaders" for their sports programs, pointing out that the compulsion to stay competitive, though it may not be their creation, isn't in their power to destroy. A reviewer of the book, Marc Horger of OSU, says of this impasse, "Unilateral disarmament is impossible, and effective collective action is highly, highly improbable."

Mark Horger, review of Ronald Smith, *Pay for Play: A History of Big-Time College Athletic Reform* (Urbana: University of Illinois Press, 2011), May 2011, http://origins.osu.edu/review/wagging-dog.

5. Branch, "The Shame of College Sports."

6. After my sophomore year, I fell ill and had to leave school for a brief while; when I returned, seventy pounds thinner, I didn't have the body mass to be a lineman and retired from the team. However, I retained my athletic scholarship, which allowed me to go on and get my degree, the bedrock of my whole later career.

7. Erik Brady, Steve Berkowitz, and Jodi Upton, "College Football Coaches Continue to See Salary Explosion," *USA Today*, November 20, 2012, http://www.usatoday.com/story/sports/ncaaf/2012/11/19/college-football-coaches-contracts-analysis-pay-increase/1715435/.

NCAA Salaries, *USA Today*, 2016, http://sports.usatoday.com/ncaa/salaries.

8. Ben Strauss, "Colleges' Shift on Four-Year Scholarships Show Players' Growing Power," *New York Times,* October 28, 2014, https://www.nytimes.com/2014/10/29/sports/colleges-shift-on-four-year-scholarships-reflects-players-growing-power.html?_r=0.

Mark Dent, "Colleges, Universities Slow to Offer Multiyear Athletic Scholarships," *Pittsburgh Post-Gazette*, May 19, 2013, http://www.post-gazette.com/sports/Pitt/2013/05/19/Colleges-universities-slow-to-offer-multiyear-athletic-scholarships/stories/201305190222.

Jamilah King, "How Scholarships Leave Student-Athletes Powerless in the NCAA Game," *Colorlines*, March 23, 2012, http://www.colorlines.com /articles/how-scholarships-leave-student-athletes-powerless-ncaa-game.

9. Branch, "The Shame of College Sports."

10. Dylan Hernandez, "College Basketball's So-Called One-and-Done Rule Needs Revisiting," *LA Times*, March 24, 2016, http://www.latimes.com /sports/la-sp-college-one-and-done-hernandez-20160324-story.html.

Gary Parrish, "NCAA's New Policy on Transfers Has Bad Unintended Consequences," http://www.cbssports.com/college-basketball/news /the-ncaas-new-policy-on-transfers-has-one-bad-unintended-consequence/.

11. "Tulane Green Wave School History," http://www.sports-reference.com /cfb/schools/tulane/.

12. Katie Thomas, "At Tulane, a Sports Revival," *New York Times*, October 8, 2008, http://www.nytimes.com/2008/10/08/sports/ncaafootball/08tulane .html?pagewanted=print&_r=0.

13. Figure is from 2014.

Jon Solomon, "College Football Attendance: Home Crowd Drops to Lowest in 14 Years," December 15, 2014, http://www.cbssports.com /collegefootball/writer/jon-solomon/24891415/college-football-attendance -home-crowds-drop-to-lowest-in-14-years.

14. It should be noted, though, that only 1 percent of college basketball players are drafted by the NBA, and only 2 percent of college football players are drafted by the NFL; moreover, getting drafted is not a cast-iron guarantee of a professional career. Branch, "The Shame of College Sports."

15. "Sports at the University of Chicago: A Rich History," The University of Chicago News Office, October 1, 1998, http://www-news.uchicago.edu /releases/98/981001.ratner.history.shtml.

16. Testosterone studies confirm the highs and lows fans experience in response to wins and losses. Paul C. Bernhardt, James M. Dabbs Jr., Julie A. Fielden, and Candice D. Lutter, "Testosterone Changes during Vicarious Experiences of Winning and Losing among Fans at Sporting Events," *Physiology & Behavior* 65, no. 1 (August 1998): 59–62, https://www.ncbi .nlm.nih.gov/pubmed/9811365.

17. Andy Thomason, "U. of Alabama at Birmingham Will Resurrect Football Program," *Chronicle of Higher Education*, June 1, 2015, http://chronicle .com/blogs/ticker/u-of-alabama-at-birmingham-will-resurrect-football -program-reports-say/.

Watts specified that institutional support would not exceed current levels, donors who have pledged $17.1 million to cover costs of reinstatement would meet prescribed deadlines, and the university would borrow no money to improve existing athletic facilities.

18. I am indebted to Tom Burish, provost at the University of Notre Dame, for his thoughts on the "Hurricane Katrina" solution to the problem of Division I athletics.

5. The Tail Wags the Dog, Part II: Medicine

1. Solutions to the spiraling cost of health care might include reducing the number of tests doctors order (which would require addressing physician anxiety and legal liability); public health initiatives devoted to prevention and behavioral change; increasing the number of palliative care programs (which might require changing public attitudes toward end of life); and more regulation of the pharmaceutical and insurance industries.
2. "Sir William Osler & His Inspirational Words," The Osler Symposia, http://www.oslersymposia.org/about-Sir-William-Osler.html.
3. Formerly, academic "safety net" hospitals were compensated by Medicaid and Medicare as Disproportionate Share Hospitals (DSH), but these payments have been phased out under the Affordable Care Act. A recent article describing the pressures on academic medicine in the current environment delineates the economic problem in detail: "PPACA establishes the Medicare Shared Saving Program (MSSP) for Accountable Care Organizations (ACOs), an approach that many AMCs [Academic Medical Centers] will undoubtedly attempt to pursue. The stated goal of MSSP is to achieve better care for individuals, better health for populations, and slower growth in costs through improvements in care. An ACO must assume responsibility for the care of a clearly defined population of Medicare beneficiaries and if it succeeds in delivering high-quality care while reducing costs, it will share in the cost savings with Medicare. However the ACO will receive less monies than it would have under the old fee-for-service reimbursement . . . One fear is that government and private payers will shift the financial risk of taking care of the sickest and most expensive patients to ACOs [Accountable Care Organizations]." Ian L. Taylor and Ross Mcvicker Clinchy, "The Affordable Care Act and Academic Medical Centers," *Clinical Gastroenterology and Hepatology* 10, no. 8 (2012): 828–30, http://www.cghjournal.org/article/S1542-3565(12)00644-1/fulltext.
4. Tamara Rosin, "Med School Deans Worry Residencies Won't Keep Up with Surging Enrollment," *Becker's Hospital Review*, May 5, 2015, http://www.beckershospitalreview.com/hospital-physician-relationships/med-school-deans-worry-residencies-won-t-keep-up-with-surging-enrollment.html.
5. Atul Gawande, "Big Med," *New Yorker*, August 12, 2012, http://www.newyorker.com/magazine/2012/08/13/big-med.
6. One model Gawande has come upon in his research is corporate cooperation with academic medical centers—"centers of excellence"—to improve

health among their employees while also reducing costs. Lowe's has one such program; Kohl's and Walmart have similar ones. They refer an ailing worker to one of these centers, like the Mayo Clinic, the Cleveland Clinic, and others on the list; fly them in, pay their hotel expenses; and then encourage the employee to follow the expert's recommendations—which turn out to be, often enough, modest things like physical therapy rather than spinal surgery.

Atul Gawande, "America's Epidemic of Unnecessary Care," *New Yorker*, May 11, 2015, http://www.newyorker.com/magazine/annals-of-health-care.

7. Gawande, "Big Med."

8. The limitations on work hours for house staff were established in the 1970s after the Libby Zion case, when it was determined that the exhaustion of residents led to clinical errors and threatened the safety of patients. Barron Lerner, M.D., "A Life-Changing Case for Doctors in Training," *New York Times*, March 3, 2009, http://www.nytimes.com/2009/03/03/health/03zion.html.

Now other problems have developed, involving errors with the handoff, when one shift ends and the next team picks up the service.

9. Not only does teaching go unrewarded in terms of professional advancement, it is largely unpaid labor. Though faculty associated with academic medical centers have higher salaries than any other member of a university's faculty, the pressure on clinical faculty to bring in money to the hospital through clinics and on medical researchers to bring in grant money means, in essence, that any teaching is a volunteer job. Most medical schools and hospitals pay little or nothing for time spent teaching.

Mary Ellen Miller, "Troubled Times for Med School Teachers," *Hopkins Medical News*, Winter 2000, http://www.hopkinsmedicine.org/hmn/W00/top.html.

More recently, a few efforts have been made to find small stipends for clinical faculty to commit time to teaching, but teaching continues to remain under siege in the current environment.

Liz Kowalczyk, "Harvard Sweetens Reward for Doctors Who Teach," *Boston Globe*, March 9, 2007, http://archive.boston.com/news/local/articles/2007/03/09/harvard_sweetens_reward_for_doctors_who_teach/.

10. A medical specialist whose role is to see hospitalized patients and to improve efficiency for the hospital.

11. Medicare, as well as Accountable Care Organizations mandated by the Affordable Care Act, now tie pay to clinical performance, using various measures to determine meaningful use of time and resources in an attempt to improve outcomes while containing costs. The upshot is considerable financial risk for academic centers that educate young physicians as well as provide patient care.

Taylor and Clinchy, "The Affordable Care Act and Academic Medical Centers."

There are also many problems with the metrics used to determine quality care and hence reimbursement, problems that plague doctors nationwide at this moment and complicate financial risks for hospitals.

John Tozzi, "Quantitative Conundrum: The Problem with Obama's Plan to Pay Doctors Based on Performance," *Bloomberg Politics*, May 8, 2015, https://www.bloomberg.com/politics/articles/2015-05-08/the -problem-with-obama-s-plan-to-pay-doctors-based-on-performance.

12. Jeff Balser, "Rounds: A Message from the President and CEO of VUMC," *Vanderbilt Medical Center Reporter*, May 10, 2016, https://news.vanderbilt .edu/2016/05/10/rounds-a-message-from-the-president-and-ceo-of-vumc/.

The slightly lower A3 bond rating (down from the university's A2 rating) may ultimately mean more capital investment. "While the high bond rating signals less risk, it also can mean less reward for investors. A slightly lower rating, like those of other hospitals, would generally lead to a higher yield for bond purchasers, luring more investors to support the medical center's plans."

Eleanor Kennedy, "Divide and Conquer: Vanderbilt Readies for Big Moves after Cuts," *Nashville Business Journal*, January 16, 2015, http://www.bizjournals.com/nashville/print-edition/2015/01/16/divide -and-conquer-vanderbilt-readies-for-big.html.

13. In contrast, Tulane University Hospital and Clinic has a "closed" system: Every physician in the TUHC network has a faculty appointment at Tulane Medical School.

14. The minutes of the Vanderbilt Faculty Senate Meeting (February 5, 2015) include Vice Chancellor Balser's remarks on care of the indigent: "Uninsured care and the growing economic burden of uninsured care on academic medical centers is a huge problem. We do half of the nation's uninsured care in 5% of the hospital beds. We are the uninsured care provider for America. We are the uninsured care provider for middle Tennessee at Vanderbilt. That is a huge economic threat to us." https://www .vanderbilt.edu/facultysenate/minutes/2-5-15facsen.pdf.

15. "I think there is much more of an open landscape in the Mid-South," Jeff Balser, dean of the Vanderbilt University School of Medicine, said. "In many places of the country, health care is already consolidated, partnerships are already set up. Whereas in this part of the country it is in evolution." Tom Wilemon, "Vanderbilt Aims to Be Agile with Medical Spinoff," *Tennessean*, November 14, 2014, http://www.tennessean.com/story/news /health/2014/11/14/vandy-reorg-mean-patients-growth-mid-south/19033233/.

16. Ron Ozio, "J. Larry Jameson Reappointed Head of Penn Medicine and Perelman School of Medicine," *Penn News*, January 17, 2017, https://news

.upenn.edu/news/j-larry-jameson-reappointed-head-penn-medicine-and
-perelman-school-medicine.

17. It should be noted that senior physicians (and medical students) at the Cleveland Clinic and elsewhere are "training" Watson by tweaking its responses to complex medical scenarios. This "machine learning" may ultimately make computers a more reliable source of diagnostic and treatment protocols than formerly.

Larry Greenemeier, "Will IBM's Watson Usher in a New Era of Cognitive Computing?" *Scientific American*, November 13, 2013, https://www.scientificamerican.com/article/will-ibms-watson-usher-in-cognitive-computing/.

18. One example of bias built into an algorithm: an analysis of Google searches for "three black teenagers" and "three white teenagers" produced biased samples reflecting stereotypes, most likely unconscious, held by the young Silicon Valley techies who created the algorithm.

Jessica Guynn, "'Three Black Teenagers' Google Search Sparks Outrage," *USA Today*, June 9, 2016, https://www.usatoday.com/story/tech/news/2016/06/09/google-image-search-three-black-teenagers-three-white-teenagers/85648838/.

And one example of a medical student habituated to typing searches into his cell phone while on rounds: when he earned a less-than-stellar grade on his medical clerkship, his professor mildly suggested that he stop looking at his smartphone and try looking at the patient.

19. The following are links to articles describing the arts-and-humanities components of medical school curricula at Harvard and Stanford:

https://www.bostonglobe.com/business/2015/11/02/harvard-joins
-growing-trend-arts-education-med-schools/nra9CQHb1h0Zfmz3x8b
PNO/story.html
http://sm.stanford.edu/archive/stanmed/2001fall/medicalscholars.html
http://news.stanford.edu/news/2012/july/humanities-medical
-students-070212.html

For an overview on the importance of such elements in medical education, see David Jones, "A Complete Medical Education Includes the Arts and Humanities," *AMA Journal of Ethics* 16, no. 8 (August 2014): 636–41, http://journalofethics.ama-assn.org/2014/08/msoc1-1408.html.

20. Ernest Boyer, *Scholarship Reconsidered: Priorities of the Professoriate*, The Carnegie Foundation for the Advancement of Learning, 1990, http://www.hadinur.com/paper/BoyerScholarshipReconsidered.pdf.

21. "Faculty Promotion and Tenure Policy and Procedures, Virginia Commonwealth University and School of Medicine," pp. 7–8, Effective April 16, 2009, http://www.medschool.vcu.edu/media/medschool/documents/promotionguide_041609.pdf.

22. Medical faculties are by far the largest contingent on any university campus—Tulane Medical School has some five hundred full-time faculty members, while Harvard Medical School, with the largest medical faculty in the United States, has over nine thousand; obviously only those with a highly distinguished and impeccable résumé should be promoted to full professor.

Table 2. Distribution of U.S. Medical School Faculty by School and Department Type, American Association of Medical Colleges, https://www.aamc.org/download/475542/data/16table2.pdf.

6. Brave New World: Innovation and Scholarship

1. One example of the intersection between scholarship and practice is a service-learning course entitled Pathways to Urban Sustainability. In partnership with the community group Green Light New Orleans, students survey community members and research local food distribution in order to develop metrics for the economic and environmental impact of urban gardens.

   http://www2.tulane.edu/cps/students/upload/ServiceLearningCourses .pdf.

2. Donald Stokes, *Pasteur's Quadrant: Basic Science and Technological Innovation* (Washington, DC: Brookings Institution Press, 1997), http://www .ebookcore.com/download/pasteur-s-quadrant-basic-science-and -technological-innovation-13759-epub.html.

3. Ernest Boyer, *Scholarship Reconsidered: Priorities of the Professoriate*, The Carnegie Foundation for the Advancement of Learning, 1990, http://www.hadinur.com/paper/BoyerScholarshipReconsidered.pdf.

4. Daniel Kahneman's *Thinking Fast and Slow* (New York: Farrar, Straus and Giroux, 2013) on the psychological mechanisms of decision making reflects this research. Kahneman's colleague Amos Tversky would very likely have been awarded the Nobel Prize as well, but he died before the award was given.

5. Richard H. Thaler and Cass R. Sunstein, *Nudge: Improving Decisions about Health, Wealth, and Happiness* (New York: Penguin Books, 2009).

6. Cass R. Sunstein, "The Council of Psychological Advisers," *Annual Review of Psychology* 67, no. 713 (2016).

   https://dash.harvard.edu/bitstream/handle/1/13031653/annualre view9_15.pdf?sequence=1.

7. David Zax, "It's Up to Social Science to Make Us Act in an Environmentally Conscious Way. But Can We Trick Ourselves into Saving Ourselves?" *Seed Magazine*, January 25, 2017, http://seedmagazine.com/content /article/the_last_experiment/.

Ho's early work was on the role of apologies in medical malpractice suits.

Elke Weber at Columbia University has focused on scare tactics; Anthony Leiserowitz at Yale University has been working on group identities, different rhetorics tailored to different audiences, and the idea of multiple strategies—"silver buckshot."

8. A recent development in economics illustrates the brisk exchange on the borders between the ivory tower and the world at large. Curricular changes are emerging—a Yale pilot course, Designing the Digital Economy, for example—to meet the demand of the tech industry for economists who study the behavior of consumers (such things as procrastination on booking sites or actual clicks on a site related to ad relevance). Academics are engaging with the public sector on issues large and small, profound and less profound—from saving the environment to enhancing online consumerism.

Steve Lohr, "Goodbye, Ivory Tower. Hello, Silicon Valley Candy Store," *New York Times,* September 3, 2016, https://www.nytimes.com/2016/09/04/technology/goodbye-ivory-tower-hello-silicon-valley-candy-store.html.

9. Karubian was, in fact, one of the faculty members asked to draft the 2013 Tulane white paper proposing a process of academic review for "engaged scholarship."

10. Karubian has also formed an NGO, the Foundation for the Conservation of the Tropical Andes (FCAT), which helps Ecuadorians expand their role in the design and management of the conservation initiative.

11. Karubian Lab: Ecology, Behavior, Evolution, and Conservation, http://karubian.tulane.edu/engagement/overview/.

12. "Innovators, Not Innovations," http://dschool-old.stanford.edu/our-point-of-view/.

13. Leticia Britos Cavagnaro and Humera Fasihuddin, "A Moonshot Approach to Change in Higher Education: Creativity, Innovation, and the Redesign of Academia," Association of American Colleges and Universities, *Liberal Education* 102, no. 2 (Spring 2016), https://www.aacu.org/liberaleducation/2016/spring/cavagnaro.

14. Such research is grounded in material reality, avoiding some of the excesses of abstruse speculation (leading to the "wrong question") that Jonathan Swift satirizes in the Academy of Lagado on the flying island of Laputa—a place where "projectors" extract sunbeams from cucumbers, build houses starting with the roof, and exhaustively study how to propagate a breed of naked sheep. Jonathan Swift, *Gulliver's Travels* (New York: The Modern Library, 1958), 143, 145.

15. David Wessel, "Tapping Technology to Keep Lid on Tuition," *Wall Street Journal,* July 19, 2012, http://oli.cmu.edu/study-of-oli-in-the-wall-street-journal/.

16. William G. Bowen, Matthew M. Chingos, Kelly A. Lack, and Thomas I. Nygren, "Interactive Learning Online at Public Universities: Evidence from Randomized Trials," *ITHAKA Report*, May 2012, http://www.sr.ithaka.org/wp-content/uploads/2015/08/sr-ithaka-interactive-learning-online-at-public-universities.pdf.

Rebecca Griffiths, Matthew Chingos, Christine Mulhern, and Richard Spies, "Interactive Online Learning on Campus: Testing MOOCs and Other Platforms in Hybrid Formats in the University System of Maryland," *ITHAKA Report*, July 2014, http://www.sr.ithaka.org/wp-content/uploads/2015/08/S-R_Interactive_Online_Learning_Campus_20140716.pdf.

17. The quality of the content also matters in assessment of the merit of online courses. Materials used in these studies came from Carnegie Mellon's excellent Online Learning Initiative, and Coursera, which offers courses designed by faculty at the University of Michigan, Stanford, and elsewhere.

18. William G. Bowen, "Academia Online: Musings (Some Unconventional)," Stafford Little Lecture, Princeton University, October 14, 2013, http://www.ithaka.org/sites/default/files/files/ithaka-stafford-lecture-final.pdf.

19. Steve Kolowich, "Online Learning and Liberal Arts Colleges," *Inside Higher Ed*, June 29, 2012, https://www.insidehighered.com/news/2012/06/29/liberal-arts-college-explore-uses-blended-online-learning.

7. Can We All Get Along?

1. I am indebted to *The Locus of Authority: The Evolution of Faculty Roles in the Governance of Higher Education* by William G. Bowen and Eugene M. Tobin (Princeton, NJ: Princeton University Press, 2015) for this phrase, as well as for important insights into the history and current state of shared governance.

2. The early colonial history of colleges was marked by latent struggles over "the locus of authority." Harvard University, established in 1636, provides a good example: The Board of Overseers at Harvard, established in 1637 and consisting of members outside the university, retained veto power and ultimate control even after Henry Dunster, the first president of the university, obtained a charter for the Harvard Corporation, a body consisting of the president, treasurer, and five fellows, in 1650. Late in the eighteenth century, the corporation became a nonresident body consisting of nonteachers, exercising powers that it had lacked when it was an academic organization.

3. Bowen and Tobin, *The Locus of Authority*.

4. I am indebted to Michael Bernstein, formerly provost at Tulane and currently provost at Stony Brook University, for this astute observation.

5. Larry G. Gerber, "College and University Governance: How the AAUP Has Established Widely Accepted Norms of Shared Governance," AAUP, *Academe*, January–February 2015, https://www.aaup.org/article /college-and-university-governance#.V—qvJMrKjS.

6. John D. Aram, Scott S. Cowen, and National Association of Accountants, *Information for Corporate Directors: The Role of the Board in the Management Process* (New York: National Association of Accountants, 1983).

7. John D. Aram, Scott S. Cowen, and Albert J. Weatherhead, "Reforming the Corporate Board from Within: Strategies for CEOs and Directors," *Journal of General Management* 20, no. 4 (Summer 1995): 23–49.

8. Andrew Rice, "Anatomy of a Campus Coup," *New York Times Magazine*, The Education Issue, September 11, 2012, http://www.nytimes .com/2012/09/16/magazine/teresa-sullivan-uva-ouster.html.

9. Coursera, a highly regarded company, provides content created by professors from Stanford, Harvard, and MIT.

10. Among other things, board members weighed in on a course entitled GaGa about Gaga: Sex, Gender and Identity.

11. Teresa Sullivan, in addition to being the first woman president in the school's history and an outsider to the closed community of UVA, is in her sixties and (according to some) didn't "look the part" of president (a comment apparently directed to her style of dress—an irrelevancy, but petty concerns are unfortunately often a part of meltdown scenarios). Her scholarship benefited from her meticulousness and her interest in numbers, but did not prepare her for the public performances and inspirational messaging demanded of a university president.
    Rice, "Anatomy of a Campus Coup."

12. Mark Feeney, "John Silber, 86, Terrain-Changing BU Leader and Political Force," *Boston Globe*, September 27, 2012, https://www.bostonglobe.com /metro/2012/09/27/former-boston-university-president-john-silber-dies /aumnrC2KARnPIBCVecGDRI/story.html.

13. Rachel Aviv, "The Imperial Presidency," *New Yorker*, September 9, 2013, http://www.newyorker.com/magazine/2013/09/09/the-imperial-presidency.

14. More than three-quarters of college faculty are currently adjuncts.

15. Sexton was also deeply engaged in solving one of the chief problems confronting higher education today, the spiraling costs of getting an undergraduate degree. He wrote an essay proposing a system of low-interest government loans that students would repay with a small percentage of their annual salary for twenty years, when the loan would be forgiven—a process that would be reduced to half the time for those entering "socially desirable" professions like nursing and teaching.

16. Such contentions tend to be less a polite difference of opinion than a full-out war. Conspiracy theories and invidious interpretations often fan the

flames; mistrust deepens, doctrinaire positions harden, and transparency and open debate become more difficult.

17. "A Bouquet of Personal Notes from Senate Chairs and Academic Secretaries for John L. Hennessy, Stanford's 10th President," "ex officio," President and Faculty Senate 2000–2016, https://facultysenate.stanford .edu/sites/default/files/jlh_master_file_0.pdf.

18. It should be noted that Sexton and Hennessy, though both rose through the ranks, came from different academic domains. Sexton was a law professor who also held a PhD in history; Hennessy was an academic engineer. It's hard to say how much these different backgrounds influenced their presidencies, though it may be (emphasis on "may") that Hennessy, by bringing engineering and technology to the fore at Stanford, was able to preside over a less fractious and more homogeneous community than Sexton could create at NYU.

19. Lisa Lapin and Brad Hayward, "Stanford University President John L. Hennessy to Step Down in 2016," *Stanford News*, June 11, 2015, http://news.stanford.edu/2015/06/11/stanford-anouncement-061115/.

20. Elsewhere I've described four roles for board members: "overseer," engaged with matters internal and external crucial to institutional strategy; "ambassador," cheerleader for the institution, spreading the word; "matchmaker," reaching out to donors and thinkers who can improve institutional quality; and "rainmaker," who can bring in big donations capable of enhancing the mission and brand of the university. The last three of these acknowledge that donations—the ability to make them personally and solicit them from the public—are almost a job requirement. But shared governance can rein in some of the corrupting effects of even the best-intentioned of gifts.

21. Jane Mayer's *Dark Money: The Hidden History of the Billionaires behind the Rise of the Radical Right* (New York: Anchor Books, 2017) describes the Koch brothers' involvement in funding the right-wing political establishment across the United States.

22. Peter Schmidt, "How One College Quelled Controversy over a Koch-Financed Center," *Chronicle of Higher Education*, October 4, 2016, http://www.chronicle.com/article/How-One-College-Quelled/237984.

23. The problem of generating enthusiasm among adjunct faculty, who will likely move a number of times in their teaching lives and have no prospect of achieving tenure, is as much a problem for the institution as are those tenured professors who have become disengaged from their university's mission in the course of a long career.

8. The Ivory Tower

1. *The Encyclopedia of Cleveland History*, s.v. "Cleveland Tomorrow," http://ech.case.edu/cgi/article.pl?id=CT5.

   In 2004 Cleveland Tomorrow became part of the Greater Cleveland Partnership, a consortium of civic organizations devoted to technological and economic development.

2. Kathryn W. Hexter, MCRP, Ziona Austrian, PhD, and Candi Clouse, MS, *Living Cities: The Integration Initiative in Cleveland*, Cleveland State University, May 2013, http://cua6.urban.csuohio.edu/publications/center/center _for_economic_development/LC_Formative_Report_Year2%20_Final.pdf.

   University Circle is home to Case Western Reserve University, including the CWRU medical school and University Hospitals, as well as the Cleveland Art Museum, the Cleveland Institutes of Music and Art, the Botanical Gardens, the Museum of Natural History, the Cleveland Orchestra, and the Cleveland Clinic. Bordering the circle are neighborhoods that have long been in decline: Hough, where race riots occurred in 1967, as well as Buckeye-Shaker, Central, Fairfax, Glenville, Little Italy, and the city of East Cleveland.

3. Among GUCI's many achievements are mixed-use retail and residential projects, incentives for home buyers and renters in the area, cooperatively owned businesses (including green construction companies) that employ local workers, workforce training programs, anchor procurement arrangements to "buy local," a health tech corridor shared by University Hospitals and the Cleveland Clinic, and other purposeful collaborations among local organizations aiming at collective impact.

   Justin Glanville, *Cleveland's Greater University Circle Initiative: Building a 21st Century City through the Power of Anchor Institution Collaboration*, The Cleveland Foundation, 2013, http://community-wealth.org/content /clevelands-greater-university-circle-initiative.

   Ziona Austrian, PhD, Kathryn W. Hexter, MCRP, Candi Clouse, MS, and Kenneth Kalynchuk, *Greater University Circle Initiative: Year 4 Evaluation Report*, Cleveland State University, May 2014, http:// engagedscholarship.csuohio.edu/cgi/viewcontent.cgi?article=2290& context=urban_facpub.

4. Scott Cowen, "Cleveland and New Orleans: A Tale of Two Cities Exemplifying Urban Resilience," *Plain Dealer*, September 9, 2015, http:// www.cleveland.com/opinion/index.ssf/2015/09/cleveland_and_new _orleans_-_a.html.

5. Boyer's scholarship of "application," as described in chapter 6.

6. Anchoring has been most thoroughly studied and applied in urban contexts. Community colleges in rural areas have some of the functions of

an anchor, but very often civic engagement is not a fully articulated strategic aim, and the partnerships and resources to support engagement are harder to come by.

7. Michael Bernstein, former provost at Tulane, quotes Rick Marksbury on the subject of Tulane's engagement with New Orleans, as being neither a "hand up" nor a "hand out," but a "hand with."

8. I am indebted, once again, to Michael Bernstein, former provost at Tulane and currently provost at Stony Brook University, who offered these perceptive observations on the impact of the Morrill Acts.

9. Henry Louis Taylor, Jr., and Gavin Luter, *Anchor Institutions: An Interpretive Review Essay*, University at Buffalo, The Anchor Institutions Task Force, 2013, http://community-wealth.org/content/anchor-institutions-interpretive-review-essay.

10. The Penn acronyms for its programs are ABCS, for Academically Based Community Service, and UACS, for University-Assisted Community Schools.

    Judith Rodin, *The University and Urban Revival: Out of the Ivory Tower and Into the Streets* (Philadelphia: University of Pennsylvania Press, 2007).

11. The Netter Center for Community Partnerships and the University of Pennsylvania, *Anchor Institutions Toolkit: A Guide for Neighborhood Revitalization*, March 2008, https://www.nettercenter.upenn.edu/sites/default/files/Anchor_Toolkit6_09.pdf.

    For more on Ira Harkavy, see https://www.nettercenter.upenn.edu/ira-harkavy-phd and https://www.youtube.com/watch?v=bCfWAQkvMbY. The YouTube video emphasizes the particular importance of anchor institutions in promoting educational opportunity and excellence at every level. Colleges and universities "educate the educators" and hence shape what is taught and learned in K–12; and they have a responsibility to embrace diversity and transmit the knowledge necessary for full participation in a democratic society.

12. *Partners for Change*, University of Pennsylvania, The Netter Center for Community Partnerships, 2014, p. 3, https://www.nettercenter.upenn.edu/what-we-do/programs/university-assisted-community-schools/sayre-university-assisted-community-0.

13. Meagan M. Ehlenz and Eugénie L. Birch with Brian Agness, *The Power of Eds and Meds*, Penn Institute for Urban Research, July 2014, http://penniur.upenn.edu/uploads/media/Anchor-Institutions-PRAI-2014.pdf.

14. Rodin, *The University and Urban Revival*, chapter 9, "Civic Leadership," pp. 167–88.

15. Susan Snyder, "College President as Urban Planner," *phillynews.com*, May 15, 2016, http://www.philly.com/philly/news/special_packages/Drexel_University_president_John_Fry_as_urban_planner.html.

16. Sonja Sherwood, "Everything You Ever Wanted to Know about Schuylkill Yards," *Drexel Now*, March 30, 2016, http://drexel.edu/now/archive/2016/March/OrrisQA/.

17. John Fry, "Class Assignment: Jump In and Help Your City Meet Its Challenges," *Higher Education Today*, March 29, 2017, http://www.higheredto day.org/2017/03/29/class-assignment-jump-help-city-meet-challenges/.

18. Michelle Caffrey, "New Chamber Head John Fry Says Phila. Lacks a Sense of Urgency: Here's What Business Leaders Think," *Philadelphia Business Journal*, October 21, 2016, http://www.bizjournals.com /philadelphia/news/2016/10/21/drexel-john-fry-chamber-complacent -philly-economy.html.

19. Drexel website describing community engagement and centers/partnerships, etc.

    http://drexel.edu/civicengagement/.

20. A pedestrian walkway over the freeway was closed and locked daily at dusk, a potent symbol of the separation between the university and the city.

21. The immediate motivation for mobilizing strategic change was a student's murder during an armed robbery in 2003, a year after Harris assumed the presidency—an echo of Judith Rodin's experience at the University of Pennsylvania.

22. President of the University of San Diego since 2015, Harris has implemented a strategic plan to make USD an anchor institution, citing Penn, Syracuse, and Johns Hopkins as inspiring models. At first hesitant to leave Widener, he says he was "smitten" by USD, a private Roman Catholic college with a social justice mission that has been cited as a "Changemaker" by Ashoka, a global organization supporting social entrepreneurship, and honored by the Carnegie Foundation for its community service.

    Gary Warth, "New USD President Settles In," *San Diego Union-Tribune*, August 17, 2015, http://www.sandiegouniontribune.com/news /education/sdut-new-university-of-san-diego-president-settles-in -2015aug17-story.html.

    Fall Convocation USD 2016, https://www.sandiego.edu/president /writings-addresses/fall-convocation-2016.php.

23. James T. Harris, III, and Marcine Pickron-Davis, "From Gates to Engagement: A Ten-Year Retrospective of Widener University's Journey to Reclaim Its Soul and Fulfill Its Mission as a Leading Metropolitan University," *Journal of Higher Education Outreach and Engagement* 17, no. 3 (2013), http://openjournals.libs.uga.edu/index.php/jheoe/article/view/1037/682.

24. The elite liberal arts school on the Chester Higher Education Council is Swarthmore College, and its presence there suggests that an anchor need not be a large research university. In 2015 Swarthmore received a Community Engagement Classification, valid for ten years, from the

Carnegie Foundation and was included on the President's Community Service Honor Roll, the highest recognition a college can earn from the federal government for civic engagement. The college's Lang Center for Civic and Social Responsibility funds Project Pericles to support students pursuing solutions to civic issues. Recent initiatives include Chester Digital, an online urban ethnography of the city, and Chester Community Fellowships, summer internships working for social service organizations in the city.

25. The mascot was Chief Illiniwek.

26. Nancy Cantor, Peter Englot, and Marilyn Higgins, "Making the Work of Anchor Institutions Stick: Building Coalitions and Collective Expertise," *Journal of Higher Education Outreach and Engagement* 17, no. 3 (2013), http://openjournals.libs.uga.edu/index.php/jheoe/article/view/1036.

27. Nancy Cantor and Christopher Howard, "Beyond the Ivory Tower," Podcast, Public Radio Exchange, https://soundcloud.com/onbeing /nancy-cantor-and-christopher-howard-beyond-the-ivory-tower?in =onbeing/sets/nancy-cantor-and-christopher-howard-beyond-the -ivory-tower.

28. Syracuse has also worked with African American residents on art projects to cement neighborhood strength, creating a digital library, including photographs, artwork, and poetry, that commemorates the cultural history of the South Side dating back to the nineteenth century.
    http://ssio.syr.edu/projects/p-2.php.

29. Robin Wilson, "Syracuse's Slide: As Chancellor Focuses on the 'Public Good,' Syracuse's Reputation Slides," *Chronicle of Higher Education*, October 2, 2011, http://www.chronicle.com/article/Syracuses-Slide/129238/.

30. Cantor's remark about traditionalists is quoted in "Striking a (Local) Grand Bargain: How cities and anchor institutions can work together to drive growth and prosperity," *National Resource Network*, p. 14 (September 2015), https://wagner.nyu.edu/files/faculty/publications/strikingbargain.pdf. The school's acceptance rate has since gone back to about 50 percent.

31. Wilson, "Syracuse's Slide."

32. For example, Cantor recruited Cliff I. Davidson, a professor of engineering and computer science at Carnegie Mellon, to Syracuse, where he is now developing "green" roofs to manage storm water—a project he said would have been impossible in the less engaged setting of Pittsburgh. Since 2014, Cantor has been chancellor of Rutgers University–Newark, where she has continued to champion engaged scholarship among other efforts to strengthen the school's anchoring capacities.

33. See the title of the article from the *Chronicle of Higher Education* in October 2011, cited above, n. 29.

34. As mentioned earlier, dating back to their origins as land-grant colleges, public universities have had a mandate to educate students in practical spheres such as the agricultural and mechanic arts.

35. Its original designation, Miami Dade Community College, underscores its primary mission as an anchor institution responsible to the needs of residents and workers within the community.

36. Low-income students are also a priority: 46 percent of Miami Dade College students live beneath the federal poverty level, 67 percent are classified as low-income, and 56 percent are the first in their family to attend college.

    Miami Dade College, Highlights and Facts, November 2013, p. 5, https://www.mdc.edu/ir/Fact%20Book/MDC%20Highlights%20and%20 Facts_Nov2013rvd.pdf.

37. Eduardo J. Padrón, "The Birth of the Book Fair," *Miami Herald*, November 8, 2009, http://www.mdc.edu/main/images/091108_Padron _Herald_tcm6-21220.pdf.

38. Eduardo J. Padrón, "Miami Dade College and the Engaging Power of the Arts," *Journal of Higher Education Outreach and Engagement* 17, no. 3 (2013), http://openjournals.libs.uga.edu/index.php/jheoe/article/view/1040/685.

39. Johanna Gilligan, the founder and executive director, came to me with the idea, and I signed Tulane on as partner and resource. My talent is knowing talent when I see it.

40. Partnership for Youth Development was the first backbone organization for the collaborative, with the Cowen Institute as "co-backbone" in 2013 and finally sole backbone in 2015.

41. To pick another example: UCLA environmental and agricultural researchers have been studying the recent California drought and have come up with an array of techniques, ranging from bioengineered drought-resistant plants to novel systems of irrigation, to combat drought wherever it occurs on the planet and to address the global effects of climate change on agriculture.

42. Emily J. Levine, "If Colleges Are Dismantled, Consider the Impact on Their Cities," *Chronicle of Higher Education*, October 16, 2016, http://www .chronicle.com/article/If-Colleges-Are-Dismantled-/238076.

    It's true that, given the wide variety of the roughly four thousand institutions of higher education in the country, not all schools will be as engaged as a Syracuse or a Miami Dade; they won't have the circumstances or leadership to develop an anchoring capacity. However, mission "tweak" might be widely possible, with a movement toward greater engagement of one kind or another across the nation.

9. Who Are We?

1. Daniel Seymour, "Higher Education Has Lost Control of Its Own Narrative," *Chronicle of Higher Education*, November 6, 2016, http://www.chronicle.com/article/Higher-Education-Has-Lost/238321.

2. *A Master Plan for Higher Education in California, 1960–1975*, Prepared for the Liaison Committee of the State Board of Education and The Regents of the University of California, http://www.lib.berkeley.edu/uchistory/archives_exhibits/masterplan/MasterPlan1960.pdf.

3. Simon Marginson, "Reforging American Higher Education," blog post, Centre for Global Higher Education, October 26, 2016, http://www.researchcghe.org/blog/2016-10-26-reforging-american-public-higher-education/.

4. In New York, for instance, SUNY has had a single unwieldy bureaucracy governing all institutional categories. In a 2007 Master Plan the New York State Commission on Higher Education recommends a restructuring similar to California's, with governing structures specifically devoted to each tier, and proposes increasing mission differentiation and strengthening its four major research universities (especially the AAU campuses at Stony Brook and Buffalo)—all difficult tasks in a fiscally constrained environment.

    "Executive Summary," New York State Commission of Higher Education, 2007, http://system.suny.edu/media/suny/content-assets/documents/faculty-senate/CHEDraftReport_ExecutiveSummary.pdf.

    https://www.suny.edu/about/mission/.

5. Clarence Hein, "Judith Ramaley: A Pivotal Presidency for Portland State University," Looking Back: Essays on Portland State, Paper 3 (2013), http://pdxscholar.library.pdx.edu/cgi/viewcontent.cgi?article=1001&context=rememberpsu_essays.

    After leaving PSU, Ramaley served as president of the University of Vermont and then as president of Winona State University, returning to PSU in 2012 as a distinguished professor of public service.

6. "Sustainable Neighborhoods Initiative," Portland State University, https://www.pdx.edu/sustainability/sustainable-neighborhoods.

    "Portland State University Partnerships EN-9: Community Partnership," Stars, a program of the Association for the Advancement of Sustainability in Higher Education, https://stars.aashe.org/institutions/portland-state-university-or/report/2015-04-08/EN/public-engagement/EN-9/.

7. Portland as a city offered some obvious advantages to the university, and the university took the step of offering reciprocal benefits to the community in the same spirit of "enlightened self-interest" that changed the failing neighborhoods of West Philadelphia, Syracuse, and Chester.

8. Seymour, "Higher Education Has Lost Control of Its Own Narrative."

Seymour's book is *Future College Fieldbook: Mission, Vision, and Values in Higher Education* (North Charleston, SC: CreateSpace Independent Publishing Platform, 2016).

9. Kellie Woodhouse, "'Breakpoint' in Higher Ed," interview with Jon McGee, *Inside Higher Ed*, February 16, 2016, https://www.insidehighered.com/news/2016/02/16/author-discusses-new-book-changes-higher-education-marketplace.

10. "Berea's Story, Motto, and the Great Commitments," *Berea College, 2014–2015 Catalog*, http://catalog.berea.edu/en/2014-2015/Catalog/The-College/Berea-s-Story-Motto-and-the-Great-Commitments.

11. *Berea by the Numbers* (2012–2014), https://www.berea.edu/about/berea-by-the-numbers/.

12. For a history of St. John's from its origins as King William's School in 1696 to its 1930s reinvention by two University of Virginia professors, Stringfellow Barr and Scott Buchanan, see Barbara K. Townsend, L. Jackson Newell, and Michael D. Wiese, *Creating Distinctiveness: Lessons from Uncommon Colleges and Universities*, pp. 43–44, http://files.eric.ed.gov/fulltext/ED356702.pdf.

    Barr and Buchanan, influenced by the educational innovations of Alexander Meiklejohn (Amherst) and Robert Maynard Hutchins (the Chicago Plan), repurposed a great books curriculum they had proposed at UVA and installed it at St. John's.

13. Roger Kimball, "An Impending Coup at St. John's College," *RealClearPolitics*, June 6, 2016, http://www.realclearpolitics.com/articles/2016/06/06/an_impending_coup_at_st_johns_college_130786.html.

14. Entitled "Flying Disk Entertainment and Education," the thesis was on the aerodynamics of the Frisbee, as well as on entrepreneurial issues associated with the championship sport.

    "Chapter 8: Student Life and the Houses," Howard F. Johnson Library, Documentary Histories, vol. 2, 1975–85, Hampshire College, https://www.hampshire.edu/library/chapter-8-student-life-and-the-houses.

15. Fox Butterfield, "She Has Hampshire Feeling Frisky Again," *New York Times*, January 4, 1987, http://www.nytimes.com/1987/01/04/education/she-has-hampshire-feeling-frisky-again.html?pagewanted=all.

16. Ibid.

    In the 1980s, under the leadership of President Adele Simpson, the college increased its endowment through fund-raising, but it has also received long-term benefits from its membership in the Five College Consortium of the Pioneer Valley. Hampshire students can use laboratories and libraries and take courses at any of the other four (including UMass, Amherst, Smith, and Mount Holyoke), thus reducing some of the college's operating costs.

17. Jonathan Lash, "Mission Is the Core Commitment," *Huffington Post*, October 2, 2014, http://www.huffingtonpost.com/jonathan-lash/mission-is-the-core-commi_b_5908068.html.

18. *Cooperative Education and Career Development Employer Handbook*, 2015, https://www.northeastern.edu/coop/wp-content/uploads/2015/05/Co-op-Employer-Handbook-2015.pdf.
    https://www.northeastern.edu/coop/.

19. Employers who are asked to rate Northeastern graduates give them much higher marks for creativity, adaptability, teamwork, tactfulness, willingness to learn, and detail orientation than they give to graduates in general.

20. "Mission Statement," University of Notre Dame, https://www.nd.edu/about/mission-statement/.

21. "Best Colleges Rankings," *U.S. News & World Report* Rankings, http://colleges.usnews.rankingsandreviews.com/best-colleges/notre-dame-1840/overall-rankings.

22. Kevin Kiley, "Coming Up Short," *Inside Higher Ed*, July 12, 2013, https://www.insidehighered.com/news/2013/07/12/loyola-new-orleans-enrollment-shortfall-will-mean-large-budget-cuts.
    Steven Bell, "Higher Ed's Enrollment Blues," *Library Journal*, October 8, 2014, http://lj.libraryjournal.com/2014/10/opinion/steven-bell/higher-eds-enrollment-blues-from-the-bell-tower/.

23. Jessica Williams, "New Courses, New Funds, New Ideas, More Collaboration Helping Revive Loyola University," *Advocate*, June 18, 2017, http://www.theadvocate.com/new_orleans/news/education/article_9d4284c8-52c9-11e7-b50b-eb0586b7bc09.html.

24. See chapter 3 on financial sustainability for an earlier discussion of college costs and market share.

25. Andrew S. Rosen, *Harvard Envy: Why Too Many Colleges Overshoot* (New York: Simon & Schuster, 2011).
    "Too many institutions suffer from Harvard Envy regardless of classification or mission. This is the genesis of mission creep, driven by marketing and competition for fewer students prepared for college work to address increasing costs. 'Creep' turns into intentional misrepresentation; my mother would call it lying, when a regional institution compares itself to a state flagship or an elite private."
    Walter Wendler (chancellor emeritus, Southern Illinois University Carbondale), "No Two Alike," *On Higher Education* (blog), April 25, 2016, http://walterwendler.com/2016/04/.

26. Niraj Dawar and Charan K. Bagga, "A Better Way to Map Brand Strategy," *Harvard Business Review*, June 2015, https://hbr.org/2015/06/a-better-way-to-map-brand-strategy.

27. Jed Lipinski, "New Orleans College Leaders Offer Campus Forecasts," *Times-Picayune*, September 22, 2015, http://www.nola.com/education /index.ssf/2015/09/new_orleans_college_leaders_of.html#incart_river _index_topics.

28. For a discussion of the balancing act between yielding to marketplace pressures and hewing to a distinctive mission, see Lee Gardner, "The Upside of Selling Your Soul," *Chronicle of Higher Education*, September 29, 2014, http://www.chronicle.com/article/The-Upside-of-Selling-Your/149019.

29. *Paul Quinn College Student Handbook, 2015–16*, http://www.pqc.edu /wp-content/uploads/2015/08/Paul-Quinn-College-Student-Handbook -revised-Summer-2015-MJS-Final-Revisions.pdf.

30. Matt Connolly, "Bringing a College Back from the Brink," *Atlantic*, September 19, 2016, https://www.theatlantic.com/education/archive/2016/09 /bringing-a-college-back-from-the-brink/500375/.

31. Ann Butler, "Fort Lewis College Determines Identity in Modern Era," *Durango Herald*, December 3, 2016, https://durangoherald.com /articles/118965-fort-lewis-college-determines-identity-in-modern-era.

10. Presidential Leadership: Character and Context

1. Joshua Rothman, "Shut Up and Sit Down: Why the Leadership Industry Rules," *New Yorker*, February 29, 2016, http://www.newyorker.com /magazine/2016/02/29/our-dangerous-leadership-obsession.

2. To clarify further, an "unfiltered" leader may come from within academia but with an atypical résumé (as in my own case), but may also come from another sector altogether—government, business, the military, the clergy. In essence, "unfiltered" suggests an outside perspective, not automatically attuned to academic culture.

3. Jason Lane, "ViewPoint: Drew Faust and Old, White Men: The Changing Role of University Presidents," *Boston Business Journal*, June 22, 2017, http://www.bizjournals.com/boston/news/2017/06/22/viewpoint-drew -faust-and-old-white-men-the.html.

4. Kenneth R. Weiss, "L.A. Times Features Magazine President Steve B. Sample on Its Cover," *USC News*, September 18, 2000, https://news.usc .edu/25648/L-A-Times-Magazine-features-President-Steven-B-Sample -on-its-cover/.

5. Part of Sample's experiment was to see if he could raise one of the metrics used by *USNWR* to rank colleges, but the five-dollar mailing was significantly different from Newman's attempt to game the system by dismissing weak freshmen at Mount St. Mary's. Sample was tossing a ball in the air; Newman was subverting the school's mission. Weiss, "L.A. Times Features Magazine President Steve B. Sample on Its Cover."

6. And another quote, also from the *LA Times* magazine profile: "As the Rev. Cecil 'Chip' Murray, of the First African Methodist Episcopal church, puts it: 'Steve Sample is what a university president should be. He brightens the corner that he is in rather than looking for bright lights.'"

7. One example of the sheer power of his personality: Alfred E. Mann, a biomedical entrepreneur, was mired in negotiations with UCLA, his alma mater, over a planned $100 million gift to commercialize research and create a pipeline for useful products and procedures. Sample simply picked up the phone and asked if he'd consider a donation to USC, an entrepreneurial private institution that would know how to achieve Mann's aims. After a lunch meeting, Mann said yes. Asked how Sample pulled this off, Mann said, "He's a very clever guy."

8. Stephen Joel Trachtenberg, Gerald B. Kauvar, and E. Grady Bogue, *Presidencies Derailed: Why University Leaders Fail and How to Prevent It* (Baltimore: Johns Hopkins University Press, 2013).

9. The Peter Principle, a concept in management theory formulated by Laurence J. Peter in a satire of business practices published in 1969, postulates that promotions based solely on prior experience ultimately lead to widespread ineptitude. "Everyone in an organization keeps on getting promoted until they reach their level of incompetence. At that point they stop being promoted. So given enough time and enough promotion levels, *every* position in a firm will be occupied by someone who can't do the job."

   Andrea Ovans, "Overcoming the Peter Principle," *Harvard Business Review*, December 22, 2014, https://hbr.org/2014/12/overcoming-the -peter-principle.

10. Rebecca Schisler and Ryan Golden, "Mount President's Attempt to Improve Retention Rate Included Seeking Dismissal of 20–25 First-Year Students," *Mountain Echo*, January 19, 2016, http://msmecho .com/2016/01/19/mount-presidents-attempt-to-improve-retention -rate-included-seeking-dismissal-of-20-25-first-year.

    Scott Jaschik, "The Questions Developed to Cull Students," *Inside Higher Ed*, February 12, 2016, https://www.insidehighered.com /news/2016/02/12/questions-raised-about-survey-mount-st-marys-gave -freshmen-identify-possible-risk.

11. Lauren Camera, "Mount St. Mary's and the Pressures of a Changing Higher Ed Landscape," *U.S. News & World Report*, February 12, 2016, http://www.usnews.com/news/articles/2016-02-12/mount-st-marys-and -the-pressures-of-a-changing-higher-education-landscape.

12. Newman asked, "Why are there so many crucifixes on campus?" and had to be told the school housed a seminary.

13. Sarah Brown, "A Year after Controversy Toppled Its Divisive President, Mount St. Mary's Forges Ahead," *Chronicle of Higher Education*, May

12, 2017, http://www.chronicle.com/article/A-Year-After-Controversy/240062.

14. In the 1990s I wrote a "Dean's Column" for *Cleveland Enterprise: The Magazine for Growing Businesses*, jointly published by Enterprise Development, Inc., and the Weatherhead School of Management at CWRU. "The Executive Maverick" appeared in the Summer 1996 issue. Other topics I discussed in the series: fundamentals of management, self-awareness and feedback ("Looking into the Mirror"), organizational life cycles, innovation and the quality of ideas, management fundamentals, the importance of values and mission, and the power of personal relationships.

15. Clara M. Lovett, "How Trustees Can Do Better at Presidential Transitions," *Chronicle of Higher Education*, November 6, 2016, http://www.chronicle.com/article/How-Trustees-Can-Do-Better-at/238322.

16. Ibid.

It should be said that other methods—meeting with senior people, talking regularly with one's predecessor, reading and mapping out plans—can help an incoming president prepare for the new job, but board assistance might be better than relying on individual initiative.

17. Susan Snyder, "College President as Urban Planner," *phillynews.com*, May 15, 2016, http://www.philly.com/philly/news/special_packages/Drexel_University_president_John_Fry_as_urban_planner.html.

18. My "posse" in 1998 and 1999 consisted of five seasoned mentors: Henry Rosovsky (Harvard), James Freedman (Dartmouth), Richard Chait (Harvard), Diana Chapman Walsh (Wellesley College), and Gordon Gee (Brown). We met in person twice a year, beginning with a book club approach—everyone had recommended a book for me to read, and we discussed them at length—moving on to the subject of dos and don'ts, formulation of goals, and an assessment of what I'd achieved to date. After Katrina, my key advisers were Harvey Fineberg (Harvard), Malcolm Gillis (Rice), Bill Bowen (Princeton), William Brody (Johns Hopkins), Jim Duderstadt and Farris Womack (University of Michigan), and Eamon Kelly (my predecessor at Tulane).

19. Barry Glassner and Morton Schapiro, "If Only I Had Known More About . . . ," *Chronicle of Higher Education*, November 20, 2016, http://www.chronicle.com/article/If-Only-I-Had-Known-More-About/238461.

20. Steven B. Sample, "The Research University of the 21st Century: What Will It Look Like?" Address to the 23rd Army Science Conference, Orlando, Florida, December 2, 2002, https://about.usc.edu/presidentemeritus/speeches/the-research-university-of-the-21st-century-what-will-it-look-like/.

21. Glassner and Schapiro, "If Only I Had Known More About. . . ."

Index

AAU. *See* Association of American Universities

AAUP. *See* American Association of University Professors

academic freedom, 128, 139–40

academic medical centers, 96–97, 102–3, 221n3, 221n6, 222n11

academic programs, finances of, 63–64, 71–72, 74

access: assessment methods and, 43–50; case examples of, 28; college readiness and, 43–44; differentiation of mission and, 165; financial aid and, 50–53; strategies promoting, 35. *See also* diversity

Access UVA, 50–51

Accountable Care Organizations, 221n3, 222n11

adjunct and part-time faculty, 63–64, 122, 229n23

affinity groups, 42

affirmative action, 36–38, 207n4, 209n13

Affordable Care Act, 96, 116, 221n3, 222n11

African American students: and application process, 206n1; athletics and, 81, 83; community colleges serving, 70; educational success of, 24–25; Syracuse University and, 233n28; Tulane University and, 32–33; at University of California schools, 208n10. *See also* historically black colleges and universities

amateur athletics, 78–79, 81, 82, 91–92

American Association of University Professors (AAUP), 125, 128, 134–35, 138, 140, 195

Amherst, Lord Jeffery, 41, 210n18

Amherst College, 28, 38, 40–41, 209n17, 210n18, 214n42

anchoring and anchor institutions, 144–61, 167, 230n6, 231n11, 232n22

applications, college, 32, 43, 206n1

Aram, John, 110

Arizona State University, 71–74, 217n24

articulation agreements, 44, 211n24

arts and humanities: discovery and innovation in, 114; importance of, 114; in medical education, 106

Case, Joe Paul, 28
Case Western Reserve University,
    7–8, 78, 94, 109–10, 143–44, 184
Cassidy, Kim, 122
Casteen, John, 131
Catholicism, 174, 177
Chait, Richard, 240n18
character, as factor in leadership,
    10, 190
Charity Hospital, New Orleans,
    96, 100
Cheesecake Factory, 97
Chester, Pennsylvania, 150–52
Chester County Hospital, 104
Chicago State University, 70
choice, 115–17
Christensen, Clayton, 69
City University of New York, 53
Civil Rights Act, 36
class. *See* socioeconomic class
Clemson University, 1, 20, 82
Cleveland, Ohio, 143–44
Cleveland Orchestra, 124–25
Cleveland Tomorrow, 143–44
climate change, 116–17
clinical rounds, 96
Cohen, George, 130
College Access Index, 28, 40
college and university presidents,
    181–201; case examples of,
    187–92; challenges facing,
    182–83; current situation for,
    199; demographic characteristics
    of, 184–85; filtered vs. unfil-
    tered, 183–85, 190, 192–93, 197,
    238n2 (*see also* inside candi-
    dates for; outsider status of);
    governance challenges facing,
    125; inside candidates for, 198
    (*see also* filtered vs. unfiltered);
    institutional fit of, 185, 190,
    194–96; mentoring of, 197–98,
    240n18; NCAA governance by,
    219n4; outsider status of, 184,
    185, 190–93, 195–96 (*see also*

filtered vs. unfiltered); qualities
    of successful, 10, 129, 185–87,
    190, 199–201; role of, 126, 129,
    138–39; selection process and
    criteria for, 142, 183–86, 189–
    90, 193–98; succession of, 182,
    196–98; tenures of, 6, 216n14;
    unsuccessful, 189–92, 194. *See
    also* leadership; transformative
    leadership
College Football Playoff (CFP), 86,
    88, 90
College of William and Mary, 80
college readiness, 43–44
colleges and universities: business/
    industry relations with, 26–27;
    challenges facing, 29; commu-
    nity/social impact of, 14–17,
    27–29, 49, 111, 147–59, 166–67;
    governance of, 124–42, 227n2;
    racial climate at, 39–42; regional
    characteristics of, 215n2. *See also*
    higher education; historically
    black colleges and universities;
    mission; research institutions;
    town-gown relations
College Track, 44
Columbia University, 38, 106
community colleges, 44, 70,
    211n24, 230n6
Confederate States, land-grant
    institutions in, 2, 29
consultants, 62
context, decision making influ-
    enced by, 7, 190–91
contingency, decision making influ-
    enced by, 7, 125, 200–201
cooperative education model, 172,
    237n19
cost-cutting measures, 62–66
costs, of higher education. *See*
    tuition
Council of Independent Colleges,
    69
Coursera, 131, 227n17, 228n9

crises. *See* timing, of educational change
critical thinking, 114
Crow, Michael, 71–74
Cunningham, Janeya, 46

Daniels, Mitch, 73, 195, 217n26, 218n28
Dartmouth College, 154
Davidson, Cliff I., 233n32
Davidson College, 42, 52–53, 76
decision making, 115–17
Delgado Community College, 159
Denison College, 42
design thinking, 119–20
digital learning. *See* online learning
Dirks, Nicholas, 64
Disaster Resilience Leadership Academy, 159
Disproportionate Share Hospitals, 221n3
diversity, 31–56; case examples of, 39–55; in college leadership, 184–85; fiscal health and, 66–69, 69, 71, 75–76; and future student population, 52; history of, 35–39; novel approaches to, 54–55; research in support of, 37; societal increase in, 33–34; socioeconomic class as criterion for, 38–39; strategies for promoting, 35, 43–55; support programs for, 34–35; Tulane University and, 31–34, 42–43
Division I athletics, 78–79, 81, 84–88, 90–91
Division III athletics, 79, 84, 87, 92
Dornsife Center for Neighborhood Partnerships, 149–50
Dowling, Jane Martínez, 47
Dragas, Helen, 51, 129–32
Dr. Bernett L. Johnson Jr. Sayre Health Center, 148
Drexel University, 149–50
d.school, 119–20, 136

Duderstadt, Jim, 137, 240n18
Duke University, 16
Dynamic Assessment Process, 45–46, 212n26

early college, 43–44
ecology, 117–18
economic man, 115
Ecuador, 117–18
EdX, 72
Eliot, Charles, 218n2
elite institutions: educational challenges facing, 74–75; fiscal challenges of, 74–76
Embrace Warmer, 120
Emory University, 43, 94
Employment and Mobility Pathways Linked for Opportunity Youth (EMPLOY), 158–59
energy conservation, 116–17
engaged scholarship, 107, 109, 111–12, 115–23, 144, 154, 226n8
Ephron, Nora, 133
equal protection clause, 36
Essex Community College, 59
ethics, in medicine, 106

faculty: conflicts of administration with, 125; conservative/defensive character of, 64, 111, 123, 153–54; employee benefits of, 74; and institutional governance, 64, 70, 124–28, 133–34, 138–40; power of, 128; as teachers, 122–23; and town-gown relations, 151, 153–54. *See also* adjunct and part-time faculty
Family Educational Rights and Privacy Act (FERPA), 204n6
Fee, John, 169
finances, college and university, 57–77; athletics and, 80–81, 83–84, 86–92, 219n3; case examples of, 64–76; challenges concerning, 58–61; difficult decisions

Sweet Briar College, 65–66, 67
Swift, Jonathan, 226n8
Syracuse, New York, 152–53
Syracuse University, 152–55, 168

teaching, as aspect of scholarship, 120–22
teaching hospitals, 95–96
television, athletics and, 80–81, 85, 219n3
Terman, Frederick, 26, 28
test-blind admissions, 48, 171–72
test-optional schools, 47–48, 213n31
Thaler, Richard, 115–16
Thrun, Sebastian, 27
TIDES (Tulane Interdisciplinary Experience Seminar) program, 22
time to degree, 54–55, 205n13
timing, of educational change, 9, 50, 65, 76, 132
tipping points: diversity as, 33, 36; in higher education development, 4; issues indicative of, 10
touch screens, 113
town-gown relations, 143–61; anchor institutions and, 144–61, 231n11; case examples of, 147–59; challenges of, 145, 150; characteristics of successful, 160; community/social impact of colleges and universities, 14–17, 27–29, 49, 111, 117–19, 147–59, 166–67; spatial divisions in, 158; Tulane University and, 14–17, 117–19, 143, 144–45, 157–59
Trachtenberg, Stephen, 189–90, 194
Trainor, Timothy E., 192
transfer students, 44
transformative leadership: characteristics of, 6; defined, 3; moments calling for, 9. *See also*

college and university presidents; leadership
Tremaine, Stephen, 43, 210n21
Trinity Washington University, 66–67, 168
tuition: alternative programs for saving, 44, 72; and best-value schools, 175–76; increases in, 60; private colleges' discounting of, 59; reliance on students paying full, 61, 71; in-state vs. out-of-state, 60, 218n28
Tulane, Paul, 16
Tulane University: athletics at, 1, 79, 82–88, 90; community/ social impact of, 14–17, 117–19, 143, 144–45, 155, 157–59; and diversity issues, 31–34, 42–43; finances of, 57–59; governance of, 124, 137–41; Hurricane Katrina and, 3, 6–7, 14–16, 20, 21, 31–32, 58, 64–65, 87, 100, 110–11, 125, 137–39, 144–45, 162–63, 200, 204n9; interdisciplinary experiences at, 22; investment strategies and ethics of, 8; medicine at, 93, 99–101, 104, 225n22; mission and identity of, 162–63; origin of, 16; presidential leadership of, 183–84, 193–94, 200; ratings and metrics for, 13, 17–21, 83, 203n5, 204n9; as research institution, 33
"Turning the Tide" (Harvard Graduate School of Education), 49–50
Tversky, Amos, 115, 225n4
Twombly, Meredith, 38

Udacity, 27
UMETRICS, 23–24
universities. *See* colleges and universities; higher education; research institutions

Wolfe, Timothy, 39
Womack, Farris, 240n18

Xavier University of Louisiana, 6, 24–25, 28, 168, 186

Yahoo, 27
Yale University, 41, 80, 210n19
youth disconnection, 158–59

Zinn, Howard, 133